Sun
Drenched
CUISINE

Sun Drenched CUISINE

Evocative recipes from warm and sunny lands

Marlena Spieler

EBURY PRESS LONDON

To Leah and Gretchen

First published in Great Britain in 1987 by
Ebury Press
Division of The National Magazine Company Ltd
Colquhoun House
27-37 Broadwick Street
London W1V 1FR

First published in 1986 in the United States of America by
St Martin's Press
175 Fifth Avenue
New York
NY 10010

ISBN 0 85223 613 1

Printed and bound in Great Britain at The Bath Press

CONTENTS

CONVERSION TABLES

The terms and measurements given throughout the book are American. Metric equivalents are given where applicable, although you may find the following charts useful in converting temperatures and terms.

TEMPERATURES

$$\text{Fahrenheit} = \frac{\text{Celsius} \times 9}{5} + 32 \quad \text{Celsius} = \frac{(\text{Fahrenheit} - 32)}{9} \times 5$$

Oven Temperature Scales

Electric Scale °Fahrenheit	°Celsius Scale	Gas Oven Marks
225° F	110° C	1/4
250	130	1/2
275	140	1
300	150	2
320/325	170	3
340/350	180	4
375	190	5
390/400	200	6
425/430	220	7
450	230	8

TERMS

bell pepper	red or green pepper
cake flour	plain flour
catsup	tomato ketchup
cilantro	coriander
eggplant	aubergine
jalapenos	substitute chilli
Japanese eggplant	substitute aubergine
laos powder	substitute fresh ginger
masa harina	substitute tortilla flour
poblanos	substitute chilli
Serrano chilli	substitute chilli
tomatillos	substitute tomatoes
yellow mustard seeds	substitute mustard seeds

"Breakfasts on the terrace amid the bees and wasps buzzing around the grape arbor. The bunches of grapes so plump, ripening daily and hung with an almost indecent sensuality. We reach out from our table at mealtime and pick a handful, nibbling on their juicy sweetness.

Café au lait in bowls. Yeasty tender croissants from the wood-burning village oven. Sweet, creamy butter and preserves tasting of the local fruit—that's it, simple and perfect. The condiment is the beautiful view from the terrace—across our valley, over the red rooftops of the village past the pudgy white sheep snacking in our field. Here we sit and eat our sunny breakfasts and also our suppers; our artichoke and potato gratin, herby salads, our spicy cassoulets, and dishes of simmered vegetables in olive oil and garlic, and we drink great quantities of dark Vin de Cahors. Complicated food would be lost out here. A delicate, subtle taste would be overshadowed by the superb rustic atmosphere. For us, intense flavors."

From the author's journal
August 1985, Varaire, Southwest France

THE SUN-DRENCHED CUISINE

Bursting with vigor, the cuisine of the sun-drenched lands is aromatic with fresh herbs and accented with colorful flavors. It is food for the senses, delicious dishes with intense, yet often playful flavors. These are not subtle dishes, fussily seasoned with the tiniest pinch of this or a soupçon of that, then presented as a work of art—this is robust fare, prepared with passion. There is nothing prim about it; it shouts out flavor! Spicy is very, very spicy, and tart is tart indeed.

These are the simple and savory meals that are so memorable—the impromptu picnic of pan-fried fresh sardines on a beach near Portofino, or the family on the hillside in Greece who beckoned me to join in their supper of olives, bread, and cucumber—these are the kinds of eating experiences that have inspired this book. The meal may soon be gone, but the memory remains in your mind to nourish your soul as the food has nourished your body.

To experience this cuisine is to feast on pasta al dente in sauce so savory it's almost astonishing. It is to nibble on tender shreds of crusty roast lamb, doused with a biting sauce of hot pepper, lemon, and olives while walking through the sun-baked souk (marketplace), or to share a huge salad of crunchy raw vegetables splashed with tart-hot dressing on a houseboat in Bangkok.

On the surface it may seem that there is little similarity between the garlic-and-olive-oil-scented dishes of Rome and the herb-strewn foods of Southeast Asia. What could the seemingly disparate flavors of Louisiana's fiery gumbos have in common with Morocco's aromatic tajines or the tomato fragrance of southern France? If you carefully consider each one, however, and think of the abundance of vegetables and fresh, vibrant flavors found in all these places, you will begin to see the similarity in their styles of cooking. This is honest cooking, flavored by and tasting of the sun itself.

Starting in the Mediterranean and North Africa, then traveling through the Middle East, India, Southeast Asia, and Latin America, you find the sun-drenched lands. There, the days are bright, and the cuisines that emerge from these lands are straightforward and full of exuberant flavors. These native cuisines have absorbed many influences, which have become reflected in the local culinary philosophy and agriculture. A great example of this is the combination of the ancient Aztec chile-based diet with that of the Spanish conquerors, which produced one of the world's glorious cuisines, that of Mexico. Of course, there are also sun-drenched lands such as Australia or New Zealand, whose culinary roots are in colonial cool climates. Although their cuisines have remained much in the British style, they have embraced native fruits and created such confections as the kiwi-based Pavlova or Mango Fool. These dishes reflect the British penchant for sweets combined with availability of exotic fruits.

The brilliance of the sun is reflected in all aspects of life in the sun-drenched lands—it is etched onto faces, and baked into the terra-cotta or adobe tile. One must cease work at midday and flee the bright, hot light for the coolness of indoors and the pleasure of the family meal.

Life is precious there, where harshness and poverty too often prevail, and the simple pleasures, which can sadly be lost in our more sophisticated lifestyles—the joy of music, companionship, good food, and drink—have an importance many of us often forget. I think of an old Yemenite man in the marketplace of Old Jerusalem enjoying his midday pick-me-up: romaine lettuce leaves, each leaf lovingly rubbed with raw garlic, then popped into his mouth and slowly, thoughtfully chewed. Or, less exotic, but no less delicious, the plump bread rolls sold on the streets of Nice. What could taste better than toting one down to the beach and devouring it to the accompaniment of the salty sea aroma, warm sand, and the view of a very calm, very blue Mediterranean sea.

Late in the day, when heat no longer oppresses, the evening soothes like a cooling balm. Everybody is out walking in the street, visiting cafés, and catching up on gossip. Late supper is the time to socialize and enjoy the food, to revel in the relief from sun heat and workday. It is not uncommon to find whole families in Rome or Buenos Aires eating in restaurants, outside under the stars, as late as midnight or even 2 A.M.

The cuisines may emanate from the sun-drenched lands of the Mediterranean, India, Asia, Africa, and Latin America, but we don't have to live there to enjoy them. Nor are the foods in this book just for summer. The lure of this cuisine transcends both seasons and locale. Though some of the foods offered here are of the gray season, the culinary attitude remains bright. Humble, cold-climate cabbage takes on new vibrancy when dressed in a cloak of olive oil and sour lemon and sprinkled with strong wild thyme. When winter casts its dreary pall on those of us in Northern lands, these foods bring warmth and cheeriness. It's like a ticket to a sunny climate during a siege of the chills. I think of coming out of the rain not long ago, drenched to the bone in body and spirit. Once inside, I feasted upon cheese fondue lavished with garlic, served with wedges of juicy red tomato, and a small pot of blazingly hot sambal olek, the Indonesian chile condiment. It was a cold-weather dish with a sunny outlook, and the chile, garlic, and tomato flavors brightened both the fondue and my mood.

There are many cookbooks that detail at length the individual cuisines of many of the areas covered in this book. I wanted instead to capture the spirit of these cuisines, the authentic classic dishes as well as some unexpected new flavors to jolt us out of our culinary ruts. In this I've tried to present a pleasing balance.

Wonderful food, served simply and warmly, while not solving all the complicated ills of the world, enhances the quality of daily living. It is one of the few things we can do consistently to make life nicer and cozier for ourselves and those around us. Whether it is a veritable still life of vegetables and fish, with huge bowls of aïoli, spread out in the village square for all to partake or an aromatic couscous resplendent with rich chunks of spicy lamb served on a table on the floor and eaten with the hands, this is celebration food. These vibrant dishes create an atmosphere that pleases and relaxes both guests and family and makes everything friendlier.

Relatively untouched by the modern corporate agricultural machine, the sun-drenched lands are still close to the soil and to traditional methods of farming. The cuisines and life-styles reflect interest in and appreciation for the locally grown produce and agriculture. Not long ago, I sat next to two young businessmen on a train from Paris to Toulouse. Although their conversation was designed to exhibit to one another the high degree of sophistication each had attained, their talk was periodically interrupted by comments on how lovely were the plump white sheep on the hillsides and the best way to hunt and prepare snails.

I suppose it is predictable, this penchant I have toward sun-drenched meals. In my childhood home of Sacramento, California, six months of the year are sunny. Summer meals consisted of picnics by the river and sweet corn and watermelon under my grandparents' orange tree. The atmosphere was often sultry and hot, but there was always lots of chile-spiced Mexican food to perk us up. We had wonderful produce then, grown by us or purchased at a farmers' market.

Marketplaces are the center of the cuisines that flourish throughout the sun-drenched lands. The visual and sensual delight of purchasing food so fresh and so directly always enlivens this cuisine. Luxuriant with fresh vegetables, fruits, and herbs, the markets also offer homemade cheese, honey from the local hives, or regional baked specialties. I remember my first glimpse into the Guadalajara marketplace: huge piles of familiar and not-so-familiar vegetables, chiles heaped next to giant baskets of garlic, a young man peeling fronds of cactus leaves to eat as nopales. The aroma of fresh tortillas and the squawking of multicolored parrots mingled with the songs of a marimba band. Large women, brown and fleshy, with warm smiles tended the stalls. Small children played with the bits and pieces of discarded vegetables.

Later, when I lived in Israel, I often wandered through the marketplace of Jerusalem, among the vats of olives, trays of sticky sweets, piles of steamy, fresh, baked pita bread. As I walked, I inhaled the fragrance of spice mixtures lying uncovered in barrels and avoided the smells of the butcher shops. I passed tables filled with golden lemons and pink grapefruit heaped next to ruby-fleshed blood oranges.

The nature of food and travel writing is to embellish the good and to discount the bad. I can wax lyrical about the marketplace but neglect to mention the 112 degree heat or the swarms of stinging insects. I describe the ideal situation, and indeed it is so—sometimes. No one should measure his or her travels with those of a cookbook writer. I really do my fair share of complaining (more, I'm told), but images and recipes of wonderful foods always call forth memories of the good times.

These wonderful foods needn't be complicated to be good. The role of a cookbook is not just to offer recipes but also to describe and remind us of those simple pleasures we may have forgotten or never known. It should stimulate our imagination as well as our palate.

Don't be afraid to be passionate about dishes or ingredients that seem unsophisticated or humble—they're often the best. This attitude is really at the heart of *Sun-Drenched Cuisine*.

Some notes on ingredients (unless otherwise specified):
All eggs called for are large.
All butter used is unsalted.
All olive oil used must have lots of olive flavor (extra virgin).
All garlic cloves specified are large.

The Fresh Herbs and Leaves

Fresh herbs add joy to your palate and your table. These fragrant green leaves are the bright accent of freshness. If you really want wonderful food you will grow or buy fresh herbs and use them with enthusiasm.

Arugula   (See Roghetta.)

Basil   No book on the cuisines of the sunny lands could be complete without homage to this sweet, fragrant herb. We know it, of course, in pesto, that emerald-colored essence of basil sauce slathered on almost everything in Genoese *cucina*. It is said that in olden days the aroma of pesto emanated so strongly from Genoa that when the weather was foggy and visibility was bad, ship captains were able to navigate their boats into the harbor by the fragrance alone.

Basil is also used in salads, soups, sautés, and pasta dishes throughout Italy; it is the main flavoring ingredient in the French vegetable soup Soupe au Pistou; strewn across many a torrid Thai dish, it lends its aroma and cooling influence. In India it is considered a holy herb, not to be eaten but to be used in sacrament; and in Greece every house keeps a pot of basil growing on the porch, not as a culinary herb but to keep away flies (it doesn't work, so it seems).

A pot of basil can grow nicely for quite a while in a sunny window, and you can continually snip off small amounts to flavor salads, sauces, and pasta.

Chives   These are delicate green-onion-like shoots; chop and add to salads, sauces, soups, or sandwiches. Delicious with creamy goat cheese or cold chicken.

Cilantro   The leaf of the coriander seed, cilantro has a controversial odor and flavor. People either love it or hate it, but most feel one way or the other. It can, however, make whatever it's served with shine. It is worth attempting to acquire a taste for this herb by starting with small amounts and working up—you will find yourself almost addicted! Also known as Chinese parsley or fresh coriander, it is available in Oriental food shops, Latin American grocery stores, and, increasingly, in local supermarkets.

Garlic   The fragrant balm for both body and spirit exudes an aroma that wafts through the medinas of Morocco and the sun-baked marketplaces of southern France; it beckons from pizza ovens in Naples. In Szechuan cuisine, it simmers with gingerroot, and chiles and Indian food would be bland without its ardent presence. Choose fresh, firm heads and use it generously. If there were one dominant flavor of the sun-drenched kitchen, it would be garlic.

Mâche   Rapidly becoming almost as well known and loved here as it has been in Europe for centuries, mâche is a tender, slightly nutty, somewhat buttery-flavored green with small oval leaves growing from a central heart. A delicate addition to salads with stronger tasting greens, and a wonderful garnish for savory sandwiches such as Bruschetta with Prosciutto. Known as *songino* in Italy; known as *lamb's lettuce* in England because the lambs feast on it in the fields in early spring (I do, too).

Mint Fresh mint leaves are refreshing and fragrant, delicious when tossed into a salad or floating atop a fiery Southeast Asian soup. Eaten throughout the Middle East, the Far East, and in India, as well as everywhere when softly crushed and added to icy lemonade.

Parsley What can possibly be said that's new about parsley except that it is delicious when used with enthusiasm and in abundance, not just as a sprig to garnish a plate. Italian parsley, the flat-leafed kind, has a strong, grassy aroma and flavor, and I heartily recommend it.

Purslane This wild green grows creeping through the garden, flat on the earth. (When I was a child, I would hop around it, for it frightened me in an inexplicable way. When I grew older and became interested in cooking, I learned that that scary weed was very good to eat.) The texture of purslane is unique—with smooth leaves, somewhat like a succulent's—and its flavor is tangy and piquant. Delicious raw in salads, it becomes a little bitter and less interesting when cooked.

Radicchio This red-leafed vegetable, grown in the Treviso and Verona area near Venice, is known as the "red lettuce of Treviso." Its leaves have a slightly (but pleasantly) bitter flavor. Radicchio can be startlingly beautiful: its colors range from scarlet to magenta to green streaked with white and pink. The radicchio we get here is generally a small, tight head, but in Italy the leaves may be larger and looser. Just a few radicchio leaves torn or cut and added to the most ordinary salad make it special indeed.

Roghetta With its dark green leaves with jagged edges and pointed ends, roghetta has a great, distinctive flavor. It grows wild and is also cultivated, much like mustard greens or dandelions. Any salad benefits from a handful of roghetta. Also known as arugula, rucula, rugula, rucola, rogetta, roquette, rocket, and arugola.

Rosemary Sweetly fragrant with a slight piny aroma, rosemary is a common ornamental bush, hedge, and ground covering. Its leaves look like green needles. When fresh, these leaves are delicious tossed in salads, soups, and sauces; but when dried, they are spiky and sharp and should be crushed when used. Since rosemary is a perennial, you can always have some growing in a sunny window. When grilling meat out-of-doors, throw a branch of rosemary onto the fire, and let the fragrant smoke perfume the food.

Sage Fresh sage leaves are distinctive and delicious when skewered into kabobs, heated in butter and poured over ravioli, or fastened (with a toothpick) onto a thinly sliced chicken breast along with a fine slice of

6

prosciutto, then sautéed. When dried, sage becomes overly strong and less desirable as a seasoning.

Tarragon   A classic herb, used in the traditional French kitchen, tarragon has flat, narrow leaves, a slight anise-like aroma, and an odd, subtle aftertaste. It is one of my favorites, and can be used in many ways. Tarragon is delicious fresh, but it is also very good when dried, and tangy and wonderful when preserved in vinegar. Try in salads, with creamy dishes, and, especially, to season your favorite puree of cauliflower. Tarragon is also quite good with lamb and fantastic with roast chicken.

Thyme   The wonderful fragrance of thyme emanates from kitchens throughout the Mediterranean, as well as from bordering placid English gardens. As with most herbs, there are myriad varieties of thyme. The most common variety are tiny grayish-green leaves growing sparsely from thin stems. There's also lemon thyme, with its unmistakable aroma of lemon wafting from its herby leaves, which makes a soothing herb tea.

Watercress   These nippy dark-green leaves growing wild on the banks of cool streams and creeks can be found in most supermarkets year-round. Watercress adds a distinctive, refreshing flavor and texture to sandwiches and salads, and is wonderful as a bed for a juicy roast chicken (in this case, the heat from the chicken ever so slightly cooks only some of the watercress). It's also delicious sprinkled on a simple, rich chicken broth or pureed with potato soup for a fresh green soup.

The Savory Oils

Oil is the cooking medium that flavors a cuisine; its aroma and character touch almost every dish. The distinctive sprinkling of olive oil on a simple salad conjures up thoughts of the Mediterranean; a drizzle of sesame oil in a stir-fry adds an unmistakably Chinese flavor.

Duck and goose fat   Although it is a solid animal fat and not an oil, duck and goose fat so form the character of the cooking of southwest France that they belong in this list. The combination of half duck fat, half olive oil from the confit recipe in this book is delicious when used to cook potatoes, sauté onions for soups and stews, and so on.

Mustard oil   The oil of the mustard seed adds a distinctive flavor to everything that cooks in it. Yellow in color, it is hot when raw, slightly sweet when cooked. In southern India and Sri Lanka it is the favored cooking medium for vegetables and fish. Try Tamatar Chatni and Sarish Bata for a taste of this unique oil.

Olive oil   To discuss olive oil in this small space would be like discussing wine: One could not do it justice. There is too much to say.

When making simple dishes, especially salads, the quality of the ingredients becomes very important. A salad with no dressing other than a kiss of olive oil demands a good olive oil indeed. A rich, robust oil with much flavor can enliven the simplest dish.

When olive oil is specified in this book, I mean the first pressing, the dark-green essence crushed from the olive fruit of which it tastes, a cold, pressed oil that has the aroma of the olive and is labeled "extra virgin."

For cooking you can use a cruder, less fine oil, so you might consider keeping at least two types of olive oil in your pantry.

Find a brand that you like and make it your staple, trying others as you discover them. As with wine, a good purveyor is a great help; find one with a good selection who knows your taste. I like Greek-style olive oil for its heaviness and body; Tuscan olive oil is like none elsewhere. Spain also produces some very good olive oils, as does California. Ratto's International grocery (see listing in Mail Order Sources) offers an excellent selection of olive oils, as well as a very good house brand.

Sesame oil Dark amber in color, and tasting of toasted sesame seeds, sesame oil is used as a seasoning rather than as a cooking oil and gives its flavor to cuisines in parts of China, Japan, and Southeast Asia. It is so fragrant only a small amount is needed, and it's generally not used in cooking, as it has a tendency to turn bitter. Try a sprinkle on stir-fried broccoli with a bit of soy sauce or on noodles.

Walnut or hazelnut oil Walnuts and hazelnuts are pressed in France into nutty tasting oils used mostly on salads. Try as a dressing for mixed wild greens tossed with shredded roasted duck, either at room temperature or slightly warmed.

Aromatics and Special Ingredients

There is a world of spices in this book from sun-drenched cuisines everywhere. I've not described them all, for to do that would take an entire book, and there are so many other books that do the job. Instead, I've described some of the more unusual spices as well as ingredients that may be new to you.

Achiote A small, hard, red seed used often in Caribbean and Latin American cooking and available in markets with large Latin American and Caribbean clients. It has a mild, distinctive flavor and must be steeped in oil, strained or simmered in water, then ground into paste before using. Sweet Hungarian paprika may be substituted.

Ancho The ripe, red, dried form of the poblano chile (see also Chile). Mild, and rich in taste, it is soaked and pureed into sauce or toasted and ground into powder (see Chile powder). Purchase in Latin American grocery shops or by mail order.

Arborio rice Plump grains of rice from Italy for making risotto. (No other rice will do!) Only Arborio cooks up creamy yet firm and has a distinctive rice aroma. Specialty food shops and international grocers carry this, as do many supermarkets.

Asafoetida A yellow-colored resin, used in Indian cooking, especially in dahl dishes. It has an unpleasant smell that is not indicative of taste, and its unique ability brightens dishes to which it's added. Asafoetida is usually sold powdered in Indian food shops. If unavailable, it can be omitted.

Banana leaves The leaf of the banana tree; sold frozen or dried in Asian and Latin American grocers. To use, you must remove the stem (use scissors), then cut into the size and shape you want (generally a rectangle). To make more pliable, lightly toast over a flame or in an ungreased frying pan. Banana leaves are traditionally used to wrap all sorts of savory and sometimes sweet ingredients. In the Yucatan they are the wrappings used for tamales; in Indonesia, plain steamed rice; in Africa, spicy rice. Try Otak-Otak, the spiced fish dish wrapped in banana leaves, for an unusual and delicious Malaysian fish dish. No other wrapping gives the subtle flavor of the banana leaf; foil, however, seals the heat in well and may be used as a substitute.

Bean sauce A Chinese savory sauce based on fermented beans used as a seasoning ingredient for stir-fries, simmered dishes, and sauces. Substitute hot bean sauce if spiciness is desired. Available in most Asian food stores. Omit if unavailable.

Blue corn An indigenous New Mexican food, occasionally available in specialty shops around the country, but grown only in New Mexico (see Mail Order Sources). It is gray-blue in color, deep in flavor, like corn, but more earthy. Traditionally, it is eaten like polenta or made into thin paper bread called piki. It is also finely ground and flattened into startlingly colored tortillas. Serve blue-corn tortillas with a side dish of chile-stewed meat, vegetables, or fish.

California chile A mild, light-to-brick-red-colored chile, steeped and pureed into the basic chile sauce that blankets dishes throughout the American Southwest and much of Mexico. Also known as New Mexico chile, chile de ristra, and, sometimes, pasilla (though pasilla can also refer to the dark-colored, wrinkled chile negro). Purchase in Latin American grocery stores or by mail order.

Capers The buds of the Mediterranean caper plant. Pickled, they are salty and distinctive tasting, good for accenting such milder, bland dishes as cold sliced potatoes in vinaigrette or sautéed veal sprinkled with lemon and chopped parsley. Available in most supermarkets. Omit if unavailable, or substitute pitted Kalamata or Niçoise olives plus a squeeze of lemon.

Cellophane noodles Also known as mung-bean noodles or bean threads. Made from the starch of the mung bean. Whitish in color and brittle in texture when dry, they become translucent and chewy when soaked and cooked. Delicious in spicy salads or stir-fries. Purchase in Oriental food shops. No substitute.

Chèvre The French name for goat or goat cheese. (see Goat cheese).

Chick-pea flour The flour of the ground garbanzo bean. Nutty in flavor, it is enjoyed in India and parts of Southeast Asia. It is high in protein and forms the basis of many Indian savory fritters, as well as multicolored sweets. It is also a delicious binding ingredient for chopped meat patties. No substitute. Buy in bags or bulk from Middle Eastern or Indian food shops.

Chile oil A fiery condiment of peanut oil steeped with crumbled, hot red chiles or chile flakes. A delicious condiment along with a dash of vinegar and soy sauce for pot stickers or other Oriental dumplings. Buy in Oriental food stores.

Or make your own: Bring 1 cup (250 ml) peanut or other vegetable oil, plus 2 tablespoons (30 ml) of well-crumbled, small, hot dried red chiles, to a boil. Remove from heat and let cool to room temperature. Strain before using. Lasts almost indefinitely.

Chile powder All dried chiles may be made into a powder by toasting and grinding. The powder makes a delicious addition to soups and stews, and it is surprisingly good when added to garlic butter then spread on French bread. Keep an array of ancho, New Mexico, pasilla, negro, and other chile powders on your shelf to use as desired. Try Ancho Gnocchi with Corn Cream.

To prepare chile powder: Place chiles on a large cookie sheet and lightly toast in a 400° F. oven for 2 to 4 minutes, until they darken only slightly. Do not let burn or they will taste bitter. Remove and cool. They will become brittle as they cool.

Remove the stems (and seeds if you wish—they have some heat and not much flavor) and crumble the chiles into a clean, electric coffee grinder. Whirl off and on, as you would for making coffee, until it reaches the consistency you desire. A food processor works too, though not as well.

[Note: To clean coffee grinder, run a handful of raw rice through, grinding it finely. Pour rice out, dusting to be rid of it all, and coffee grinder will be ready to grind spices. Do the same to recleanse for coffee. If you grind spices often, it pays to invest in a second grinder: keep one for coffee, one for spices.]

Commercial chile powders vary a great deal. Avoid those that are pre-mixed with other spices and choose a pure one ground only from the chile. May be purchased in Latin American and international markets or by mail order.

Chile sauce The sauce prepared from steeping and pureeing the mild chiles. This is the basis for much of southwestern and Mexican cooking.

Although it is available in cans, it is too thin and acidic and is good only in emergencies. Far better to make it yourself.

Lightly toast 8 to 10 New Mexico or California chiles (or ancho or negro) over an open flame or in an ungreased frying pan over medium heat. Do not let burn. Pour boiling broth (or water) over the chiles in a saucepan or heavy bowl, cover and let steep for 30 minutes. Remove stems and puree in processor or blender. Chopped garlic and cumin and a squeeze of lime may be added as a seasoning. Strain sauce to rid it of the coarse bits of chile.

Chipotle chiles   The dried, ripe ancho chile, smoked then put up into a rich, red adobo sauce (which may also be used as a condiment or in cooking). Chipotles are very hot and full of smoky flavor. Buy them in Latin American grocery stores in small cans. No substitute.

Coconut milk   The liquid extracted from pressing and squeezing the flesh of the coconut, not the liquid contained inside (though that makes a refreshing drink on a hot day). Coconut milk may be purchased in a can, unsweetened, in sizes of approximately 6 and 12 ounces (186 and 372 ml). Although quality varies from one brand to another, they are generally quite good. Be sure to buy it unsweetened, however, as the sweetened coconut milk is good only for desserts and drinks.

If you wish to make coconut milk yourself, here is how to do it:

Choose a fresh coconut that makes a noise when you shake it. That means it has liquid inside, and it is a sign of freshness. Also, avoid moldy eyes, as that is a sign your coconut is less than optimum.

Open your coconut with an ice pick and a hammer: Puncture two of the eyes, then drain out the liquid and reserve for another use. Next, take the hammer and hit the coconut shell hard, about a third of the way down all the way around the shell. There is a sort of "fault line" here—something like the equator—which runs around the shell, and when you hit the right spot, a crack will form, opening the coconut right up.

Peel off the tough skin and shred or cut the coconut into 1- to 2-inch (25- to 50-mm) chunks. Place in food processor and puree, slowly adding very hot (just below boiling) water. You will need about as much water as coconut flesh. When mixture is thick and chunky, you are ready to extract the coconut milk. Set a strainer over a large bowl; line strainer with cheesecloth. Pour in as much of the mixture as possible, pressing hard with a large spoon to extract as much liquid as possible. Twist the cloth and squeeze the coconut hard, extracting the coconut essence. Repeat until all coconut mixture is gone. As it sets, it will separate and the top will be thick like cream; but you need only stir it together to recombine. Coconut milk can be made with dried coconut instead of fresh. Be sure to use the unsweetened kind, available in health-food and Middle Eastern or Indian food shops. Follow above directions, substituting dried coconut for fresh,

2 parts liquid to 1 part coconut. Using milk instead of water produces a richer product, more like the fresh. Coconut milk lasts about 3 days in the refrigerator and may be frozen very well.

Corn husks   The husks of the corn plant, dried and used to wrap tamales in Mexico and in parts of Latin America. They must be soaked about 1 hour, then wiped dry before using. Purchase in Latin American grocery stores. Banana leaves may be used to wrap tamales if corn husks are unavailable.

Couscous   The staff-of-life dish for much of North Africa, couscous is a type of milled wheat mixture much like tiny pasta. It is served ladled with spicy stews of meat and/or vegetable in Morocco, fish stews in Tunisia and Sicily, and, when mixed with milk and sugar, eaten as a sweet or for breakfast in Egypt. Available in Middle Eastern food shops and many supermarkets.

Dried chiles   Dried red chiles come in a dizzying array, and can be divided into two groups: hot and mild. There are two basic types of mild, dried red chiles: the smooth, thinner-skinned lighter and brighter in color chiles such as California, New Mexico, and, sometimes, pasilla; then there are the darker, thicker, and wrinkled-skin ones, rich and deep in flavor, such as ancho, negro, mulatto, and, sometimes, pasilla. The small, dried red chiles are generally the hot ones, called hontaka, cayenne, tepín, pequín, árbol, japonés, and, often, just hot peppers or hot dried chiles. The mild chiles are used to make sauces and as the basis for such dishes as chile con carne, stews, soups, enchiladas, and tacos, while the hot chiles are used as seasoning (see Ancho, California chile, and New Mexico chile). May be purchased in Latin American markets or by mail order. For a more complete listing and description, refer to my other book, *Hot & Spicy*, also published by Jeremy P. Tarcher, Inc.

Dried shrimp   Small shrimp salted, dried, and used as a condiment and cooking ingredient in Chinese, Latin American, and Southeast Asian cooking. They may be crushed into a salty sea-tasting powder and sprinkled over noodles, simmered into jalapeño-seasoned rice, or added to seafood stir-fry. Purchase in Oriental or Latin American food shops.

Feta cheese   The fresh, salty sheep's milk cheese that is eaten throughout the Middle East. In Cyprus it is lightly flavored with mint and black onion seeds; in Israel and Jordan it is spread over a chewy flat bread, drizzled with olive oil, and sprinkled with a mixture of thyme, cumin, sumac, and crushed hazelnuts called za'atar. In Iran it is eaten on bread for breakfast, perhaps with a handful of fresh herbs. Of course, throughout Greece and the Balkans it is a staple food eaten in salads, savory pastries, and on bread. Though it may be made from goat's or cow's milk, the best feta is made with sheep's milk and comes from Greece, Bulgaria, or Roumania. I do not care for the Scandinavian varieties at all.

A Cypriot brand, seasoned with mint and onion seeds, is occasionally available and delightfully different.

Filé powder   Also known as gumbo filé, this is the powdered, dried sassafras root. It is used in gumbos to give that traditional flavor and texture; but never use it together with okra, or the gumbo will be unpleasantly stringy.

Fish sauce   The seasoning liquid from the Far East made by fermenting fish in large vats. It is amber brown in color, with a salty, fishy tang and aroma. It is the main seasoning ingredient used throughout Southeast Asia and is also enjoyed in the Philippines. Purchase in Asian food stores. Chinese light soy sauce may be used as a substitute.

Ful misri   The small, brown fava beans that have been eaten in Egypt since the days of the Pharaohs. Used in the national dish, ful midammis. Purchase dried from Middle Eastern or international grocers. Ful midammis is sold in cans, and once you add extra seasoning is quite good.

Gingerroot   A pungent, knobby root, golden in color, with a strong but pleasing aroma and flavor. It has a spicy, hot quality and is also used dried, to mix with other spices, or as an ingredient in baked goods. Generally, fresh gingerroot is preferable to dried. To use, simply chop up and add to any stir-fry, along with the garlic and other seasonings. Although some recipes suggest peeling first, I generally don't. Fresh gingerroot lasts at room temperature in a dry climate for several weeks, and though some say it lasts longer frozen or refrigerated, I do not like its consistency then. Purchase in the fresh-produce section of most supermarkets and Oriental food stores.

Goat cheese   There are so many goat cheeses available to us these days that I scarcely know where to begin describing them. There are wonderful chèvres from France, caprino from Italy, and California chèvre from Sonoma County. When I refer to goat cheese in this book, I'm referring to a fresh, white cheese, slightly salty and tangy, occasionally covered with herbs. Though many supermarkets carry goat cheeses, the quality will be better at a cheese shop where they can monitor the conditions of the cheese more closely and where you can taste before you buy.

Grape leaves   The leaf of the grapevine. Best known in stuffed grape leaves, but also good stewed with lamb or wrapped around trout, then grilled. The leaves have a slightly tart, piquant flavor and aroma. Buy packed in salty brine from Middle Eastern grocers, or pick fresh in the spring (choose the smaller, more tender leaves). Also known as vine leaves. If using vine leaves from a jar, rinse well to remove the excess saltiness; if using fresh, blanch for 4 to 5 minutes, then rinse and dry before using.

Hominy   Corn soaked in lye to loosen the skins and swell the kernels. When ground, it is known as grits, a staple of the southern kitchen. Hominy is eaten throughout the American Southwest, simmered into spicy soups and stews, and served alongside savory grilled meats. Sold in cans, hominy is available in supermarkets; it is sometimes available fresh or frozen in Latin American food shops.

Hot bean sauce An incendiary paste of fermented beans and chiles, this sauce is used as a condiment and cooking ingredient in Chinese, Southeast Asian, and Korean cooking. Purchase in Oriental food stores. Some brands are much hotter than others so taste should guide you regarding amounts to use.

Jalapeño chile About 2½ inches (62 mm) in length, ¾ inch (18 mm) wide at top, and light to deep green in color, this fresh chile is hot. It is the most commonly available of the fresh chiles, and it is occasionally available in its ripe, red stage, when it is slightly sweeter and a bit less hot. It is glorious as a garnish then, or in a festive-looking salsa chopped finely and combined with green chiles, dressed with no more than a little lemon and salt. Available in Latin American and Asian produce markets as well as many supermarkets.

Jalapeños en escabeche Pickled jalapeño chiles, often with bits of carrot, onion, and so on. These are tangy and hot; a wonderful condiment or addition to simmering stews or soups. Try them tucked into any taco or on a sandwich made with a crusty French roll. Serrano chiles are also available en escabeche. Latin American grocery stores and most supermarkets sell these.

Kimchee Korean fiery pickled cabbage or other vegetables, often available in jars in the Oriental section of your supermarket. Sour and hot, enjoy a bit to season strips of grilled meat rolled up in a lettuce leaf with a spoonful of bland rice and a handful of cilantro or sukkat leaves.

Laos Also known as galangal, this flavoring is a root much like ginger-root, both in flavor and appearance. It is used fresh, dried in slices, or dried and ground into powder. Used often in Southeast Asia and North Africa. Purchase in Southeast Asian or Middle Eastern food shoips.

Lavender It blankets the hillsides of Provence, echoing its aroma in the dishes prepared there. Not just for sachets and bath oils, lavender buds add a flowery fragrance to cooking, and when used with thought, add a mysterious, exciting touch. Used in Herbes de Provence, the Provençal mixture of dried herbs, and also in the Moroccan spice mixture, Ras al Hanout. It is often sold loose, as herb tea.

Lemongrass (See Sereh.)

Light soy sauce A light, thin Chinese soy sauce with a clear, salty taste. Purchase in Asian food shops. May be used as a substitute for fish sauce. (See also Soy sauce.)

Masa harina Dried corn, finely ground into flour. Used as the basis for tortillas, tamales, and as a thickener for chile sauces and stews. It has a distinctive corn flavor and may be purchased in Latin American food shops. Quaker also makes a masa harina that is available in many super-markets.

Masoor dahl   Small, red lentils that cook up to a golden yellow mass. They have a wonderful hearty flavor and are used frequently in Indian cooking and in some Arabian cooking. A handful of masoor dahl makes a savory, earthy-tasting thickener for a spicy curry. Available in Indian or Middle Eastern food shops. Yellow split peas may be substituted for masoor dahl but must be cooked longer.

New Mexico chile   Also known as California chile, or chile de ristra, and, sometimes, pasilla. This brick-colored, mild-tasting chile is the basis for the chile sauces that form much of the cuisine of Mexico and the American Southwest. Available in Latin American food shops or by mail order.

Olive paste   Sold in small jars in Italian or international markets, most often made from black olives, but occasionally from green. It is strong and full of olive flavor, lovely when spread on a slice of bread buttered with unsalted butter and a little chopped raw garlic, or tossed in spaghetti with goat cheese and chopped fresh basil or thyme. Try Olive Sauce Provençal for an exquisite homemade version.

Olives   According to mythology, the olive tree was the gift of Athena to her adored city of Athens. Olives are an ancient food, beloved in the Mediterranean since the beginning of recorded time. For anyone who loves olives, there is a huge variety of tastes, textures, sizes, and colors to choose from, each a variation on the same basic fruit. I think of the endless rows of vats filled with olives in the marketplaces at Jerusalem, Toulon, or Cahors, where they were sold by small Arab boys, or at the monastery up the hill from where I lived in Greece. There, a wiry old woman cared for the precious icons, and in addition, she grew and preserved her delicious, small black olives. In this book I usually call for a Mediterranean-type olive to distinguish it from the California ripe kind, which does not really belong in any of these dishes. When I specify a fleshy black olive, choose which-ever is available at your local specialty or international food shop, or you might like to ask for Salona or Royal (also called Royal Victoria) olives. Firm olives generally mean a Kalamata type of olive, oval-shaped, with firm flesh and a strong, olive flavor. Niçoise olives are tiny and have the most wonderful flavor and aroma but very little flesh, so they are hard to pit. When using Niçoise olives in a dish, you really have to leave the pits in and warn your guests. Though there are uncountable varieties available throughout the Mediterranean, where they are the sustenence in a diet that can be very meager, there is only a small sampling of these olives here.

Orange-flower water   A flavoring ingredient made from distilling the flowers of the orange tree. It is fragrant and heavenly, delicious sprinkled over fruits and pastries, couscous, and spicy stews. (See also Rose water.)

Available in international grocery stores. It's also sold in liquor stores, since it is a flavoring ingredient in Ramos Fizzes.

Pancetta   The bacon cut of the pig, salted and peppered, and rolled into a cylinder. It's not smoked like our bacon but dry-cured. Purchase in Italian food shops and delicatessens and use in spreads, sauces, and soups.

Peppers   One of the most exciting things that has happened in the produce department of our supermarkets is the appearance of multicolored peppers in hues of red, yellow, green, purple, and even white. They brighten our table immensely, both in appearance and flavor. Raw, cooked, or roasted and peeled, they add a savory, festive touch. When buying, look for firm peppers with no soft spots, which indicate spoilage. For a festive and simple dish, arrange multicolored pepper halves in a baking dish, fill with your favorite stuffing, and bake until peppers have softened. The combination of colors and flavors is especially appealing.

For salads and hors d'oeuvres, the peppers should be roasted and peeled: Place over an open flame, directly on the heat of the stove, or broil under a high heat in the broiler, turning occasionally to char all sides. When charred evenly, remove and place in a plastic or small brown paper bag. Seal the end and let peppers steam for about 15 to 20 minutes. Remove from bag, one by one, and rinse in cold water. The skin should have separated from the flesh and should peel off easily (you don't have to remove every tiny bit of skin).

Plantains   Larger and less sweet than its cousin the banana, plantains *(plátanes)* must be cooked to be eaten. Cut into strips or slices, sauté, and serve alongside spicy black beans and rice; or boil until tender, then mash, and either fry into savory cakes or simmer in stews. Plantains are eaten throughout Latin America as well as parts of Africa. Purchase in Latin American or Caribbean food stores.

Poblanos   A medium-large, wide chile, the poblano looks much like a flat green bell pepper with a rich, meaty flavor and a thick flesh good for stuffing, as in chiles rellenos, or roasting and cutting into strips, simmering in sauces, or adding to chicken or vegetable dishes. Anaheim chiles, the large, long, green chiles may be substituted for poblanos, but they lack the poblano's depth. Available in Latin American produce stores and in some supermarkets.

Popadums   Crisp and savory, these lentil wafers are a favorite condiment in India, where they are enjoyed with meals or as a savory snack with tea. No feast would be complete without at least one variety of popadum. There is a huge variety available, each with its own flavoring and seasoning such as chile, black pepper, or garlic; some varieties are large, and some are quite small. They may be purchased in Indian or international grocers, and even in India they are store bought, since the preparation of popadums is long and involved.

When you purchase popadums look for flat wafers wrapped in cellophane or plastic. They must be cooked first to be eaten. For a crisp, potato-chip-like texture, popadums should be deep-fried: Simply fry briefly, one at a time, in a wok or other heavy frying pan with 1 to 2 cups of hot oil. They may also be heated in an ungreased frying pan (I sometimes heat popadums over a direct flame, taking care not to let them burn), and they may be broiled as well. Frying, however, produces the best texture. Try Chicken Shacutti.

Porcini Porcini mushrooms are fragrant and totally wonderful. Dried, they are savory; fresh, they are sublime. Used often in Italian cuisine. To reconstitute the dried porcini, place them in a bowl and pour very hot, but not boiling, water over them to cover; place a plate over the bowl and let stand for 15 to 25 minutes. Remove mushrooms and squeeze to remove any pieces of grit (though most should have soaked out and fallen to the bottom of the bowl); strain liquid to remove grit, then use as desired. Mushrooms may then be sliced and sautéed, made into a sauce, and eaten on pasta, chicken, veal, fish, or in soup (delicious in onion soup). Try Porcini Pasta, which incorporates porcini into the dough itself. Purchase in Italian markets or specialty food shops.

Raspberry vinegar Vinegars steeped with raspberries, blueberries, pear slices, and other fruits have enjoyed great popularity over the last several years, but their use actually dates back to Renaissance times. The tart vinegar is permeated with the aroma of fresh, sweet fruit, and it makes a fragrant salad dressing. Try raspberry vinegar with a little garlic and olive oil or pear vinegar with hazelnut oil. Purchase in specialty food shops.

Rice flour Finely ground rice used in Far Eastern and Middle Eastern cooking. Buy in Oriental, Middle Eastern, or international food shops. In Indian cooking, fritters are made of chickpea-and-rice flour, the chickpea to give flavor, the rice flour to give a certain crispness and lightness.

Rice noodles Also called rice sticks. Noodles made from the flour of rice, available dried and, occasionally, fresh. Fresh, they are thick and soft; dried, they are chewier. Dried rice noodles are available in a variety of widths. There are very thin vermicelli-like noodles, and ¼-inch (6-mm) wide, flat ones. I have usually specified the width a recipe calls for. Purchase in Oriental food shops.

Rose water The perfume-like essence of rose petals. Aromatic and flowery, it is nonetheless delicious when sprinkled onto couscous and savory North African and Indian dishes. Try a little sprinkled over fresh-fruit salad for an exotic touch. (See also Orange-flower water.) Available in Middle Eastern grocery shops; also in liquor stores, since the flower essences are used in certain alcohol-mixed drinks.

Sereh Also known as lemongrass, this looks much like a green onion, but is woodsier and drier. To use, peel up to the white base where the leaves branch out, then slice or chop the peeled part. Lemongrass is also available dried and ground, and is sold in small bottles labeled "sereh." Used in Southeast Asian cooking, and available wherever Indonesian, Thai, and Vietnamese ingredients are sold.

Serrano chile Small and narrow, usually sold green, but occasionally red is available. This is a very hot fresh chile. Use as you would a jalapeño. Buy in Latin American and Asian food shops as well as many supermarkets.

Soy sauce There are many types of soy sauce available, so when I refer to soy sauce I mean the medium-bodied one that is easily found, unless otherwise specified. Definitely sample tamari, with its rich flavor, or Chinese dark soy, with its heavier flavor and bouquet, as well as the Indonesian sweetened dark soy sauce. Each has its own distinctive character. Most Asian food stores will have a large selection of soy sauces.

Shiitake Large, woodsy mushrooms sold dried in Oriental food stores and used throughout Japan, China, and much of the rest of the Orient. Shiitake mushrooms have become quite popular in California over the last several years, and are often combined with Western ingredients for Western cuisine. Occasionally they are available fresh. Reconstitute the dried shiitake mushrooms the same way you would the porcini, or any other dried mushroom, by soaking in hot water.

Sukkat A fresh herb from the Korean cuisine, tasting somewhat like a cross between chervil and watercress. Can be eaten fresh, tucked into lettuce, rolled around savory meat and rice, or strewn atop salads, steamed rice and bulgogi, marinated shortribs of beef. Occasionally available in Korean markets. Watercress, chervil, or cilantro may be used in its place.

Sun-dried tomatoes Salty, like olives, and with the intense flavor of tomatoes. I prefer imported Italian tomatoes, although I have eaten wonderful Sonoma county homegrown and preserved ones. It's the domestic commercial ones that I find lacking in flavor, sweet when they should be vibrantly savory. Purchase imported sun-dried tomatoes in specialty food shops or international grocery stores, and enjoy in sauces, on pasta, in sandwiches, and especially on goat cheese. They are available in both dry-pack and in jars, marinated in flavored olive oil.

Sumac The spice made from the powdering of the dried, sour sumac berry (related to poison sumac but perfectly harmless!). Used in Middle Eastern cooking (especially Iranian) to give a slightly sour flavor; it adds a lively accent sprinkled onto steamed rice, topped with a juicy, marinated and grilled chicken breast kabob. Available in Middle Eastern grocery stores.

Szechuan peppercorns Slightly piny in aroma with a complex, almost minty heat. Szechuan peppercorns are delicious when added crushed into stir-fries, especially in tandem with the hotter chile. As the name suggests, this is eaten in the province of Szechuan, where fiery food is favored. Purchase in Oriental food stores.

Tahini   Also known as tahina, it is the paste of finely ground sesame seeds and oil so beloved throughout the Middle East as a savory sauce and dip when combined with garlic, herbs, and lemon. It is the basis for the ubiquitous sweet, halvah, as well. Buy in tins or jars in Middle Eastern food shops and some supermarkets.

Tamarind   Tart and sweet, tamarind is the pulp of the tamarind pod. It is used in Indian, Latin American, and Middle Eastern cooking, for a tart, sweet accent; it is stronger than lemon but not as sour. To prepare tamarind pulp from the whole pod, peel the husk and separate the seeds from the pulp (the pulp is gooey and thick). Place this in a bowl and cover with boiling water. Soak an hour or so, then mash with a spoon or your fingers and put it through a sieve. You can also buy the pulp semidried and pressed into a block. I find this very convenient to use—simply cut off the amount desired, simmer for 10 minutes or so in water (about 2 cups [500 ml] for a 2-inch [50-mm] chunk), then sieve. Tamarind concentrate is also very good and the simplest of all. It is of roughly the same strength as the pulp and should be thinned out with the same proportion of water as you would if using the pulp—depending on how much tamarind flavor you want. Use 1 part tamarind to 4 parts water as a guide. Purchase in Middle Eastern, Indian, or Latin American food stores.

Tomatillos   Also known as miltomates, this is the green-husk tomato of Mexico and Latin America, with a tart flavor that is so compatible with chile cuisine. May be purchased in cans if unavailable fresh, but fresh is preferred. Choose tomatillos that appear firm and are not dried-looking or soft. Remove their papery husks and wash well (they tend to be a little sticky under their husks). Cut into halves or quarters and bring to a boil in a small amount of water or broth. Simmer only a few minutes, until tender. Most recipes call for you to puree the tomatillos, because when cooked they become quite mushy. If using canned, drain and treat as cooked tomatillos. Available both canned and fresh in season at Latin American produce stores and in many supermarkets.

Wonton wrapper   Noodle squares sold in Oriental food shops for preparing your own wontons. They come in varying sizes, large ones for preparing egg rolls and round ones for gyoza (the Japanese dumpling). These easily available noodles are fantastic for preparing ravioli, dumplings, and all sorts of stuffed noodle dishes.

SALADS AND COLD DISHES

When I think of sun-drenched foods, my first image is of platters heaped with crunchy raw, and barely cooked vegetables, glistening with olive oil and just touched with lemon. I think of the simplicity of a scattering of pungent herbs or a plate filled with greens and seafood in spicy dressing. There are fresh aromatics, picked from the hillsides not many minutes ago, and marketplaces where the produce is scarcely older. Tender beets are pulled from the ground, the scarlet roots boiled and sliced, and served with the quickly steamed beet greens—all splashed with olive oil pressed by the old lady up the hill who took care of the monastery.

These are the sorts of everyday foods, honest and straightforward, that taste extraordinary. From the unexpected seasoning of fresh mint in Insalata di Patate Siciliano to the extravagant garnish of prosciutto and foie gras in Salade Auvergne and the humble but so delicious shredded cabbage in Lachano Salata, salads are platters of freshness, with flavors to awaken and enliven your palate.

Insalata alla Giovanni

Fresh Fennel, Radicchio, and Orange Salad

Italy

Fennel, radicchio, and orange combine so unexpectedly well in this rustic salad, the bitterness of the radicchio balancing the sweetness of the fennel, the fruitiness of the orange complementing the olive-oil dressing. It is a very refreshing salad, endearing in its simplicity and memorable for its fine flavor.

Usually served in winter around Christmastime, when oranges are at their sweetest and juicy best, its vivid colors are particularly festive. I like to serve it with chunks of crusty bread that are used to scoop up bits of the salad.

Serves 4

2 cups (500 ml) fennel bulb (finocchio), diced
1 to 2 heads radicchio, coarsely cut up
3 tablespoons (45 ml) extra-virgin olive oil
1 large sweet orange, peeled and cut into ½- to ¾-inch (12- to 18-mm) cubes

1. Combine fennel with radicchio and toss well with the olive oil.
2. Add orange pieces (and any of the accumulated juice), toss, and serve immediately. The small amount of orange juice combines with the olive oil for a delicate yet flavorful dressing.

ADVANCE PREPARATION: All ingredients may be cut up to 3 hours ahead of time and stored, lightly wrapped in the refrigerator. Combine just before serving.

Sabzi Khordan

A Plate of Fragrant Herbs

Iran

No Iranian meal is complete without a plate of herbs, fresh and fragrant, which each diner nibbles on between bites of richly cooked foods. In addition to tasting wonderful, their appearance on the table—a plate of green leaves and tender shoots—is so pleasing.

The variation that follows the recipe is a delightful salad that pairs the fresh herbs with salty feta cheese, and dresses it in rich olive oil and tart vinegar. Delicious with grilled meats and kabobs.

Serves 4

½ cup (125 ml) fresh mint leaves
4 to 5 green onions, trimmed
½ cup (125 ml) cilantro leaves
  Fresh tarragon leaves
½ (125 ml) cup watercress
6 to 8 tiny red radishes, still sprouting leaves

Simply wash and dry all the herbs; leave them whole. When dry, place on a plate for all to take as desired.

VARIATION: Make a delicious salad with the herbs listed above, coarsely chopped. Combine with coarsely chopped tomatoes, cucumbers, and feta cheese, and dress with olive oil and vinegar. If all the fresh herbs are not available, prepare the dish with those that are. Wonderful with simple grilled foods and crusty bread or soft pita.

Warm Peppers
Stuffed with Two Cheeses
Served on a Bed of Greens

I love the taste and texture of roasted and peeled peppers, tangy with marinade, stuffed plumply with creamy cheese, and heated to melting. The dish depends upon the peppers—yellow, red, green, or even poblano —each has a different flavor. The type of cheese you choose also determines the flavor—goat cheese for tartness, Jack or other mild white cheese for creaminess and soft melting.

This recipe pairs marinated peppers with soft, melted cheese filling. Served on a bed of mixed greens and herbs, it's quite delicious.

Enjoy as a first course, accompanied by crusty bread, and followed with Rôti de Porc Provençal or Weta Ki (Burmese Lemon-Baked Pork), or serve as a main dish along with a lively soup such as Soupe de la Nuit des Noces (see Index for each).

Serves 4 to 6

4 to 6 medium-sized red or yellow bell peppers, or a combination of both
3 tablespoons (45 ml) extra-virgin olive oil
1 tablespoon (15 ml) red-wine vinegar
1 clove garlic, chopped
4 cups (1000 ml) mixed greens and herbs (or, in season, a handful of fresh basil, 2 [30 ml] tablespoons chopped chives, and a few leaves of radicchio or Belgian endive, romaine, red-leaf lettuce, mâche, roquette, or arugula, torn up)
5 ounces (140 g) Montrachet cheese (chive, herb-coated, or plain)
4 ounces (112 g) mild cheese, such as Doux de Montagne or Jack, diced
Additional olive oil and vinegar
8 Kalamata olives

1. Roast peppers by laying them directly on the burners of a gas stove or broiling close to the heat source in an electric oven, until peppers are blistered and somewhat blackened; place in a plastic or small brown paper bag, seal the end and let stand for at least half an hour. Remove peppers one by one, and run under cold water. Blackened skin should peel right off. Remove stems and seeds, and discard.

2. Place roasted peppers in bowl. Add olive oil, wine vinegar, and garlic. Set aside to marinate while you prepare rest of dish, about 5 to 10 minutes. Letting it marinate longer can only make it more delicious.

3. Wash and trim greens and herbs. Dry and arrange on plates. Mix the two cheeses with a fork.

4. Stuff each marinated pepper with several tablespoons of the cheese mixture. Lay the stuffed peppers in a baking dish side by side and drizzle the rest of the marinade over them.

5. Broil or bake at the highest heat for 5 minutes or just until the cheese melts.

6. Serve immediately, each pepper atop a portion of the mixed greens and herbs. Dress with an additional bit of olive oil and vinegar, and garnish with Kalamata olives.

ADVANCE PREPARATION: Peppers may be roasted and marinated several days ahead of time. Stuff them several hours before serving, if desired. The salad greens may be prepared several hours ahead of time as well, but do not add dressing until ready to eat.

Fattoush

Salad of Cucumber, Tomato, Mint, Parsley, and Pita

Lebanon

Much like tabbouli, this salad combines fresh vegetables and herbs with a grain. But rather than bulgar wheat, fattoush is made with pita bread. This traditional dish no doubt originated as a way to use up leftover pita gone stale. Though the individual ingredients are familiar and easy to find, the dish itself is uncommon. It is lively with the flavor of juicy cucumber, tomato, and fresh mint, and a dressing of lemon and olive oil. A sprinkle of sumac adds a tart accent, and served with a dollop of yogurt this makes a delicious summer lunch.

Serves 4

2 medium-sized cucumbers, peeled and diced
2 medium-sized tomatoes, diced (1 cup [250 ml])
½ cup (125 ml) chopped fresh parsley
½ cup (125 ml) chopped fresh mint
3 green onions, thinly sliced
½ cup (125 ml) greens (Belgian endive, watercress, or curly endive), coarsely chopped
1 teaspoon (5 ml) salt
3 cloves garlic, chopped
⅓ cup (85 ml) extra-virgin olive oil
Juice of 3 lemons (⅓ cup [85 ml])
1 teaspoon (5 ml) sumac
3 pita breads
⅔ cup (170 ml) yogurt

1. Combine cucumbers with tomatoes, parsley, mint, green onions, and greens. Season with salt, garlic, olive oil, lemon juice, and sumac.

2. Break pita into 1½-inch (37-mm) pieces and lightly toast in 400° F. oven. Cool.

3. Toss vegetables with toasted pita just before serving and top each portion with a dollop of yogurt.

ADVANCE PREPARATION: The vegetables may all be chopped up to 2 hours ahead of time, but should be combined within half an hour of serving.

Zucchini Fritti Cotti

Marinated Zucchini with Mint

Italy

I once had a Hebrew teacher who kept the class's attention by reading aloud rather "spicy" novels in serial form. It worked well. I soon had mastered verb tenses I never knew even existed—just to know what was happening in the next installment. I am currently submerged in the Italian language, and my teacher does not read to us from questionable novels, but he keeps my attention by describing all sorts of enticing dishes his mother makes.

This is one of them, and it couldn't be simpler or more delicious. The mint lends a wonderful flavor to the zucchini, garlic, and vinegar. Serve as part of an antipasto or keep in the refrigerator to nibble on any time of day.

Serves 4

4 small- to medium-sized zucchini, thinly sliced
8 cloves garlic, chopped
¼ cup (60 ml) extra-virgin olive oil
2 tablespoons (30 ml) red-wine vinegar
3 tablespoons (45 ml) thinly sliced fresh mint leaves
    Salt and pepper to taste

1. Sauté zucchini with half the garlic in the olive oil, until zucchini is slightly golden-flecked but still crisp. Do not let the garlic brown too much or it becomes bitter.

2. Remove from pan and let cool. Then add remaining garlic, sliced mint leaves, vinegar, and salt and pepper.

3. Serve whenever you like, at room temperature or chilled.

ADVANCE PREPARATION: May be stored, covered in the refrigerator, for 3 to 4 days.

Insalata di Patate Siciliana

Potato Salad with Mint, Onion, and Capers

Italy

The fresh mint seasoning in this Sicilian salad reflects an Arab influence on Sicily's cuisine, which dates back to Phoenician traders and reveals itself also in Sicily's couscous and very sweet desserts.

This is the freshest of potato salads, aromatic with mint and savory with pungent onions and salty capers. A plateful with several slices of red tomato nestled next to it will convince you that outside your window the Italian fishermen are returning with their nets full.

This would be a great salad to accompany grilled salmon (especially a whole grilled salmon), or cold, thinly sliced rare roast beef or lamb.

Serves 4 (small portions)

6 to 8 medium-sized waxy new potatoes, red or white
½ medium-sized onion, finely chopped
¼ cup (60 ml) extra-virgin olive oil
¼ cup (60 ml) red-wine vinegar
1 clove garlic, chopped
　Salt and coarsely ground black pepper to taste
¼ teaspoon (1.5 ml) dried oregano leaves, crushed between your fingers
3 tablespoons (45 ml) chopped fresh mint leaves
1 teaspoon (5 ml) capers
1 medium-sized tomato, cut into wedges or slices for garnish

1. Boil or steam potatoes in their skins. When cool enough to handle, slice ¼- to ½-inch (6- to 12-mm) thick. (Peel only if desired.)

2. Toss with onion, olive oil, vinegar, garlic, salt and pepper, oregano, mint, and capers. Serve immediately, at room temperature, or let cool and serve chilled. Garnish with tomato wedges or slices.

ADVANCE PREPARATION: May be prepared up to two hours ahead of time and left at room temperature or chilled.

Insalata Gorgonzola

Italy

The combination of fresh greens and rich, pungent blue cheese is one of the world's best taste sensations. Gorgonzola is particularly smooth and elegant, but any blue cheese may be used instead.

Enjoy as a sunny lunch dish accompanied by crusty bread, or for supper followed by Vitello con Peperoni (see Index).

Serves 4

1 medium-sized Belgian endive, cored and cut into ½-inch (12-mm) slices
½ head of butterhead lettuce, torn into bite-sized pieces
¼ cup (60 ml) chopped chives, or ¼ cup (60 ml) chopped green onions
½ cup (125 ml) fresh basil, coarsely cut or left whole if not too large
3 tablespoons (45 ml) extra-virgin olive oil
1 to 2 tablespoons (15 to 30 ml) wine vinegar
4 ounces (112 g) Gorgonzola cheese, crumbled with a fork

1. Combine the endive, butterhead lettuce, chives, and basil.
2. Just before serving, toss well with the olive oil, then with the vinegar. Add crumbled Gorgonzola and serve immediately.

Panzanella

Italian Salad of Bread, Tomatoes, Olives, and Herbs

Italy

This rustic salad combines dry bread, rich, ripe tomatoes, fresh basil, garlic, and olive oil. Tote it along on a picnic without worry of ingredients spoiling. The robust tomatoes and herbs taste perfect amidst grass, sun, and sky.

Panzanella is prepared as a salad in Tuscany, but in Rome it is served as an open-faced sandwich, with the vegetables piled atop slices of crusty bread (see Variation). Since bread is eaten with almost every meal in Italy, and since there is always a bit remaining to go stale in the sultry air, no doubt this dish evolved as a way to use up those leftovers. If you have no leftover bread, this dish is delicious enough to warrant using fresh bread, dried in the oven.

Serves 4 to 6

⅔ pound (300 g) French or Italian bread (stale preferred), cut into 1½-inch (37-mm) cubes
2 cups (500 ml) water
2 medium-sized red (or 1 red and 1 yellow) bell peppers, toasted, peeled, and sliced thinly

8 cloves garlic, chopped

½ cup (125 ml) each of fresh basil and parsley, coarsely chopped

½ cup (125 ml) black Italian or Greek-style olives, pitted and halved

5 medium-sized ripe, red tomatoes, each cut into about 8 chunks

½ rib celery, minced

½ cup (125 ml) extra-virgin olive oil

3 tablespoons (45 ml) red-wine vinegar

Dash cayenne pepper, or ½ jalapeños en escabeche (see Aromatics and Special Ingredients)

Salt to taste

1. Place bread cubes in baking dish and bake at low temperature (250° F. to 300° F. oven) for 30 minutes or until dried out. When cool, pour water over them. Let the water stand 2 to 3 minutes, then drain and gently squeeze dry.

2. Combine the soaked bread chunks with the other ingredients.

3. Serve immediately, or even better, several hours later, after flavors have melded.

VARIATION: Roman Style Panzanella

1. Slice the bread about ½- to ¾-inch (12- to 18-mm) thick instead of cutting into cubes. Dry in the oven for only 10 to 15 minutes; if bread is already stale do not oven-dry at all, but lightly toast.

2. Combine the rest of the ingredients and spoon onto the slices of bread a few minutes before serving.

Provençal Chicken Salad

France

Juicy chicken, crisp-tender green beans, Mediterranean black olives, and roasted red peppers all tossed together in aïoli, the garlic-infused "butter of Provence." This is a fabulous chicken salad—my favorite!—and easy enough to throw together since I often rely on a neighborhood store that daily roasts succulent, crisp-skinned chickens. (I object to no shortcut as long as the ingredients are pure, and the finished product excellent.)

The intense garlic flavor belies the fact that it contains only one clove of garlic. Garlic possesses an aromatic oil that is released into the air as the walls of the cells are broken. Therefore, the more you crush it, the stronger the aroma will be. Cooking dissipates the aroma, so, because this one clove is raw and well crushed, it has robust garlic flavor.

Serve the salad on tender leaves of lettuce, garnished with wedges of tomatoes or strips of roasted red pepper, and accompany with crusty bread and a plate of boiled potatoes doused with an herb vinaigrette.

Serves 4

½ pound (225 g) green beans, trimmed and cut into 2-inch (50-mm) lengths
1 juicy chicken (about 2½ to 3 pounds)
½ cup (125 ml) Niçoise olives (see Note)
8 to 10 large leaves of butterhead lettuce
1 medium-sized red bell pepper, roasted, peeled, and cut into strips, or 1 ripe medium-sized tomato, cut into wedges

Aïoli:
1 clove garlic, peeled
1 egg
1 tablespoon (15 ml) mustard (Maille, Dijon, or Meiux)
Juice of ½ lemon (1 tablespoon [15 ml])
Dash cayenne pepper
½ cup (125 ml) extra-virgin olive oil
½ cup (125 ml) vegetable oil
Salt to taste

NOTE: Since Niçoise olives are too small to pit easily, you may choose a delicious Kalamata, pitted and halved

1. Steam or boil green beans quickly until crisp-tender and bright green. Rinse with cold water to stop the cooking process, and drain well.
2. Remove chicken from bones and cut into bite-sized pieces.
3. Make aïoli: In blender or processor puree garlic; add egg, mustard, and lemon juice and combine well. With motor running, slowly add vegetable oil and olive oil, until sauce is thick and lemon colored. Season to taste with salt.
4. Toss green beans and chicken together with the aïoli and add the olives.
5. Serve on a bed of lettuce, garnished with either the roasted red pepper strips or tomato wedges. Serve immediately.

ADVANCE PREPARATION: May be prepared several hours to a day ahead, although the final presentation on lettuce leaves and garnish of pepper or tomato should be done just before serving.

VARIATION: Add 1 bunch (about 1 to 1½ cups [250 to 375 ml] fresh sweet basil leaves to aïoli mixture and puree until a lovely green color.

Alu Ka Raita

Indian Potato and Yogurt

India

Fiery Indian curries need something to quell the flames, and cool yogurt raitas do just that. Sometimes fruit, other times spices, seeds, or nuts are added. I particularly like this combination of smooth boiled potato, crisp raw onion, startling chile, and herbal cilantro mixed together with cool, creamy yogurt.

Fewer potatoes make this an Indian-style condiment, more potatoes turn it into a potato salad. As a condiment, serve alongside Cumin Roast Lamb, perhaps accompanied by Sweet-and-Sour Tamarind Sauce. Alu Ka Raita is delicious dabbed with a spoonful of mango chutney—the sweet, spicy, and sour flavors achieve perfect balance (see Index for each).

Serves 4

6 medium-sized waxy new potatoes for a potato salad, or 3 waxy new potatoes for a condiment
1 small-sized white or yellow onion, finely chopped
1 to 2 fresh green jalapeños, thinly sliced
½ cup (125 ml) coarsely chopped cilantro
3 cups (750 ml) plain yogurt
Pinch turmeric
Cayenne pepper to taste
Black pepper to taste
Salt to taste

1. Steam or boil potatoes until just tender. Cool, then peel and dice.
2. Mix potatoes, onion, jalapeños, and cilantro in bowl. Mix yogurt into vegetable mixture.

3. Season to taste with turmeric, cayenne pepper, black pepper, and salt.
4. Serve chilled.

VARIATION: Indian-Flavor Burrito
The combination of lemony lentils, cool potatoes, and yogurt with spicy-sweet mango chutney all wrapped in a chewy flour tortilla is deliciously satisfying.
Heat a soft flour tortilla on an ungreased or lightly greased pan and wrap around Nimbo Dal; thick in consistency, add several spoonfuls of Alu Ka Raita, a dab of mango chutney, and roll up tightly. Serve immediately.

Karnabit bi Tahini

Arabian Cauliflower Tahini

Syria, Lebanon, and Jordan
My formative years in the Middle East left me with lifelong affection for tahini sauce. My first look at it horrified me—it had all the visual appeal of library paste—but I was soon won over by its creamy, nutty sesame flavor enhanced with spices and hot peppers.
Tahini, also called tahina, is sold in tins and jars. It is simply sesame seeds ground with a little bit of oil. The spicy sauce and dip made from this sesame paste is called tahini too, or tahini bi taratour, depending upon which country you are in.
Cold cauliflower has an affinity for this spicy sesame sauce. This dish is an authentic Arabian salad: Its rustic character perfectly suits my gaily painted red earthenware plates. Enjoy a small amount, served on a few leaves of lettuce, decorated with wedges of lemon and studded with black Middle Eastern olives. Excellent for a picnic.

Serves 4

1 large (or 2 small) heads of cauliflower, broken into florets or sliced ¾-inch (18-mm) thick
3 cloves garlic, finely chopped
½ cup (125 ml) tahini (see Aromatics and Special Ingredients), mashed with a fork to smooth lumps
1 teaspoon (5 ml) cumin
1½ teaspoons (8 ml) hot salsa, or to taste
Juice of 1 medium-sized lemon

3 tablespoons (45 ml) water
Salt to taste
6 to 8 butterhead lettuce leaves

1. Boil or steam cauliflower until just tender. Drain and set aside.
2. Mix garlic with tahini, then add cumin, salsa, and lemon juice and stir to a thick paste. Lighten by stirring in the water.
3. Combine cooled cauliflower with tahini mixture, season to taste with salt, and serve chilled or at room temperature on a bed of lettuce leaves.

ADVANCE PREPARATION: May be prepared from an hour to several days ahead. Place on the lettuce leaves just before serving.

VARIATION 1: Taratorlu Karnibahar
A Turkish way to prepare this salad is to steam a whole cauliflower, then spread it with the tahini sauce and decorate with black Greek olives, roasted and peeled red bell peppers, lemon wedges, and chopped parsley.

VARIATION 2: Lebanese Avocado Tahini Salad with Pistachio Nuts
My editor, Janice Gallagher, suggested this dish of avocado and tahini. It is rich and wonderful. Mash an avocado and combine with tahini sauce as in Karnabit bi Tahini. Serve topped with toasted unsalted pistachio nuts and accompany with fresh, soft pita bread.

Southeast Asian Vegetable
Salad with Cucumber Dressing

Southeast Asia

Throughout Southeast Asia raw and cooked vegetables are heaped onto platters and doused with bright savory dressings—some fiery from chile, some tart with lime. These dishes are the mainstays of the diet, eaten every day in one form or another, accompanied by rice and, often, fish.

This salad is my version of such a dish—crunchy, fresh, tart, and savory, a beautifully colorful still life.

Serves 4

Salad:
½ head of red cabbage, thinly sliced (about 2 cups [500 ml])
1 bunch raw spinach, washed and torn into 1-inch (25-mm) pieces

1 medium-sized cucumber, thickly sliced (remove peel only if it is bitter)
1 medium-sized carrot, shredded on the large holes of a shredder
1 medium-sized red bell pepper, thinly sliced

Cucumber Dressing:
2 cloves garlic, chopped
1 medium-sized cucumber, peeled and diced
¼ cup (60 ml) vegetable oil
⅓ cup (85 ml) red- or white-wine vinegar
3 tablespoons (45 ml) sugar
Salt and pepper to taste
Nuoc Nam or light soy sauce to taste
Garlic-chile paste or hot salsa to taste
½ cup (125 ml) coarsely chopped dry roasted peanuts, preferably unsalted

1. Arrange red cabbage, spinach, cucumber, carrot, and red bell pepper on platter.

2. Prepare dressing: In blender or processor puree garlic and cucumber. Add oil, vinegar, sugar, and salt and pepper. Blend until smooth. As it stands, dressing will separate and need only be stirred to recombine.

3. Serve salad with cucumber dressing and nuoc nam and other hot condiment. Top with a sprinkling of roasted peanuts. Enjoy immediately.

ADVANCE PREPARATION: Dressing may be made up to 2 days ahead of time and stored tightly covered in refrigerator.

VARIATION: Any fresh raw vegetable is delicious in this salad, as are cubes of golden-fried tofu. Toasted sunflower seeds may be used instead of peanuts.

Diced Eggplant in Spicy-Tart Sauce

Morocco

The variety of eggplant dishes seems endless; just when I think I've tasted or heard about all the possible eggplant combinations I discover another delicious one! Cooks in the Mediterranean and Middle East excel in preparing this smooth, rather bland vegetable. There, they roast their eggplant and mash with seasonings, or fry it and layer it with vinaigrette. This eggplant appetizer is strikingly unusual in taste. Diced and sautéed in olive oil until tender, it is then tossed with a tangy sauce made from chopped lemon, olives, pepper, and cumin. Serve at room temperature, tucked into warmed pita bread.

Serves 4

    1 **large-sized eggplant, or 2 small- to-medium-sized eggplants, unpeeled, cut into ¾-inch (18-mm) cubes**
  ½ to ¾ cup (125 to 180 ml) olive oil, or as needed
    1 cup (250 ml) prepared lemon-chile-olive sauce for Pinchitos (see Index)

1. In skillet, sauté eggplant cubes in olive oil until lightly browned, turning and mashing slightly as they cook.
2. Combine browned eggplant with sauce from Pinchitos and toss to coat completely. Serve at room temperature.

ADVANCE PREPARATION: Lasts 3 to 4 days tightly covered in refrigerator.

Thai Salad

Thailand

All the world loves wild herbs. Foraging for them gives reason and delight to an afternoon walk. In Greece such greens are cooked and doused with extra-virgin olive oil and freshly squeezed lemon, then eaten at room temperature. In France, wild herbs are frequently tossed with the cullings from a garden, the tiny vegetables that must be picked to make room for the others to grow.

The following delicate tangle of greens is from Thailand, where the vegetation is lush and the assortment of wild edibles is incredibly varied. These bits and pieces—tiny shoots, tropical leaves, and flowers—are added to the evening's salad. Sometimes the Thais even enjoy fragrant flowers such as rose petals scattered atop their greens. Of course, you must know the flora of your area, for some plants are poisonous. If you have a garden, though, the little thinnings are particularly delicious—tiny carrot tops (and tiny carrots, too), baby lettuces, onion shoots, spinach or chard leaves, citrus leaves, sweet basil, and so on.

What could be a more enticing dish for entertaining than a large Thai Salad, resplendent with crisp textures, savory tastes, and spicy chile, and festooned with flowers?

Serves 4

1 ounce (28 g) cellophane noodles, also called mung-bean noodles or bean threads (see Aromatics and Special Ingredients)
4 ounces (112 g) ground pork
1 chicken breast (4 ounces [112 g] of meat)
4 ounces (112 g) shrimp, peeled and cleaned
2 tablespoons (30 ml) cloud ears or tree fungus
6 large leaves of lettuce (romaine, butterhead, or red-leaf)
2 green onions, finely sliced
1 medium-sized cucumber, peeled and diced
10 to 15 fresh mint leaves
½ cup (125 ml) torn or coarsely cut up wild greens and whole
  tiny trimmings (or substitute shredded raw spinach)
¼ cup (60 ml) coarsely chopped dry-roasted, salted peanuts

Dressing:
3 tablespoons (45 ml) fish sauce or light soy (see Aromatics and
  Special Ingredients)
1 fresh red or green serrano chile, chopped or thinly sliced
1 clove garlic, chopped
  Juice of 2 limes (about ¼ cup [60 ml])
1½ teaspoons (8 ml) sugar

Garnish:
3 Thai Chile Flowers (see my other book, *Hot & Spicy,* for
  directions) (or substitute 1 fresh red jalapeño, sliced into
  long, thin strips)
6 cloves garlic, coarsely chopped and lightly fried until golden
6 shallots, chopped and lightly fried until golden
¼ cup (60 ml) cilantro leaves
  Several fresh nasturtiums, if available (optional)

1. Soak cellophane noodles in cold water to cover for 5 to 10 minutes
to soften. Drain, then add to boiling water and cook until tender, about
5 minutes. Some brands will take longer to cook, and some will be tender
almost immediately. Drain and cut into 2-inch (50-mm) lengths. Set aside.
2. Simmer pork in water to cover until pork is no longer pink inside.
Drain, then break up into small pieces and set aside. Simmer chicken until
opaque and tender. Drain and set aside. Cook shrimp by covering with
cold water, bringing to boil, cooking for 1 minute, then turning off heat
and letting them steep in the water, cooling as the water cools.
3. When chicken is cool, shred or cut into matchsticks; when shrimp is
cool, chop coarsely
4. Soak cloud ears in water to cover (cloud ears come in large and small

size—if using the large one, cut into ½- to ¾-inch (12- to 18-mm) pieces. Set aside.

5. Arrange lettuce leaves on a platter. Top with noodles, pork, chicken, shrimp, onions, cucumber, cloud ears, mint leaves, shredded greens, and peanuts.

6. Combine dressing ingredients and pour over salad.

7. Garnish with chile flowers (or sliced red chile), fried garlic and shallots, cilantro leaves, and nasturtiums, if available.

VARIATION: Instead of the tiny thinnings, wild greens, or shredded spinach, strew the salad with unsprayed rose petals—use the petals from 2 to 3 fragrant roses.

Salade Auvergne

Lettuce and Roghetta with Tarragon, Prosciutto, and Foie Gras

France

How wonderful are the extravagant garnishes of prosciutto and foie gras on a bed of rustic greens! The bits of rich meat combine with the light fresh greens, tossed with flavorful oil and tart tarragon vinegar, to create a special salad indeed. This balance of rich and slightly acidic is a traditional taste in this region of France, the Auvergne. Here, you will find salads based on duck or pork confit, grilled duck breast, warm sautéed poultry livers, or mussels paired with vegetables such as the homey cabbage or elegant wild mushroom. While this recipe calls for prosciutto, in the Auvergne you would use a local salt-cured ham, unavailable here.

The striking simplicity of this salad charms completely, and begs to be served on its own with no other accompaniment, except crusty bread for spreading with bits of the foie gras, dipping into the dressing and sandwiching tiny pieces of the green. Though at its best with fresh tarragon, I've happily prepared it with tarragon preserved in vinegar. If roghetta is nowhere to be found, you could substitute watercress leaves, although then it will be a different salad.

Serves 4 to 6

1 small- to medium-sized head of curly endive, cleaned and cut into 2- to 3-inch (50- to 75-mm) pieces

¼ to ½ cup (60 to 125 ml) roghetta leaves (see Aromatics and Special Ingredients)

2 teaspoons (10 ml) fresh tarragon, or 1 teaspoon (5 ml) tarragon leaves preserved in vinegar (do not substitute dried)

2 ounces (56 g) prosciutto, cut into thin slices, then torn into 2- to 3-inch (50- to 75-mm) pieces

2 to 3 ounces (56 to 84 g) foie gras, diced or sliced (be sure to buy the foie gras whole, or more likely, in pieces and re-formed. Do not use pâté de foie gras for this salad)

3 tablespoons (45 ml) extra-virgin olive oil

1 tablespoon (15 ml) tarragon vinegar

1. Arrange curly endive on a platter or on individual plates. Garnish with roghetta, tarragon, prosciutto, and foie gras.

2. When ready to serve, drizzle with the oil and vinegar.

Lachano Salata
Cabbage Salad

Greece

I once spent an entire winter on the island of Crete, deep under the spell of life in Greece. As the thermometer dipped (though the sun remained brilliant and the sky a deep blue) tender lettuce became scarce in the village shops. Cabbage took its place in those wonderful Greek salads. I never truly appreciated crunchy raw cabbage until then.

Here is the simplest of salads—unpretentious, and very, very good. The humble cabbage is thinly sliced, lavished with fruity olive oil, and topped with crumbled feta cheese and wild, mountain oregano or thyme. Serve with fresh, crusty bread to soak up any dressing left on the plate.

An excellent salad to accompany anything grilled: lamb, trout, or brochettes, or something savory in a sauce, such as Kefta (Moroccan Meatballs; see Index).

Serves 4

1 medium-sized green cabbage

½ cup (60 ml) Greek-style black olives, either firm Kalamatas or the fleshier Salonicas

2 to 4 ounces (56 to 112 g) feta cheese, cubed or coarsely crumbled

3 tablespoons (45 ml) extra-virgin olive oil

1 tablespoon (15 ml) wine vinegar (or lemon juice to taste)

¼ teaspoon (1.5 ml) dried oregano, or ¼ teaspoon (1.5 ml) thyme leaves

1. Remove cabbage core and slice thinly.

2. Make a bed of the sliced cabbage. Garnish with the olives and feta cheese.

3. Dress with olive oil and vinegar or lemon juice, then sprinkle with the oregano or thyme, crumbling the herbs between your fingers to release their full aroma.

4. Serve immediately.

Pommes de Terre Antiboise

France

From the Côte d'Azur town of Antibes comes this dish of salty, silky anchovies draped over creamy potatoes, drizzled with olive oil and a bit of vinegar. It is one of those simple, but perfect combinations. The recipe serves 1 rather than 4, since it's a dish I usually eat alone or with a close friend.

Serves 1 to 2

2 to 3 medium-sized waxy new potatoes, boiled creamy, firm, and peeled

4 or 5 anchovy fillets, or as desired

1 or 2 tablespoons (15 or 30 ml) olive oil

1 or 2 teaspoons (5 or 10 ml) red-wine vinegar

Chopped parsley to taste

1. Arrange boiled potatoes on a plate, cut into wedges or slices, or leave whole. Garnish with anchovy fillets, drizzle with olive oil and vinegar, then sprinkle with parsley.

2. Serve immediately.

Roasted Red Peppers with Fennel

Italy

While driving along the coast, crossing the lonely mountaintop border, and catching my first glimpse of Italy long ago, we came upon a village and marketplace. We bought provisions for a seaside picnic, and there we feasted on tiny, pan-fried fresh sardines and this salad, with the sharp scent of the sea in our nostrils and damp sand between our toes.

Serves 2

1 red bell pepper, roasted, peeled, and thinly sliced
1 large bulb fresh fennel, thinly sliced (tossed with lemon juice
   to prevent browning)
3 tablespoons (45 ml) extra-virgin olive oil
1 tablespoon (15 ml) red- or white-wine vinegar or lemon juice
4 to 5 black Greek- or Italian-style olives, whole

1. Arrange peppers on a platter next to sliced fennel. Dress with olive oil and vinegar or lemon juice.
2. Garnish with olives and enjoy immediately.

VARIATION: If you have no time to roast and peel the pepper, slice and enjoy raw. Its sweetness will accent the flavor of the fennel.

Roasted Red Peppers with Chick peas, Anchovies, and Carrot

France

A sunny hors d'oeuvre salad reeking with garlic. Serve with a selection of other salads, accompanied by crusty bread for a sensual and satisfying lunch. As a first course, follow with a tureen of rustic soup or a rare roasted leg of lamb.

Serves 4

  1 cup (250 ml) cooked chick peas
  4 cloves garlic, finely chopped
  ½ cup (125 ml) extra-virgin olive oil
  ¼ cup (60 ml) red-wine vinegar
  ½ teaspoon (3 ml) dried oregano leaves, crumbled between
     your fingers, or ½ teaspoon (3 ml) fresh thyme leaves
  3 tablespoons (45 ml) chopped parsley
     Salt and pepper to taste
  3 to 4 red bell peppers or a mix of red and yellow peppers
  1 medium-sized carrot, coarsely grated
 10 anchovy fillets

1. Combine chick peas with 2 cloves garlic, ¼ cup (60 ml) olive oil, 2 tablespoons (30 ml) vinegar, oregano or thyme, parsley, and salt and pepper to taste. Let marinate for at least ½ hour.

2. Roast peppers over direct flame or under a broiler on high heat until blistered. Place in plastic or small brown paper bag and seal end. Let steam in bag for 30 minutes, then remove and run under cold water. Rub off the skin; it should remove easily where charred. Slice peeled peppers thinly.

3. Arrange peeled peppers on a platter, next to them arrange the chick peas, and next to them the carrots. Garnish with anchovy strips in a crisscross pattern.

4. Sprinkle with marinade, and serve.

ADVANCE PREPARATION: May be assembled an hour or so before serving. The chick peas and peppers last up to 1 week, marinated and tightly covered in the refrigerator.

Salad of Mango, Chile, and Peanuts

South Pacific

Sweet mango combines exotically with volatile chile oil and crunchy, salty peanuts. Serve with grilled fish and rice, Pollo Pibil, or Sopa de Mariscos (see Index for both).

> 2 ripe but firm mangos, peeled and cut into slices
> Juice of ½ lime (2 teaspoons to 1 tablespoon [10 to 15 ml])
> ¼ teaspoon (1.5 ml) chile oil (see Aromatics and Special Ingredients)
> 1 tablespoon (15 ml) coarsely chopped dry-roasted peanuts

1. Arrange mango slices on plate. Sprinkle with lime juice and chile oil.
2. Top with a scattering of peanuts and serve immediately.

VARIATION: Steamed shrimp would be a delicious as well as beautiful addition to this salad.

Some Simple Salad Ideas

Pantaria Salata   This makes a nice part of the Greek selection of tidbits called mezes. Steam beet roots and beet greens separately, each until just tender. Let cool, then arrange on the same platter, drizzled with olive oil, salt, and a squeeze of lemon. Serve at room temperature, along with some olives, a few anchovies, some taramosalata, and a few chunks of feta.

Sliced sweet orange with thin red onion slices, dressed with olive oil, and sprinkled with chopped fresh rosemary.

From southwest France   A splash of red wine on any mixed green salad, dressed with olive oil and a dash of salt.

Insalata Caprese   When tomatoes are ripe and sweet this is on nearly every menu in Rome—the richly red tomatoes are sliced and arranged next to buttery, soft, fresh mozzarella cheese (nothing like the rubbery domestic stuff), drizzled with extra-virgin olive oil, and seasoned with fresh oregano or basil.

Surprisingly, throughout Italy you'll find avocado salad on nearly every restaurant menu, but it's not surprising really, when we think of how Italy has embraced that other New World food, the tomato. Arrange slices of avocado next to roasted red pepper slices; dress with a vinaigrette made with whole-seed mustard.

Belgian Endive and Roquefort   The slight bitterness and astringency of endive (or radicchio) is perfect with rich, pungent blue cheese. Toss the endive, cut up or whole, with blue cheese of choice, and dress with olive oil and vinegar.

Hearth-roasted potatoes, cold, are delicious spread with Olive Sauce Provençal (see Index).

Marouli Salata   Thinly slice, almost shred, romaine lettuce leaves and toss with chopped fresh dill and green onions. Then toss with olive oil and lemon juice, and salt and pepper to taste. A favorite everyday salad on Crete.

For a salad from the Spanish countryside, toss curly endive with fresh tarragon leaves (or those preserved in vinegar) and lots of pimento-stuffed green olives. Dress with fruity olive oil, wine vinegar, and 1 or 2 cloves of chopped raw garlic.

All-American Potato Salad with Purslane   To your favorite simple potato salad add lots of (1 cup [250 ml] for 4 servings) purslane (see The Fresh Herbs and Leaves).

SOUPS

The soups of Northern climes are long-simmered affairs, with chunks of simmering meat, hearty grains, and filling legumes, often smoothed with great quantities of sour or sweet cream.

Sun-drenched soups are lighter and brighter in flavor. They are smooth essences of vegetables such as Artichoke Soup à la Alice B. Toklas or a flavorful broth with bits of tiny pasta floating on it such as Soupe de la Nuit des Noces. They may be filled with fresh leaves of salad as in a Vietnamese soup-salad, Phõ Bò, or based on a grain but enlivened with a flurry of fragrant herbs and a jolt of lemon, such as the Armenian Tanabour. These soups are full of flavor, not meant to stick to the ribs and protect against the cold, but to delight the palate and nourish the body.

Initially, a cauldron of simmering water or broth was the perfect way of stretching a few vegetables, a leftover bone, or the fish from the bottom of the net that were too small to make a meal of by themselves. It was an economy, yes, but as necessity is the mother of invention, so has this economy given birth to a rich variety of soups.

When making soup, the hard-and-fast rules evaporate. Perhaps a few leeks would be nice . . . a handful of rice . . . a bunch of wild herbs, and a lone, sulking tomato. In Europe, and probably most of the world, soups are often based on water, and the flavor of the broth does not interfere with the taste of the vegetables. Of course, this is an economy, too, but the vegetables are so flavorful, tasting fresh and sun-ripe, that the soups become rich and flavorful as well. Here, I need to cook a soup in broth since store-bought vegetables have less flavor, but if you grow your own vegetables, and they sing with flavor, you might use water instead of broth in some of the lighter vegetable soups.

Iced Triple-Garlic Soup from the Midi

France

It was oppressively hot that day in Provence. The air seemed thick and stifling. I couldn't imagine how anything could pick me up from my stupor, least of all food. Everything irritated me, especially how cool and chic the French women looked in the heat, while I was pink and shiny and very wilted. Ever the gracious guest, I did my best to appear enthusiastic when the first course was served. *"Comme le gazpacho,"* my hostess said, "wonderful for days such as this." The cool garlic essence was accompanied by a plate of garlic croutons, finely chopped celery, and diced tomatoes to add to the soup as desired. It was wonderfully refreshing, and a delight to discover, for I'd tasted many garlic soups, but they had always been served warm.

This fragrant bowlful is called Triple-Garlic Soup because of the three types of garlic used—long simmered and sweet; raw, pungent chopped garlic; and the garlic croutons. The wallop in this soup is stronger than it tastes—enjoy it with people who are aficionados of the aromatic bulb. The other morning I poured myself a big mugful for breakfast, leftover from the night before. It was heavenly for me, but I smelled like a delicatessen for several days.

Serves 4

Garlic Croutons:
   ¼ to ½ loaf French bread
   3 tablespoons (45 ml) extra-virgin olive oil, or as needed
   2 cloves garlic, chopped

Soup:
   1 large head of garlic, cloves separated and peeled, but left whole
   1 quart (1 l) rich chicken or vegetable broth
   2 eggs, beaten

½ clove garlic, finely minced
⅓ cup (85 ml) whipping cream
  Juice of ¼ lemon (1½ teaspoons [8 ml])
2 tomatoes, chopped
1 stalk celery, finely chopped
  Garlic Croutons

1. To make Garlic Croutons: Cut French bread into ½- to ¾-inch (12- to 18-mm) cubes. Toss with olive oil and garlic.
2. Cover the bottom of a shallow baking dish with 1 layer of croutons, then bake at 350° F. until golden brown, about 15 minutes. I often make a larger batch of garlic croutons than needed for this dish, since they are delicious added to salad, fish soups, omelets, or just to nibble on.
3. To make soup: Simmer whole garlic cloves, covered, in broth for 15 minutes or until garlic is tender and soft.
4. Remove garlic cloves to a blender or processor and puree with eggs, ½ clove minced uncooked garlic, and cream. Remove from stove and slowly stir mixture into the hot broth. Return to heat, stirring constantly until slightly thickened. Season with a dash of lemon juice. Strain, then chill.
5. Serve accompanied by a platter of tomatoes, celery, and Garlic Croutons for each person to take as desired.

Puree of Corn and Red-Chile Soup

Arizona and New Mexico

Seldom have I tasted a soup so mysterious—both suave and gutsy at the same time. Fresh sweet corn, yes, but thickened with bits of earthy corn tortilla. Deep spiciness and red color are created by adding mild New Mexico red chiles, and this smooth, unusual bowlful is topped with a dollop of thick sour cream. If I close my eyes when I eat this soup I am transported to a mesa at dusk.

Serve with crusty bread as a first course and follow with Pollo Pibil, and for dessert, Sunset Sorbet (see Index for both).

Serves 4

4 cups (1 l) rich chicken or vegetable broth
4 New Mexico dried red chiles
1 medium-sized onion, chopped

3 cloves garlic, chopped
2 slices bacon, diced
¼ teaspoon (1.5 ml) cumin
2 cups (500 ml) corn
3 corn tortillas, cut into small pieces
1 cup (250 ml) milk
½ cup (125 ml) sour cream, or as desired, for garnish

1. To make chile sauce, heat 1 cup (250 ml) of broth and pour over chiles. Cover and let soak to soften, about 30 minutes. Puree in blender or processor.

2. Then sauté onion and garlic lightly together with the diced bacon. When soft, sprinkle in the cumin and cook 1 or 2 minutes longer. Add the corn, cut-up tortillas, reserved chile sauce, and remaining broth, then bring to a boil. Reduce heat and simmer until tortillas soften.

3. Puree soup, then strain. It is important to strain this soup, as its smooth consistency combined with robust flavor are what make it so intriguing.

4. Add milk to strained soup, return to heat, and warm to almost boiling, then serve immediately, each serving garnished with a spoonful of sour cream.

ADVANCE PREPARATION: Soup may be prepared up to a day ahead of time.

Minestra alla Zingara

Pureed Red-Pepper Soup with Lemon Cream

Italy

Sun-sweetened, ripe, red peppers, sautéed with tomatoes and simmered in rich broth, are the basis of this incredibly good soup. Unlike most purees this one has texture; you can taste the tiny bits of juicy sweet pepper and tomato. Floating atop this scarlet bowlful is a spoonful of lemon-scented cream, just the right accent for this vividly flavored soup.

The name means "gypsy soup" in Italian, although it is not a traditional Italian soup—I named it to conjure up a flamboyant image that would describe this lively soup.

Serve for a sun-drenched lunch or supper accompanied by a salad of tomatoes, avocado, and crisp-tender green beans on a bed of salad leaves, strewn with a few herbs, and dressed in extra-virgin olive oil and vinegar. Also, enjoy crusty bread and a rich cheese such as St. André.

Serves 4

Soup:
1 medium onion, chopped
3 cloves garlic, chopped
2 tablespoons (28 g) unsalted butter
2 medium-sized red bell peppers, coarsely chopped or sliced thinly
1 cup (250 ml) chopped tomatoes (canned is fine)
1 tablespoon (15 ml) ouzo or Pernod
2 teaspoons (10 ml) paprika
½ teaspoon (3 ml) Herbes de Provence (see Index)
2 cups (500 ml) rich chicken or vegetable broth
½ cup (125 ml) sour cream
Lemon Cream

Lemon Cream:
½ cup (125 ml) sour cream
Juice of ½ lemon (2 teaspoons [10 ml])
Grated rind from ¼ lemon (about ⅛ teaspoon [.5 ml])
Dash cayenne pepper

1. Lightly sauté the onion and garlic in butter until softened, then add peppers and cook over medium heat until peppers are softened.

2. Add tomatoes, ouzo, paprika, Herbes de Provence, and broth and cook over medium-high heat until mixture comes to a boil.

3. Puree soup, leaving a little texture of the red peppers. Stir sour cream in a bowl and add several spoonfuls of the soup to it, stirring until it is smooth. Add this to the soup, continuing to stir the soup until it is smooth.

4. Meanwhile prepare Lemon Cream: Stir together all ingredients.

5. Serve soup immediately, each portion topped with a spoonful of Lemon Cream.

ADVANCE PREPARATION: Soup is just as good the next day, reheated. Store tightly covered in the refrigerator, and top with lemon cream just before serving. Lemon cream may be prepared up to 3 days ahead of time.

Potage de Cahors

Pureed White-Bean Soup with Woodsy Mushrooms

France

Pureed bean soup may not sound very sun drenched, but when I tasted this soup at a sunny terrace luncheon in southwest France I revised my opinion of what a Northern, wintry soup was. The thyme, the unexpected mushroom essence, and the smooth texture will forever remind me of sitting beneath a red-and-white umbrella, gazing out onto the medieval town of Cahors.

The soup I had that day was made with smoked goose carcass, the mushrooms were cèpes, and the garnish was extravagant—strips of smoked goose. Here in California I use a ham bone, and the mushrooms are shiitake. Adding the garnish of smoked goose is up to you, but I prefer the rich taste of a tiny pat of butter. It smooths the soup nicely and, since there are no other fats in the dish, it feels more sinful than it really is.

Serves 4 to 6

1½ cups (375 ml) white beans, presoaked overnight and drained, or covered with water, brought to a boil, removed from the heat, and allowed to stand for 1 to 2 hours, covered
1 quart (1 l) beef or rich vegetable broth
1 ham bone with a bit of meat still left on, but not much fat
2 teaspoons (10 ml) fresh thyme leaves, or 1 teaspoon (5 ml) dried (see Note)
1 medium-sized carrot, diced
1 large baking potato, peeled and diced
3 cloves garlic, coarsely chopped
1 to 2 ounces (28 to 56 g) dried shiitake mushrooms (about ¼ cup [60 ml]) (see Aromatics and Special Ingredients)
1 cup (250 ml) very hot, but not boiling, water
1 cup (250 ml) milk
Salt, pepper, and additional thyme to taste
2 tablespoons (28 g) unsalted butter

NOTE: Fresh thyme leaves really do make a difference in the soup.

1. Place soaked beans, together with the broth, ham bone, and thyme in a large pot, then cover and bring to a boil. Reduce heat and simmer for 2 hours.

2. Add carrots, potatoes, and garlic and simmer another hour.

3. Soak mushrooms in hot water for about 30 minutes. Strain the liquid to remove any sandy particles. Cut mushrooms into thumb-sized pieces, then puree in processor with just enough of the soaking liquid to make a smooth paste.

4. Remove ham bone from soup. Trim off any bits of ham still clinging to the bone and add to the soup. When bone is picked clean, discard. Puree soup in small batches until smooth, combine with pureed mushrooms, and stir in milk.

5. Heat through and season to taste with salt, pepper, and more thyme. Top with butter and serve immediately.

Puree de Carottes Provençale

Provençal Carrot Puree

France

This carrot soup is vibrant with the bright flavors of Provence: red and green peppers, tomatoes, onions, and garlic. It's not overly subtle or sweet like many of the carrot soups I've tasted in the North. The garnish of shredded raw carrot is a fresh contrast to the rich, smooth soup. Try it—carrots never tasted so good!

Serves 4

1 medium-sized onion, chopped
3 cloves garlic, chopped
½ medium-sized green pepper, diced
½ medium-sized red bell pepper, diced (canned pimentos or roasted peppers are fine)
1 teaspoon (5 ml) fresh thyme leaves, or ½ teaspoon (3 ml) dried thyme
2 tablespoons (28 g) unsalted butter
2 medium-sized carrots, sliced ¼-inch (6-mm) thick
1 medium-sized baking potato, peeled and diced
2 cups (500 ml) chicken broth
½ cup (125 ml) tomato sauce
1 cup (250 ml) milk
Salt and pepper to taste
Thyme to taste
2 tablespoons (30 ml) chopped parsley
1 medium-sized carrot, shredded
3 tablespoons (45 ml) sour cream or crème fraîche

1. Sauté onion, garlic, red and green peppers, and thyme in butter until limp and fragrant, 3 to 5 minutes. Add carrots and potatoes and continue cooking a few minutes longer.

2. Stir in broth and tomato sauce. Bring to a boil, then reduce heat and simmer, covered, until the vegetables are tender, about 20 minutes.

3. Puree mixture to smoothness in blender or processor; add milk. Season with salt, pepper, and more thyme, if needed. Heat until very hot but not boiling.

4. Garnish with a sprinkling of chopped parsley, a pinch of shredded carrots, and a spoonful of sour cream or crème fraîche. Serve immediately.

Tanabour

Barley, Herb, and Yogurt Soup

Armenia

Armenia . . . the land of the Tigris and Euphrates, where Noah's ark is said to have come to rest after the deluge. Though an ancient nation, it now lies sadly divided, with many of its people scattered throughout the world. But no matter where they live, Armenians cling to traditional customs and cuisine. They are proud of their food and share it lovingly. Indeed, their hospitality is so great that as their guest your bowl will be constantly replenished, and you must place your hand over the top to stop the endless refilling.

A peasant cuisine, it is also one of delicacy, and bears a Turkish influence as does much Middle Eastern food. Armenian food is flavored with tart and sweet accents rather than hot spices. This hearty soup is tangy with yogurt and lemon, rich with creamy barley, and delicately scented with cinnamon, dill, and cilantro.

Serves 4 to 6

½ cup (125 ml) dry barley
1½ cups (375 ml) water
1 large or 2 small leeks, cleaned and diced
2 tablespoons (28 g) unsalted butter
6 cups (1.5 l) rich chicken or vegetable broth
1 egg, slightly beaten
1½ cups (375 ml) plain yogurt
Juice of 1½ lemons (3 tablespoons [45 ml])
¼ to ½ teaspoon (1.5 to 3 ml) cinnamon

2 tablespoons (30 ml) snipped fresh dill leaves, or ½ teaspoon (3 ml) dried dill

3 tablespoons (30 ml) chopped cilantro, or fresh mint to taste
Salt and pepper to taste

1. Place barley in saucepan and cover with water. Bring to a boil, cook several minutes, then turn off heat and let stand, covered, for 30 minutes.

2. Sauté leeks in butter until wilted, then add broth and soaked barley; bring to a boil, then simmer, covered, until barley is tender and soup thickened, about 30 minutes. Remove from heat.

3. Beat eggs into yogurt, then stir several spoonfuls of hot soup into mixture. This will keep it from curdling or becoming scrambled eggs when it's added to the hot soup. Add egg mixture to the soup, stirring well.

4. Return to the heat and warm through, being careful not to let it boil. Season with lemon juice, cinnamon, dill, and cilantro. Serve immediately.

VARIATION 1: For a meaty flavor, cook ½ pound (225 g) lamb stew meat in the chicken broth until tender, adding more water if necessary to keep the amount of liquid close to 6 cups (1.5 l). Skim the fat from the flavorful broth, then proceed with the basic recipe.

VARIATION 2: A Syrian version substitutes broken vermicelli for barley. Add to leeks and broth as in step 2 of the basic recipe, but simmer only until noodles are cooked.

VARIATION 3: Tanabour may be served chilled on a hot summer day. Add lots of chopped herbs, such as scallions and mint, and increase its tartness with more lemon juice.

Puree of Artichoke Soup
à la Alice B. Toklas

France

Inspired by a recipe in Alice B. Toklas's wonderfully evocative cookbook, this soup recalls the soft, silken essence of artichoke that Toklas and Gertrude Stein enjoyed on one of their many jaunts to the French countryside. This recipe is quite a bit easier and quicker than the original, and I could not resist adding the wallop of garlic. I think Toklas would approve!

Serve followed by a juicy roast chicken or Poulet à la Chilindrón (see Index).

Serves 4

4 large or **6** small artichokes, peeled of their thistles (see Note);
   or **1** package frozen artichoke hearts, thawed
2 to **3** cloves garlic, chopped
3 tablespoons (42 g) unsalted butter
1 medium-sized baking potato, peeled and diced
3 cups (750 ml) chicken or vegetable broth
   Salt and pepper to taste

NOTE: To prepare fresh artichokes, pull back the leaves of the artichoke individually. Each leaf will give a little snap, which shows that the flesh of the artichoke remains on the vegetable and that the leaf you discard is only waste. Peel stem and pare away the bits of thistle around the base.

When you reach the tender leaves near the heart, stop removing them. Quarter the artichoke, and with a small paring knife remove the sharp leaves inside and the furry choke.

Keep artichokes from discoloring by placing them in a bowl of water to which you've added a squeeze of lemon juice.

1. Lightly sauté prepared artichokes (or frozen artichoke hearts) and garlic in 1½ tablespoons (21 g) butter.

2. Add potatoes and broth, bring to a boil, then reduce heat. Cover and simmer until artichokes and potatoes are tender, about 10 minutes.

3. Puree in blender or processor until smooth. Salt and pepper to taste. Top each portion with a tiny pat of butter to enrich the soup. Serve immediately.

Sajoer Lodeh

Thick, Spicy Vegetable and Peanut Soup

Indonesia

Indonesia dots the map between Australia and Southeast Asia like a scattering of jewels—as if a treasure box had been up-ended, flinging its precious stones to the sea.

The islands are lush and balmy, bathed in the warm, moist sunshine, steaming in the tropical rains. The vegetation grows with abandon, the greens and leaves seem to be in continual wild growth. It's no wonder then that vegetables of all kinds play such an important role in the Indonesian cuisine.

This soup is almost like a stew: an assortment of mixed vegetables—cabbage, green beans, corn, carrot, bean sprouts, and more—simmering in rich broth, spiked with hot pepper, and smoothed with creamy peanut butter. I especially like the way the vegetables all become tinted yellow from the turmeric and contrast with the spicy red soup. Authentically, the soup would be enriched with coconut milk, but the peanut butter is a particularly delicious variation.

Sajoer would traditionally be served with the rest of the meal, instead of as a separate course, the way we enjoy soup. It is sipped in between bites of the solid foods, a few spoonfuls used as a sauce for rice if desired. You might try it that way, accompanied by a whole, spicy grilled fish, bowls of steamed rice, a plate of the most exotic greens and herbs you can find (cilantro, chervil, green onions, and nasturtium leaves), and a small amount of sambal olek, the incendiary pureed chile condiment (buy or make your own—a recipe appears in my other book, *Hot & Spicy*).

Serves 4

1 medium-sized onion, chopped
4 cloves garlic, chopped
1 tablespoon (15 ml) vegetable oil
2 teaspoons (10 ml) turmeric
½ teaspoon (3 ml) cumin
¼ teaspoon (1.5 ml) ground fenugreek
1 jalapeño, chopped
1 medium-sized waxy new potato, unpeeled and cut into eighths
2 cups (500 ml) vegetable or chicken broth
1½ cups (375 ml) chopped tomatoes (canned is fine)
1 cup (250 ml) tomato juice
½ medium-sized white or green cabbage, thinly sliced
¼ pound (112 g) green beans, trimmed and cut into 1½-inch (37-mm) lengths
1 cup (250 ml) corn, coarsely pureed in blender or processor
1 medium-sized carrot, shredded
2 cups (500 ml) bean sprouts
¼ cup (60 ml) creamy peanut butter
Juice of 1 lemon (2 tablespoons [30 ml])
1½ tablespoons (23 ml) soy sauce
Cayenne pepper to taste (optional; taste first, because some jalapeños can be very, very hot, others too mild)

1. Sauté onion and 3 cloves garlic in vegetable oil until softened, not browned. Add turmeric, cumin, fenugreek, jalapeño, and potato chunks; toss with the onion mixture and cook 1 or 2 minutes over medium heat.

2. Pour in broth, tomatoes, and tomato juice; simmer 10 minutes. Add cabbage and green beans, and cook until green beans are crisp-tender, about 10 minutes. Add corn, shredded carrot, and bean sprouts.

3. In a separate bowl, stir in peanut butter until smooth, adding a few spoonfuls of the soup to thin the peanut butter somewhat and help it melt into the soup more easily.

4. Add the softened peanut butter, remaining garlic, lemon juice, and soy sauce, stirring into the soup until soup is smooth. Taste for seasoning and add extra soy sauce, lemon, or cayenne if needed.

ADVANCE PREPARATION: Lasts for 3 to 4 days tightly covered in the refrigerator. When reheating, taste for seasoning and add extra lemon or cayenne if needed.

Phō Bò

Spicy Soup with Rice Noodles and Salad

Vietnam

Phō Bò is often the dish a homesick North Vietnamese will prepare to conjure up warm feelings of home. The steamy soup is ladled over bits of beef, noodles, salad, and herbs. Its aroma beckons from food stalls in the streets and marketplaces where it is served with a generous dose of potent chile paste, a squeeze of tart lime, and a scattering of crunchy, chopped peanuts.

Authentically, this soup is made with fresh beef stock, prepared by simmering meat and soup bones together with cinnamon stick, ginger, and onions for many hours. This is rich and delicious, but alas, takes far more time than most of us have. I've found an acceptable shortcut by using a combination of canned chicken broth and canned beef broth. Home-made broth that you may have frozen is also fine. In Vietnam raw meat is added to the soup and slightly cooked by the hot liquid, but I find that marinating the beef strips, then lightly stir-frying them is tastier. (Indeed, you might wish to triple the amount of marinated meat, and make another meal of the stir-fry, accompanied by steamed rice.)

Phō Bò is a full meal, and a cool citrus sorbet or sherbet, along with a few crisp cookies, is a nice ending.

Serves 4

1 pound (450 g) fresh rice noodles, ¼-inch (6-mm) thick and ¼-inch (6-mm) wide (if unavailable, choose dried rice noodles, ¼-inch [6-mm] wide)

Soup:
6 shallots, chopped (⅓ cup [85 ml])
3 cloves garlic, chopped
1 tablespoon (15 ml) vegetable oil
4 medium-sized tomatoes, chopped (canned is fine)
1 cup (250 ml) chicken broth
2 cups (250 ml) beef broth
1 cinnamon stick, 2 inches (50 mm) long
2 teaspoons (10 ml) chopped gingerroot

Meat and Marinade:
6 to 8 ounces (168 to 224 g) sirloin or any tender cut of beef, thinly sliced
3 cloves garlic, chopped
2 tablespoons (30 ml) fish sauce or light soy sauce
½ teaspoon (3 ml) sereh (see Aromatics and Special Ingredients)
½ teaspoon (3 ml) hot chile-garlic paste (or substitute Tabasco)
1 tablespoon (15 ml) vegetable oil

Salad and Garnishes:
4 large leaves of lettuce (butterhead, romaine, or other), thinly sliced
1 medium-sized cucumber, peeled and diced
1 medium-sized lime, cut into wedges
½ cup (125 ml) fresh mint leaves, coarsely chopped or left whole (do not use dried)
½ cup (125 ml) cilantro, coarsely chopped
⅔ cup (170 ml) coarsely chopped peanuts
1½ cups (375 ml) raw or blanched bean sprouts
Vietnamese hot chile or chile-garlic paste to taste

1. If using dried rice noodles, prepare by soaking in warm water to cover for about 30 minutes, then boiling for 2 to 3 minutes, only until tender, not mushy. (If using fresh rice noodles, no advance preparation is necessary; simply add them to the hot broth.)

2. To make the soup: In saucepan, sauté shallots and garlic in oil until soft. Add tomatoes and continue cooking until tomatoes become a bit

mushy. Pour chicken and beef broth into pan, add cinnamon stick and gingerroot, then gently simmer while you prepare the rest of dish.

3. To prepare the meat and marinade: mix meat with garlic, add fish sauce or soy sauce, sereh, and chile paste. In wok, heat oil and stir-fry the spiced meat (it only needs to marinate 1 or 2 minutes). Stir-fry only until barely cooked. Set aside.

4. Then add rice noodles to the soup. Cook only for 1 or 2 minutes, to heat through and absorb the flavors. Do not overcook!

5. To serve: Set out a platter of the lettuce, cucumber, lime wedges, mint, and cilantro; a bowl of peanuts; and a plate of the stir-fried meat. Into each person's bowl, place a handful of bean sprouts; over this, ladle a portion of the soup and noodles. Each person then adds his or her own bits of salad, herbs, and peanuts, along with wedges of lime and chile paste, if desired. (I like mine very tart with lime and fiery with chile paste.)

ADVANCE PREPARATION: The broth may be prepared up to a day ahead, and the meat cut an hour or two earlier. You need only marinate and stir-fry at the last minute. The vegetable platter may be prepared up to 2 hours ahead of time and kept tightly covered in the refrigerator.

VARIATION: Cool and Spicy Noodles

Cook extra rice noodles in the flavorful broth and remove noodles from the broth. Serve them cool the next day, topped with chopped mint leaves, sliced green onions, diced cucumber, and chopped peanuts; season with lime wedges and chile paste. Wonderfully refreshing in sweltering weather.

Soupe de la Nuit des Noces

Tomato Broth with Small Pasta

France

My daughter and I sampled variations of this soup throughout the Périgord and in Quercy—sometimes the soup was thick with tomato, other times the broth was merely tomato scented. The curious title translates to "wedding night soup" because it is traditionally served to newlyweds. I'm not even going to speculate on why, since the only effect it had on me was to make me feel well fed.

This memorable soup combines tomato-flecked broth seasoned with thyme, and floating rounds of pasta the size of black peppercorns. The shape of acini de pepe offers a unique, delightful texture, and it is well worth searching for in international food stores. If unavailable, you could substitute orzo or semone de melone. While the shape will be different, the soup will still be delicious.

Serve sprinkled with Parmesan cheese and follow with Tarragon Veal Patties, a green salad, and then a creamy cheese. For dessert, Fresh Fruit in Fraises de Bois Sauce (see Index), and voilà: a lyrical French countryside menu.

Serves 4 to 6

1 medium-sized onion, chopped
3 cloves garlic, chopped
2 teaspoons (10 ml) fresh thyme leaves, or ½ teaspoon (3 ml) dried thyme
1 medium-sized carrot, diced
2 to 3 tablespoons (30 to 45 ml) extra-virgin olive oil
4 to 5 medium-sized ripe tomatoes, coarsely chopped (canned is fine)
1 cup (250 ml) tomato juice
3 cups (750 ml) chicken or vegetable broth
4 to 6 ounces (112 to 168 g) acini de pepe (small peppercorn-shaped pasta) or other small pasta, such as orzo or semone de melone
Freshly grated Parmesan as desired

1. Sauté onion, garlic, thyme, and carrots in olive oil until softened and lightly golden. Add tomatoes and continue cooking another 3 to 5 minutes.

2. Add tomato juice, broth, and pasta. Bring to a boil, then reduce heat and let simmer until pasta is tender, about 10 minutes, depending on the pasta you choose. Be very careful not to overcook the pasta.

3. Serve immediately, offering each person freshly grated Parmesan to sprinkle on his or her soup.

Some Simple Soups

Broccoli in Garlic Broth Cook broccoli florets in chicken broth with several cloves coarsely chopped garlic, until the broccoli is just cooked, but still brightly colored and crunchy. Serve with a dusting of freshly grated Parmesan cheese.

Asparagus Puree Lightly sauté several cloves of garlic in unsalted butter. Add a chopped, peeled potato, and when that is almost tender, add

1 pound (450 g) cut-up asparagus and 3 cups (750 ml) of chicken or vegetable broth. Cook until asparagus is tender, then blend in processor or blender until smooth. Serve, enriched with a few spoonfuls of cream or a pat of sweet butter.

Faire Chabrot In southwest France, in Bordeaux, Limousin, and in a region known as Quercy, there is an ancient custom called *"faire chabrot,"* which consists of pouring a glass of wine into your soup bowl when only a few spoonfuls of soup remain. It is then swirled around, put directly to the lips, and drunk down. This is an old, traditional breakfast, and the custom is still practiced, especially during the season of grape harvest when work is hard. In Basque Country they *faire chabrot* with the hearty vegetable and meat soup, Garbure.

Pureed Potato and Garlic Cook 3 large baking potatoes, peeled and diced, along with 1 or 2 heads of garlic, broken into cloves and peeled, in 3 cups (750 ml) of rich broth. When potatoes and garlic are tender, puree until smooth. Enrich with several pats of butter and a jolt of cream or half-and-half. Salt and pepper to taste.

Crumble tart goat cheese into your favorite red or yellow bell pepper or tomato soup, or minestrone.

EGGS AND CHEESE

A nyone who can keep a few eggs need never go hungry" is an old Basque saying. Courtesy of the chicken, the egg is easily available, and its versatility is amazing. It combines with both extravagant and humble ingredients to make satisfying, sustaining meals.

I love eggs; when I am very hungry nothing else quite satisfies my survival need. When my palate is jaded, an egg dish, preferably spicy, is what I crave as a restorative.

If I were to recount the best meals of my life, they would include feta cheese and eggs sizzling in olive oil, eaten while watching the drizzle of the Mediterranean winter at the window, or soft-poached eggs in a pool of spicy sauce, at breakfast somewhere in Mexico.

In addition to chicken eggs, we have rich duck eggs and ostrich eggs large enough to make a 12-person omelet (though I've heard their shells are virtually impregnable). There are also tiny quail eggs, elegant miniatures of our familiar chicken egg, which are delightful as an hors d'oeuvre when a larger egg would be too much.

Cheese is not as prevalent in the sun-drenched kitchen as it is farther north, but the cheese used in this cuisine is wonderful—strong, salty feta, pungent Roquefort, buttery mozzarella, sharp, dry Parmesan, crumbly Mexican *queso fresco*, tangy goat cheese. Melt them with herbs and vegetables, enjoy as a snack or informal meal. See Sandwiches, Breads, and Savory Snacks for some wonderful egg and cheese sandwiches. Try the Taco de Rajas y Queso, oozing spicy peppers and melted cheese, or the zesty goat cheese, layered with pesto and sun-dried tomatoes. Enjoy these dishes with a glass of sturdy red wine.

Pastel de Tortillas

Layered Vegetable Omelet Gratin

Spain

In Spain, *tortilla* means "a flat omelet," and this dish is a stack of three vegetable omelets covered with a cheese sauce, then broiled until the cheese sauce lightly browns.

It is a colorful dish from Catalonia, full of garden hues and fresh vegetable tastes. Serve for brunch, cut into wedges, accompanied by Middle Eastern Fruit Compote with Pistachios, or for supper, accompanied by a crisp little salad of mixed greens and Olive-Rosemary Bread (See Index for both).

Serves 4

3 small cloves garlic, chopped
3 tablespoons (45 ml) cooked spinach, squeezed dry (frozen is fine)
6 eggs
2 tablespoons (30 ml) vegetable or light olive oil
½ medium-large red bell pepper, chopped
2 ounces (56 g) ham, diced
5 to 6 spears asparagus, sliced ⅛- to ¼-inch (3- to 6-mm) thick
1 tablespoon (14 g) unsalted butter
1 tablespoon (15 ml) flour
1 cup (250 ml) milk
1 cup (250 ml) shredded Gruyère or Appenzeller cheese
  Salt and cayenne pepper to taste
2 tablespoons (30 ml) freshly grated Parmesan

1. To make three flat omelets, using 2 eggs each: First omelet: Combine 1 clove garlic and spinach with 2 eggs, mix well, and fry in a small omelet pan in about 2 teaspoons (10 ml) oil. Turn and cook the other side, then transfer to plate.

2. Second omelet: Sauté red bell pepper with 1 clove garlic and cook until pepper is softened. Add ham and 2 beaten eggs and cook flat, then turn and cook the other side. Transfer to plate.

3. Third omelet: Sauté asparagus with remaining garlic and cook until asparagus is tender; pour 2 beaten eggs over asparagus and cook until done on first side, then turn and cook the other side. Transfer to plate.

4. To make sauce: Melt butter in saucepan, then sprinkle with flour and cook 1 or 2 minutes over medium to low heat until flour begins to turn golden. Remove from heat and add milk, stirring to mix well. Return to heat and stir as it cooks, thickening the sauce. Stir in cheese and season with salt and cayenne pepper to taste.

5. Layer omelets, one on top of the other, taking care not to break any of them. Pour cheese sauce over the omelet stack, sprinkle with grated Parmesan, broil until lightly browned, and serve immediately.

ADVANCE PREPARATION: Vegetable omelets should not be made any sooner than an hour before assembling, but sauce may be made several hours ahead, and the vegetable mixtures (cooked spinach, sautéed peppers, and sautéed asparagus) may be made as much as a day ahead and refrigerated.

Tacos de Rajas y Queso

Soft Tacos of Mixed Peppers, Chiles, and Cheese

New Mexico

It was the late '60s and we had succumbed to the lure of the open road —a mad, wonderfully romantic journey through America's Southwest, heading toward Old Mexico. Along a particularly desolate stretch of land we stopped at the only restaurant that appeared on that long, empty, cactus-studded horizon—ANITA'S its peeling sign proclaimed.

An old Spanish-speaking woman with curlers in her hair and a cigarette dangling from her mouth came scurrying toward us. "Seat down, seat down. Now, red or green?" With that she disappeared, leaving us feeling more than a little spooky.

Green appeared first: a plate of meat chunks simmered to tenderness in a sauce of green chiles and tomatillos. We scooped up the last bits of sauce with sopaipillas, those crisp pillows of fried dough ubiquitous in New Mexico. We doused the spicy flames with gulps of beer. Never, I swore, had more delicious food passed my lips.

The red arrived. Red was a platter of soft tacos filled with sauteed chilis

—rajas—and melted cheese, than splashed with savory red chili sauce. This food was *good*.

Serve as a luncheon dish accompanied by a salad of crisp shredded greens, or enjoy for supper with a salad and steamed rice topped with savory simmered black beans. Offer your favorite salsa or other hot condiment on the side.

Serves 4

2 poblanos, stems and seeds removed, cut into ½-inch (12-mm) strips
1 medium-sized green pepper, stem and seeds removed, cut into ½-inch (12-mm) strips
1 medium-sized red bell pepper, stem and seeds removed, cut into ½-inch (12-mm) strips
4 cloves garlic, chopped
2 tablespoons (30 ml) vegetable oil
Dash salt to taste
1½ teaspoons (8 ml) cumin
1 cup (250 ml) red-chile sauce (canned is okay since it's one of many ingredients, but homemade is best)
8 to 10 ounces (224 to 280 g) Gruyère, Lappi, or similar cheese, cut into ½-inch (12-mm) chunks
1 jalapeño en escabeche (see Aromatics and Special Ingredients), finely chopped
½ cup (125 ml) sour cream
Squeeze of ¼ lemon or lime
8 to 10 corn tortillas

1. In skillet, sauté poblanos, green and red bell peppers, and garlic in 1 tablespoon (15 ml) vegetable oil until softened.

2. Sprinkle with cumin and cook for 1 minute to give the cumin a toasted flavor, then stir in the red-chile sauce and cook 1 or 2 minutes. Add salt to taste.

3. Stir cheese and jalapeño en escabeche into sauce and cook, stirring over low-medium heat until cheese melts, about 4 to 5 minutes. Remove from heat and stir in the sour cream. Add a squeeze of lemon or lime.

4. Warm tortillas in another skillet in the remaining oil, or use a nonstick pan with only the tiniest bit of oil. I find also that wetting the tortillas lightly before warming them makes them softer.

5. Spoon a portion of the chile mixture onto each tortilla and roll up.

6. Serve immediately, offering extra jalapeños en escabeche, as well as extra sour cream.

ADVANCE PREPARATION: Sauce may be prepared a day ahead of time and stored tightly covered in the refrigerator. Reheat gently to melt the cheese, then warm tortillas and roll up tacos.

Salata Feta

Herbed Feta Salad or Spread

The Mediterranean

Feta salad is a quintessential sun-drenched food. Each bite conjures up the Mediterranean sun and its white-washed villages. As with most simple dishes, the flavor depends entirely upon the quality of the ingredients. Be sure to use Greek or Bulgarian feta, the kind made from sheep's milk, and choose a rich, fruity extra-virgin olive oil. Since you're using only a small amount, you want the flavor to sing out. I've included directions for 2 separate flavorings, oregano and mint, because I can't decide which is better; each contributes a distinctive taste. I often prepare half the recipe with mint and half with oregano, and serve a tiny mound of each on every salad.

Serves 4 as a salad

½ pound (225 g) sheep's milk feta
2 tablespoons (30 ml) plain yogurt
2 tablespoons (30 ml) extra-virgin olive oil
2 cloves garlic, chopped
2 teaspoons (10 ml) dried oregano leaves, crumbled (or ⅓ cup [85 ml] fresh mint leaves, coarsely chopped, or 1 tablespoon [15 ml] dried mint)
1 head butterhead lettuce, washed, and the leaves separated
1 to 2 ripe tomatoes (or substitute 1 red bell pepper, roasted, peeled, and cut into strips)
1 medium-sized cucumber sliced, or cut into ½- to 1-inch (12- to 25-mm) chunks
8 black olives such as Kalamata
Sprigs of fresh oregano, mint, or parsley as garnish (optional)

1. Crumble feta cheese into bowl, and with a fork, mash in the yogurt, olive oil, garlic, and either oregano or mint. Mixture does not have to be very smooth, it should, in fact, retain a bit of texture.
2. Arrange leaves of lettuce on each plate. Top with a small mound of

the cheese and garnish with tomato wedges (or pepper strips), cucumber, black olives, and herb sprigs.

ADVANCE PREPARATION: Cheese mixture with oregano may be prepared several days in advance, but if using fresh mint, you should add it the day you plan on serving it, as the leaves do wilt.

VARIATION 1: As a spread, serve with crusty French bread. Combined with roasted pepper strips and/or cucumber chunks it makes a great sandwich.

VARIATION 2: Spread the inside of warm pita bread with the creamed feta salad, then stuff with thin strips of grilled lamb or Roast Cumin Lamb and a salad of chopped cucumber and tomato.

VARIATION 3: As an hors d'oeuvre, hollow out cherry tomatoes and fill with the feta mixture, or drop it onto fingers of Belgian endive or slices of cucumber.

Vine-Leaf–Wrapped
Goat Cheese and Green Olives

France

Each component of this dish has such a strong, distinctive flavor it is surprising how complementary they taste when combined. Though this dish appears as a mere lump of leaf-covered cheese, its aroma and taste magically evoke the Mediterranean. Its appeal lies in its disarming simplicity.

I once stayed in a huge, ancient stone house in the southwest of France, where the terrace was covered with a grape arbor. The tender leaves continually found their way into my kitchen, stuffed with savory brown rice and served with yogurt or stewed with meat and red wine, and as a fragrant wrapper for many different foods.

Many of our neighbors kept goats, and produced chèvres. Since some were wrapped in grape leaves, this recipe was almost inevitable. Although it must be baked, the baking is for combining the flavors, not for warming it to serve hot. It tastes much better cool rather than warm, so don't be tempted to eat it hot from the oven.

Serve as an appetizer, as part of a cheeseboard, or accompanied by fresh, ripe tomatoes and several slices of pâté or terrine for a picnic lunch.

Serves 6

12 to 15 grape leaves (the amount you need will depend upon their size)

3 tablespoons (45 ml) extra-virgin olive oil or Garlic-Herb Oil (see Index)

1 log (about 12 ounces [336 g]) goat cheese, such as Montrachet, Lezay, Royal, or Provence

⅔ cup (170 ml) pitted Mediterranean-style green olives

1. If using canned grape leaves, rinse well with running water and wipe dry. If using fresh, blanch them for several minutes to make them tender and pliable. Dry well.

2. Oil baking dish such as a 1-quart (1-l) soufflé dish with 1 tablespoon (15 ml) olive or garlic-herb oil. Line with grape leaves.

3. Place one third of the cheese in the bottom of the leaf-lined container, patting it in tightly. Top with half the olives, then repeat.

4. Fold edges of leaves over to enclose cheese, then top with several more grape leaves. Sprinkle 1 tablespoon (15 ml) oil over top. Bake at 325° F. for 10 to 15 minutes. Remove from oven and cool until cheese becomes firm.

5. Serve cool, drizzled with the remaining olive oil. To serve, cut a slice, making sure to include a small portion of the vine leaves, and spread on crusty bread. If grape leaves are tough, push aside the leaves and scoop out the savory cheese.

ADVANCE PREPARATION: Keeps about 1½ weeks tightly covered in the refrigerator.

Eggs Scrambled with Asparagus, Garlic, and Fontina

California

After a dreary, gray winter there is no more reassuring sight than the first pile of green, ferny asparagus in the stores. No matter how hard the winds blow or the rain falls, that asparagus is a harbinger that the days will soon be soft and warm, blanketed with gentle sun.

Asparagus season is short, but while it's in its glory, we feast on it so often that I am always seeking new ways to prepare it. The first batch is eaten with heady delight, steamed, with no more than a squeeze of lemon and a kiss of unsalted butter. Soon we eat pureed asparagus soup, chow mein made with stir-fried asparagus in black-bean sauce, even ravioli stuffed with asparagus. Sometimes it feels like a race against the swiftness of the season—to happily eat our fill because soon it will be over. Of course, then we have juicy summer fruits and vibrant vegetables as consolation.

In this recipe, the scent of pungent garlic cooking in sweet, melting butter permeates this soft scramble of delicate asparagus and melted fontina cheese. Serve for a sunny, informal brunch, accompanied by a basket of fresh croissants, pots of sweet butter and fruit preserves, and rich, dark coffee with a pitcher of hot milk to make café au lait. Since asparagus season coincides with the beginning of strawberry season, I'd offer a big basket of glorious berries with a bowl of red wine to dip them in and sugar to sprinkle over them. The red wine does something indefinable to the berries and makes them even more berry-flavored.

Serves 4

   6 eggs
   8 ounces (224 g) fontina (preferably Italian fontina), cut into
      ½-inch (12-mm) cubes
   1 pound (450 g) asparagus spears, tough ends snapped off, cut
      into ⅔-inch (16-mm) lengths
   ½ stick (4 tablespoons [56 g]) unsalted butter
   3 to 4 cloves garlic, chopped
   ¼ cup (60 ml) freshly grated Parmesan
   2 tablespoons (30 ml) of either fresh sweet basil, chopped, or
      thinly sliced prosciutto, cut into ribbons (optional)

1. Beat eggs and add fontina cubes. Set aside.

2. Gently cook the asparagus in half the butter over low heat. When barely tender and bright green, add garlic and rest of butter and cook 1 or 2 minutes.

3. Pour in egg-and-cheese mixture, stirring into scrambled egg curds. Don't overcook.

4. Sprinkle with Parmesan and serve immediately, garnished with basil or prosciutto, if desired.

Migas

Eggs Scrambled with Fried Tortilla Strips

Mexico

The Mexican kitchen prepares superlative egg dishes combining the creamy, bland taste of egg with the sharp bite of chile and earthy flavor of corn tortilla. These dishes are simple, and their balance of flavors is, I think, perfect. Huevos rancheros is a classic example of this, a spicy tomato sauce ladled over delicate fried eggs, all of which tops a corn tortilla.

The following is a lesser-known dish. It could not be simpler, yet the taste is far from ordinary. The savory chile and tomato blend with the creamy scrambled eggs, and contrast with lightly toasted tortilla strips, slightly softened in the egg mixture.

Migas are wonderful for brunch, with their vivid colors and festive flavors. Serve accompanied by an avocado salad such as Tomatillo-Guacamole (see Index) or perhaps avocado halves filled with lobster or crab meat with a dash of fresh salsa and a wedge of lemon.

Serves 4 to 6

10 to 12 corn tortillas, cut into ½-inch (12-mm) strips
½ cup (125 ml) vegetable oil, for frying the tortilla strips
6 cloves garlic, chopped
2 poblano or Anaheim chiles, roasted, peeled, seeded, and thinly sliced (if fresh poblanos or Anaheims are unavailable, substitute 1 green bell pepper plus 2 jalapeños)
3 tablespoons (42 g) unsalted butter
1½ teaspoons (8 ml) cumin
4 ripe medium- to large-sized tomatoes, coarsely chopped
8 eggs, lightly beaten
½ cup (125 ml) cilantro, chopped
3 to 4 green onions, chopped

1. Fry tortilla strips in oil until golden but not dark brown. Remove from oil and drain tortilla strips on paper towels.

2. Sauté garlic and poblano strips in 1 tablespoon (14 g) butter for just a minute; do not let garlic brown. Sprinkle in cumin, then add the tomatoes and cook over medium heat for 3 to 4 minutes until tomatoes are no longer runny. Remove from pan and set aside.

3. Over low heat, melt remaining butter in pan. Pour in beaten eggs. Cook over low heat and stir until eggs begin to set. Add reserved chile-tomato mixture and tortilla strips, and continue cooking, stirring once or

twice, until eggs are the consistency you desire. The tortilla strips should be neither crisp nor soggy, but pliable and chewy. Top with cilantro and green onions.

4. Serve immediately, accompanied by a fresh hot salsa or other spicy condiment.

Parsee Omelet

Omelet with Cilantro-Spice Puree and Feta

India

The Parsees are an Indian religious sect that originally came from Iran. Hence the name Parsee (Farsi), the Iranian word for Persian. Although they live mostly in the north, they are known throughout India for their variety of egg dishes.

This dish is traditionally made with small pancake-like omelets, but I like it better with one large, flat omelet, or even, softly scrambled. The large amount of cilantro is pureed with the rest of the spices and is surprisingly subtle.

Serve with crusty French bread, soft, chewy flour tortillas, or whole wheat chapatties; offer a spicy condiment on the side.

Serves 2 to 3

2 cloves garlic, chopped
½ medium-sized onion, chopped
2 to 3 green onions, chopped
1 jalapeño, chopped
1 tablespoon (15 ml) chopped gingerroot
½ teaspoon (3 ml) turmeric
½ teaspoon (3 ml) cumin
½ teaspoon (3 ml) coriander
1 cup (250 ml) cilantro, chopped and loosely packed
4 eggs, lightly beaten
2 to 3 tablespoons (30 to 45 ml) extra-virgin olive oil or vegetable oil
¼ pound (112 g) feta, sliced or coarsely crumbled
Salt to taste

1. In processor or blender, mix garlic, onion, green onions, jalapeño, gingerroot, turmeric, cumin, coriander, and cilantro until it is all well chopped and mixed. Add eggs and mix again.

2. Heat oil in skillet, then pour in spiced egg mixture. Crumble feta over eggs, salt to taste, and cook over medium-low heat until bottom is cooked through. To cook other side pop under broiler. (I often just turn it in sections, or turn it into scrambled, spiced eggs with feta.) Serve immediately.

Omelette Pipérade

Omelet with Red and Green Peppers

Basque Country

Where the Pyrenees mountains separate France from Spain live an ancient, hearty people known as Basques. They make their way in the world as fishermen or shepherds, and they hold strong to tradition. They speak a language unrelated to the languages of the region, and no one is really certain of their origins.

Peppers grow in profusion in the *pays basque* (Basque Country). In the hills behind Biarritz, a tiny village, Esplette, hosts a pepper festival each October. Every house displays huge strings of peppers hung in the sun to dry, giving a festive atmosphere to the village. Esplette peppers have bite to them, adding piquancy to the Basques' rustic fare.

Pipérade, beaten eggs cooked with sautéed peppers, is probably the most famous Basque dish. It may be made three ways—as a rolled omelet filled with peppers; flat and cooked until firm, much like a Spanish tortilla; or my favorite: slowly, softly scrambled into a creamy, peppery mélange. My first taste of pipérade remains etched in my mind—the creaminess of the egg, the slight sharpness of the peppers, and the tang of tomato, with thin pink slices of ham languidly draped over one side of the plate, half covering the eggs. I nibbled bites of salty ham with mouthfuls of the pipérade—one of the world's perfect combinations.

Serves 4

½ medium-sized onion, chopped
1 medium-sized red bell pepper, thinly sliced
1 medium-sized green pepper, thinly sliced
1 tablespoon (15 ml) extra-virgin olive oil, more if needed
3 cloves garlic, chopped
2 medium- to large-sized tomatoes, coarsely chopped
6 eggs, lightly beaten
½ teaspoon (3 ml) fresh thyme (or 2 tablespoons [30 ml] basil leaves, coarsely chopped, or to taste)

Salt and cayenne pepper to taste
4 ounces (112 g) high-quality, raw ham (jambon de Bayonne,
Serrano ham, or the more readily available prosciutto), thinly
sliced

1. Sauté the onion and the red and green peppers lightly in olive oil until slightly softened. Add the garlic and tomatoes and cook over low heat until mixture is of a thick, saucy consistency and vegetables are quite soft; this will take about 30 minutes.

2. Pour in beaten eggs, stirring into soft curds, until they reach the firmness you prefer. In France they would be a bit softer than we usually prefer here. Don't overcook. Stir in the fresh thyme or basil and salt and cayenne pepper, and serve immediately, draped with slices of ham.

Ricotta al Forno

Baked Ricotta Cheese

Italy

Ricotta cheese, seasoned and baked, is one of those dishes that seems too simple to be good. Yet it has a subtle, quite refined flavor that tastes fantastic. It is reminiscent of dishes prepared in Roman times.

Serve it at room temperature, alongside roasted sweet peppers, Greek olives, a drizzle of extra-virgin olive oil, and several leaves of fresh basil or thyme leaves. Any sort of bright accent, such as a few leaves of mâche or sun-dried tomato, is delicious next to the ricotta's creaminess.

Serves 4 to 6

3 cups (750 ml) ricotta, preferably whole-milk type
⅓ cup (85 ml) Parmesan, freshly grated
3 cloves garlic, chopped
1 teaspoon (5 ml) dried thyme or fresh rosemary, crushed
2 eggs, beaten
1 to 2 tablespoons (14 to 28 g) unsalted butter, for buttering
dish
½ to ¾ cup (125 to 180 ml) fine bread crumbs

1. Combine ricotta, Parmesan, garlic, and thyme or rosemary with eggs; mix well.

2. Butter a 1-quart (1-l) soufflé dish or other similarly shaped and sized

baking dish. Place bread crumbs in dish and turn dish to coat the sides with crumbs. Pour off excess.

3. Pour in cheese mixture and bake at 325° F. for 40 minutes until slightly puffed on top but firm to the touch and lightly browned. Remove and let cool. Do not be tempted to eat it now, even though it will smell rich and buttery. It really is best cool.

4. Serve at room temperature, garnished with olives, peppers, and olive oil, as desired.

ADVANCE PREPARATION: This dish is excellent the day after it is made.

VARIATION: Spinach and Red Bell Pepper Torta
The ricotta mixture is also delicious as a basis for a sort of crustless vegetable pie. My version has two layers, one of spinach and one of red peppers, but you could have as many layers as you like, including such ingredients as sautéed, sliced mushrooms, zucchini, or yellow bell peppers.

1. Divide ricotta mixture into two parts. To one part add 1 cup (250 ml) cooked, drained, and chopped spinach, squeezed dry. To the other part add 2 red bell peppers, chopped and sautéed.

2. Bake according to recipe, adding the vegetable mixtures each in their own layer.

3. Bake at 325° F. for 40 minutes.

Some Simple Egg and Cheese Dishes

Yarali Ioa   Parsee-style dish of sunny-side up eggs lightly fried in unsalted butter with a sprinkling of turmeric, cumin, ginger powder, coriander, salt, and cayenne pepper (or with homemade Curry Powder [see Index], a dash of Tabasco, and a sprinkling of cilantro).

A thick slice of crusty bread, lavishly spread with unsalted butter and topped with a sliced, warm, freshly cooked hard-boiled egg, the heat of the egg melting the butter into both the egg and bread. Sprinkle with salt and pepper.

Salata Feta spread onto soft pita bread and wrapped around thinly sliced grilled lamb or flank steak.

Cover hard-shelled, hard-cooked egg with spicy ground meat mixture such as the one for Kefta, and fry or grill until browned. Serve sliced in halves, accompanied with a spicy peanut sauce such as the one from Thai Grilled Chicken with Peanut Sauce (see Index).

Grilled Radicchio with Mozzarella   The slightly bitter quality of this red lettuce of Treviso pairs perfectly with the creaminess of melted cheese. Simply lay out a single layer of radicchio and drizzle with olive oil. Grill briefly over high heat, then remove from oven, top with a slice of mozzarella or Italian fontina, and broil until bubbly and lightly browned. Enjoy with toasted bread rubbed with garlic.

Thinly sliced smoked mozzarella, drizzled with extra-virgin olive oil and a few coarse grindings of black pepper.

Sunny Egg-and-Watercress Sandwich   Season egg salad with lots of tangy mustard, capers, and tart tarragon. Spread generously onto a piece of whole-wheat bread and top with lots of peppery watercress.

Serve poached or lightly fried eggs blanketed with the spicy tomatillo sauce from Pollo en Jacón, or cooked in the simmering green sauce.

Torta di Caprina   Mix goat cheese (such as Lezay or Montrachet) and cream cheese in equal proportions. Season with a generous sprinkling of thyme, garlic, and salt and pepper to taste; layer with pesto and pureed sun-dried tomatoes; chill until firm; then unmold. Or spread the cheese mixture on a flat plate and garnish lavishly with fresh basil leaves and marinated sun-dried tomatoes.

VEGETABLES

Whereas in the Northern lands vegetables may be relegated to a role as side dish, in the sunny lands vegetables are a culinary celebration. The variety of vegetables is amazing, whether you are in a marketplace in Italy marveling at the mounds of green shoots of asparagus or in Thailand feasting your eyes on the huge pile of elaborately carved vegetables brought to the table. When the sun shines in abundance, the vegetables grow with great flavor, and are savored at every meal.

In these lands vegetables follow the seasons, So does life, mingling holidays and celebrations with the natural rhythm of nature and the harvesting of the crops.

The following dishes are both exotic and homey. They will grace a dinner party as easily as an informal family supper.

Peperoni all'Italia

Multicolored Baked Peppers with Olive Oil and Vinegar

Italy

In restaurants in Italy, antipasto tables are laden with platters of savory morsels—black salty olives, thinly sliced peppered salami next to billows of sweet fluffy butter, pink octopus cooked with garlic and olive oil, small creamy balls of juicy fresh mozzarella, and cubes of vegetable frittata. Multicolored baked peppers were a part of many an antipasto table I sampled recently. They are so very delicious and easy to prepare, I've been making them ever since.

In fact, the disarming simplicity of this dish was one of the inspirations for this book. The ingredients are the same as those we see in any number of other recipes, but baking the peppers together with garlic, olive oil, and vinegar creates from these humble ingredients a bright new dish. It is best when all three colors of peppers are available, but it is also good with just red and green, and I often substitute some ripe, sweet, and slightly hot Anaheim chiles for the yellow peppers.

Served warm, this dish accompanies almost anything, or let cool and enjoy as an antipasto, with crusty bread to dunk in. It's terrific tucked into any sort of sandwich, too.

Serves 4 to 6

> 2 medium-sized red bell peppers, seeded and cut into 1½- to 2-inch (37- to 50-mm) pieces
> 2 medium-sized green bell peppers, seeded and cut into 1½- to 2-inch (37- to 50-mm) pieces
> 2 medium-sized yellow bell peppers, seeded and cut into 1½- to 2-inch (37- to 50-mm) pieces
> 6 cloves garlic, peeled and coarsely chopped
> 3 tablespoons (45 ml) extra-virgin olive oil
> 1 tablespoon (15 ml) red-wine vinegar
> ¼ teaspoon (1.5 ml) dried oregano leaves, crumbled
>   Salt to taste
> 1 tablespoon (15 ml) chopped fresh parsley (or 2 tablespoons [30 ml] chopped fresh basil)

1. Place peppers in a single layer in a shallow baking dish. Toss with garlic, then drizzle with olive oil and vinegar. Sprinkle with oregano and salt.

2. Bake at 400° F. for about ½ hour, turning once or twice. Remove from oven and top with fresh parsley or basil. Serve hot, warm, or at room temperature.

ADVANCE PREPARATION: Store tightly covered in refrigerator for up to 4 days.

VARIATION: In addition to the multicolored peppers, or instead of the yellow ones when they are not available, I add several Anaheim or poblano chiles, or just 1 sizzling jalapeño, chopped.

Gulai Malabar

Rich and Spicy Eggplant and Green-Bean Stew

Indonesia

Gulai is a type of soupy stew from Indonesia, made with meat, fish, or just vegetables. This dish is creamy with coconut milk, sweet and spicy at the same time. It is not dominated by any one flavor but is a subtle and complex mix.

Serve in bowls, just as is, or as a main course, accompanied by steamed rice. Offer several condiments, such as chopped green onions, toasted cashews, and fried onion flakes, if desired.

Serves 4

> 2 medium-sized onions, chopped
> 10 cloves garlic, coarsely chopped
> 2 tablespoons (30 ml) vegetable oil
> 2 teaspoons (10 ml) homemade curry powder
> 1 teaspoon (5 ml) cumin
> ½ teaspoon (3 ml) turmeric
> 4 small hot dried red chiles
> 1½ tablespoons (23 ml) chopped fresh gingerroot
> ½ teaspoon (3 ml) coriander
> ½ teaspoon (3 ml) laos powder
> ½ cup (125 ml) Coconut milk (see Aromatics and Special Ingredients)
> ½ cup (125 ml) rich vegetable or chicken broth
> 2 Japanese eggplants (the long, narrow kind), cut into ½- to ¾-inch (12- to 18-mm) chunks

2 cups (500 ml) green beans, cut into 1½-inch (37-mm) lengths
2 tablespoons (30 ml) brown sugar or honey
2 tablespoons (30 ml) chick-pea flour
1 to 2 teaspoons (5 to 10 ml) soy sauce, or to taste
Juice of 1 lemon (2 tablespoons [30 ml])

1. Sauté onion and garlic in vegetable oil until lightly browned; sprinkle with curry powder, cumin, and turmeric. Add red chiles, gingerroot, coriander, and laos powder, and cook for 1 or 2 minutes.
2. Pour in coconut milk and broth, then add eggplant and cook a few minutes. Add green beans and cook until crisp-tender and bright green.
3. Add brown sugar or honey, chick-pea flour, soy sauce, and lemon juice, and heat through until sauce thickens, about 3 minutes.
4. Serve immediately, with condiments, such as chopped green onions, toasted cashews, or fried onion flakes, as desired.

ADVANCE PREPARATION: May be prepared as much as a day ahead and kept covered in the refrigerator.

Puree de Pommes de Terre à l'Ail

Garlic Mashed Potatoes

France

I love garlic passionately. I yield to its voluptuous presence often, even at the pain of destroying my social life. There's almost no dish that I don't find improved by a touch of the aromatic bulb, though garlic is so delicious it can overshadow the rest of the dish.

Garlic is versatile, too. Raw, it's potent and strong, more so as it is chopped or pounded. But cooked whole, garlic's flavor is tender and mild.

Here, whole garlic cloves are cooked with chunks of potato, then mashed with a bit of sweet butter and cream. It's smooth and aromatic, and utterly irresistible.

Enjoy with rare roast lamb, studded with cloves of garlic before being put to roast, and accompany with spinach sautéed in a little olive oil with lots of chopped—you guessed it!—garlic.

Serves 4

2 heads garlic
6 to 8 medium-sized baking potatoes, peeled and cut into 1-inch (25-mm) cubes

2 cups (500 ml) water
½ stick unsalted butter
3 to 4 tablespoons (45 to 60 ml) whipping cream
   Salt and freshly ground black pepper

1. Separate garlic into cloves and peel.
2. Place garlic and potatoes in saucepan and cover with water. Cook over medium-high heat until potatoes and garlic cloves are just tender, adding more water if needed.
3. Drain potatoes and garlic, saving the cooking liquid for soup. Mash with a fork or potato masher and stir in butter and cream. Season to taste with salt and pepper, and serve immediately.

VARIATION: Garlic mashed potatoes are a good topping for a spicy meat mixture, much like an exotic shepherd's pie.

Gratin Varaire

Casserole of New Potatoes and Artichokes

France

This combination of potatoes and artichokes was conceived in the marketplace of the medieval French town of Cahors and named after the village I was staying in. There were at least 7 different types of potatoes to choose from—each a different size, color, and texture. I chose small potatoes that seemed creamy and tender, even when still raw.

The dish emerged from the oven fragrant and bubbling, and creamy indeed in its flat, oval ceramic casserole. We ate it with a salad of greens and herbs with a mustard vinaigrette. By the time we finished supper the sun had set. As we drank the last of a large bottle of Vin de Cahors we watched the expansive, starry black sky overhead, and counted shooting stars.

Serves 4

½ stick unsalted butter
8 medium-sized, red, waxy new potatoes, peeled and thinly sliced
3 large artichokes (see Note)
2 tablespoons (30 ml) chopped shallots
3 ounces (84 g) raw ham (prosciutto, Westphalian, and so on)

¼ pound (112 g) Gruyère, Appenzeller, dry Jack, or similar
   cheese, diced or thinly sliced
6 cloves garlic, chopped
1 teaspoon (5 ml) fresh thyme leaves, or ½ teaspoon (3 ml)
   dried, crushed
¼ cup (60 ml) milk
   Salt and freshly ground coarse black pepper to taste

NOTE: To prepare artichokes, peel off leaves by pulling them backward until they snap off. Discard. Don't worry about losing too much of of the flesh, since when raw it is hard and crisp and does not come off with the leaves. Cut artichokes into quarters, and remove fuzz and thistles with a paring knife. Slice ¼- to ½-inch (6- to 12-mm) thick, then place in saucepan containing several cups of boiling water.

Boil artichokes 2 to 3 minutes, until barely tender, then drain and set aside.

1. Butter a 1½-quart (1.5-l) ceramic baking dish with 1 or 2 tablespoons (14 or 28 g) of the butter. Make a layer of half the potatoes, then the artichoke slices, shallots, ham, cheese, and half of the garlic and thyme. Top with remaining potatoes.

2. Dot top with remaining butter, moisten with milk, sprinkle with remaining garlic, and salt and pepper.

3. Bake uncovered in 350° F. oven for 45 minutes, or until the potatoes are tender, and the top is golden brown. Serve immediately.

ADVANCE PREPARATION: Casserole may be assembled up to a day ahead of time and baked just before serving. Be sure to warm up the casserole to room temperature before baking so that it cooks evenly, and so that the ceramic casserole does not break.

VARIATION: Pastel de Patata con Romero

From Spain we have this rosemary-scented potato gratin. Try it with Rôti de Porc Provençal or Canard aux Olives et Vin Rouge and a lettuce salad with a mustardy vinaigrette.

Omit artichokes and thyme. You can omit ham, as desired. Proceed with the previous recipe, increasing the amount of potatoes to 10 to 12 and adding 3 tablespoons (45 ml) fresh rosemary leaves to the casserole, sprinkled in as you add the shallots and garlic.

Imam Bayildi

Eggplant Stuffed with Tomatoes, Onions, and Eggplant

Greece and Turkey

This is one of those traditional peasant dishes that breaks no new culinary ground, a dish you can find in other cookbooks, but one I had to include because it is so delicious, and because I think this version is more delicious than any of the others.

The ingredients could not be humbler—eggplant, tomato, parsley, and lots of onions, but combined, they become a dish that sings of the sun-drenched shores of the Mediterranean, a dish of tender sautéed eggplant that is more honestly flavorful than any nouvelle dish could possibly be.

The name of the dish translates as "the priest fainted"—with pleasure over the tastiness of it all, I suppose.

Serve warm or at room temperature, accompanied by a bowl of cool yogurt, and rice pilaf topped with chopped fresh mint. Leftover Imam Bayildi makes a splendid sandwich on thickly sliced French bread, for a lazy sunny-day picnic.

Serves 4 to 6

> 1 large-sized eggplant
> ⅓ cup (85 ml) extra-virgin olive oil, more if needed
> 2 medium-sized onions, thinly sliced
> 5 to 8 ripe medium-sized tomatoes, chopped (canned is fine)
> 1½ tablespoons (23 ml) tomato paste
> 2 teaspoons (10 ml) sugar
> Salt to taste
> 1 cup (250 ml) chopped parsley
> 3 cloves garlic, chopped

1. Cut eggplant in half. Slice half the eggplant into ¼- to ½- inch (6- to 12-mm) slices, the other half into small ½-inch (12-mm) cubes.

2. Sauté eggplant slices in olive oil until lightly browned, then place in baking dish.

3. Lightly sauté the onions until softened, not browned. Add eggplant cubes, tomatoes, tomato paste, sugar, and salt to taste, and simmer for 5 to 10 minutes or until thickened. Add parsley and garlic.

4. Cover each slice with a portion of the eggplant-onion-and-tomato filling.

5. Bake uncovered in a 350° F. oven for approximately 20 minutes or until lightly browned on top.

6. Serve hot, cool, or at room temperature. Accompany with cool yogurt and a salad of cucumbers and mint.

ADVANCE PREPARATION: Refrigerated, this dish lasts up to 4 days.

Mofongo

Fried Patties of Mashed Plantain and Sausage

West Indies

Plantains are one of the staple foods of the Caribbean, indeed, in much of Latin America. They are a cousin of the banana, but larger, less sweet, and more starchy. Plantains are cooked many ways—sautéed and eaten as an accompaniment to black beans and rice or grilled meat. Sometimes they are first boiled, mashed, and rolled into balls, then simmered in stews. Here, they are first boiled and mashed, then combined with sautéed bits of sausage and garlic, formed into cakes, and fried. These are delicious as a snack or alongside rice and black beans.

Serves 4

2 medium-sized green plantains, peeled and diced.
3 cups (750 ml) water
    Pinch salt
6 ounces (168 g) smoked sausage (kielbasa or smoked beef sausage), diced
3 tablespoons (45 ml) olive oil
3 cloves garlic, chopped
    Several shakes Tabasco or cayenne pepper
1 teaspoon (5 ml) cumin
    Tabasco or other very hot condiment, to taste

1. Boil plantains in water with pinch of salt until tender, just about 5 minutes. Drain and mash with a potato masher.
2. In skillet, sauté the sausage bits, adding 1 or 2 teaspoons (5 to 10 ml) olive oil if needed to keep from sticking. When just about browned add the garlic, Tabasco, and cumin, and cook a minute or two longer.
3. Mix mashed plantains with spiced sausage bits and form into flat cakes. Let cool.
4. When ready to eat, fry patties in olive oil until browned on each side. Eat immediately, sprinkled with Tabasco or other hot condiment.

Xinxim

Bahian Tomato–Coconut Stew with Red Beans, Broccoli, and Rice

Brazil

Bahia—where native Indian, African, and Portuguese cuisines and cultures combine to the sultry sounds of the samba—is the exotic Brazil of movies and books: balmy, sexy, mysterious, and bursting with life.

The cuisine reflects the diverse cultures that make up Bahia. Coconut milk, seafood, hot peppers, palm oil, and peanuts are prominent in the Bahia kitchen. As for the peanuts, did they go to Africa with the explorers from Peru, and then back again to the New World? Did they come directly to Brazil, long before, in the trade between the Indian tribes? Nobody seems to know when they became a dominant flavor in the Bahian kitchen.

While Xinxim is often made with shrimp or chicken, I like the sauce so well with red beans, broccoli, and rice that my recipe does not include fish or fowl. While more Cajun than Brazilian, the flavor of red beans is nonetheless very compatible with the rest of the dish. When elephant garlic is available I use it in the red beans and broccoli. It has a mild flavor, somewhat like a combination of garlic and leek.

Palm oil is a favorite oil of Brazil and parts of Africa. Also known as dênde oil it is bright orange in color. Achiote oil or olive oil with paprika are fine substitutes.

Serves 4

Sauce:
- 2 medium-sized onions, chopped
- 3 cloves garlic, chopped
- 2 to 3 jalapeños, chopped
- 2 tablespoons (30 ml) palm oil or achiote oil (see Note)
- ¼ teaspoon (1.5 ml) powdered ginger
- ¼ teaspoon (1.5 ml) cinnamon
- Pinch nutmeg
- 2 cups (500 ml) chopped tomatoes (canned is fine)
- 1 cup (250 ml) chicken or vegetable broth
- ½ cup (125 ml) cilantro, coarsely chopped
- ½ cup (125 ml) fresh mint leaves, coarsely chopped
- 1 cup (250 ml) coconut milk (see Aromatics and Special Ingredients)
- ½ cup (125 ml) smooth peanut butter

Juice of ½ to 1 lemon (1 to 1½ tablespoons [15 to 23 ml], or to taste)

¼ cup (60 ml) coarsely chopped, dry-roasted unsalted peanuts

Red Beans, Broccoli, and Rice:

1 small-sized green bell pepper, coarsely chopped

2 cloves elephant garlic, diced (or substitute 2 cloves garlic, chopped, plus ½ onion, chopped)

2 tablespoons (30 ml) olive oil

1 tablespoon (15 ml) flour

½ cup (125 ml) chicken or vegetable broth

Salt and coarsely ground black pepper to taste

1 bunch broccoli, cut into florets, about 1½ cups (375 ml), or equal amount of broccoli-type greens such as broccoli de rabe

2 cups (500 ml) cooked kidney beans or red beans

3 cups (750 ml) cooked white or brown rice

Salsa, jalapeños en escabeche, or other hot condiment, to taste

NOTE: To make achiote oil: Heat 1 tablespoon (15 ml) achiote seeds in 3 tablespoons (45 ml) olive oil until bubbles form around the edge of the pan and the oil turns a reddish color; let stand 10 minutes to cool, then strain. If achiote seeds are unavailable substitute paprika, taking care not to burn it. Pour off the red-colored oil to use and discard the solids.

1. To make the sauce: Sauté onions, garlic, and jalapeños in the palm or achiote oil until softened. Sprinkle with ginger, cinnamon, and nutmeg, then stir in tomatoes and broth, and cook uncovered over high heat for 10 to 15 minutes, or until a saucy consistency.

2. Stir in cilantro, mint, coconut milk, peanut butter, and lemon juice, and cook over medium heat until sauce is thickened, only a few minutes. It will be soupy. Set aside while you prepare red beans, broccoli, and rice.

3. Sauté green bell pepper and elephant garlic or garlic and onion in olive oil until softened. Sprinkle in flour and cook until golden, about 3 minutes. Remove from heat, add broth, then return to heat and cook, stirring, over medium heat until smooth and thickened, about 5 minutes.

4. Add broccoli or broccoli de rabe and kidney or red beans and cook about 5 minutes longer, just until the broccoli is tender.

5. Sprinkle peanuts over Xinxim sauce. Serve broccoli-bean mixture ladled over rice accompanied by Xinxim sauce. Offer salsa or other hot condiment at the table.

ADVANCE PREPARATION: Xinxim sauce may be prepared as much as a day ahead of time, and keeps well for several days tightly covered in the refrigerator.

VARIATION: With shrimp: Soak ½ cup (125 ml) dried shrimp in 1 cup (250 ml) water for ½ hour; drain and add to the sauce, along with the tomatoes. Add about ½ pound (225 g) fresh shrimp when you add the mint and cilantro, and cook only a few minutes, until the shrimp turn pink.

Alu Kofta

Potato Cutlets with Spinach–Yogurt Sauce

India

In a land where so many eschew meat there is an imaginative vegetarian cuisine. Vegetable cutlets are a favorite dish because there are so many ways you can vary them, depending on what vegetable is available. The chopped vegetables are bound together with mashed potatoes and/or chick-pea flour. This cutlet is a golden fried patty of mashed potato, savory chick-pea flour, and potent chile-onion paste. Served with tart spinach-yogurt sauce, it is a shock of delicious flavor.

These cutlets are traditionally served as a snack, with afternoon tea, or as part of a buffet.

Serves 4

  1 medium-sized onion, finely chopped
  6 cloves garlic, chopped
  2 tablespoons (30 ml) chopped gingerroot
  ½ teaspoon (3 ml) turmeric
  1 teaspoon (5 ml) cumin
  1 tablespoon (15 ml) chopped cilantro
  1 tablespoon (15 ml) chopped mint leaves
  2 jalapeños, chopped
    Juice of 2 lemons (about ¼ cup [60 ml])
  1 teaspoon (5 ml) salt
  1 cup (250 ml) cooked mashed potatoes (with on added butter or milk)
  ¼ cup (60 ml) chick-pea flour
  ¼ cup (60 ml) vegetable oil, more if needed

Spinach-Yogurt Sauce:
½ cup (125 ml) cooked spinach, drained and chopped (frozen
   is fine)
2 cloves garlic, chopped
¼ teaspoon (1.5 ml) turmeric
2 cups (500 ml) plain yogurt
   Salt and cayenne to taste

1. In blender or processor puree onion, garlic, gingerroot, turmeric, cumin, cilantro, mint, and jalapeños. Add lemon juice and salt.

2. Combine this spicy mixture with potatoes and chick-pea flour. Cover and chill until ready to use, at least an hour (chilling makes it easier to handle).

3. For Spinach-Yogurt Sauce, combine spinach, garlic, turmeric, and yogurt by hand, or in blender or processor. Add salt and cayenne pepper to taste. Chill until ready to serve.

4. Heat oil in skillet. Using about 2 tablespoons (30 ml) potato mixture per patty, fry until golden, then turn over and fry other side. The patties are very tender, so use care in turning.

5. Drain each patty on paper towels and serve immediately, accompanied by a dollop of cold Spinach-Yogurt Sauce.

ADVANCE PREPARATION: Unfried potato mixture may be kept covered in refrigerator for up to 2 days. Once fried they should be served immediately, or placed on a cookie sheet and reheated in a 350° F. oven. The sauce will keep covered in the refrigerator for about 3 days.

Papas y Ejotes Chorreadas

Potatoes and Green Beans in Tomato–Chile Sauce

Colombia

Tinted brilliantly yellow from turmeric, this tomato-flecked cheese sauce is at once spicy and creamy. It is somewhat reminiscent of Papas Huancaina, the Peruvian creamy cheese sauce spooned over boiled potatoes and garnished with ears of corn, black olives, wedges of tomato, and egg. Chorreada sauce, a spicier, more tomatoy version, comes from Colombia, where it is not reserved for potatoes, but is poured over many kinds of vegetables such as Brussels sprouts and green beans, and even grilled chicken and steak.

The name refers to both the sauce and dish. Here, we have whole, tender potatoes and crisp green beans topped with this intriguingly flavored tomato-cheese sauce. This would traditionally be an accompaniment to thin, grilled steaks seasoned with lime juice, but it is delicious and substantial enough to serve as a main course as well. Begin with shrimp steamed in their shells, tossed with a garlic vinaigrette and a shake of cayenne pepper, and have something sinful for dessert, such as Teresa's Mexican Chocolate Cake (see Index).

Serves 4 as a main course,
6 as a first course

8 to 12 small-sized waxy new potatoes, whole and unpeeled, but washed
½ pound (225 g) green beans, trimmed and cut into 2-inch (50-mm) lengths
2 medium-sized onions, chopped
3 cloves garlic, chopped
2 jalapeños, chopped
2 tablespoons (30 ml) olive oil
1½ teaspoons (8 ml) turmeric
1 teaspoon (5 ml) cumin
¼ teaspoon (1.5 ml) powdered ginger
2 cups (500 ml) chopped tomatoes (canned is fine)
¼ cup (60 ml) chopped cilantro
1½ cups (375 ml) cubed mild cheese (Jack, Muenster, Lappi, or Danish fontina)
1 cup (250 ml) sour cream

1. Place potatoes in steamer or saucepan filled with water. Steam or boil until just tender, 15 to 20 minutes. Drain well and keep warm while you prepare the green beans and sauce.

2. Steam or boil green beans until they are crisp-tender and bright green. Set aside.

3. Sauté onion, garlic, and jalapeños in olive oil until softened. Sprinkle with turmeric, cumin, and ginger, stir together, and cook 1 or 2 minutes. Add tomatoes and cilantro and cook over medium-low heat until most of the liquid has evaporated, about 10 minutes.

4. Stir in the cheese and sour cream and slowly heat until it forms a cheesy, creamy mixture.

5. Serve spooned over the boiled potatoes and steamed green beans.

ADVANCE PREPARATION: Sautéed onions, spices, and tomatoes may be prepared up to a day ahead, but cheese and sour cream must be added just before serving. Potatoes and green beans can be prepared an hour or two ahead of time and briefly reheated before serving, or can be served at room temperature.

Nimbo Dahl

Curried Lemon Lentils

India

Dahl, a spicy preparation of lentils, is eaten at almost every meal in Indian homes. Its high-protein content is especially appreciated in this land of many vegetarians. While dahl is described basically as a porridge of spiced lentils, this does nothing to convey its huge variety of flavors, colors, and textures. Dahl may be made from any legumes—kidney beans make a delicious, deep red-colored dahl; chick pea's distinctive flavor is enhanced by the sharp Indian spices; and masoor dahl or yellow split peas cook into a mushy consistency, perfect for rich soups or sauces to ladle over rice.

This dahl is flavored strongly with lemon, not just the juice, but the entire lemon shell. It imparts its citrus fragrance as it simmers with the legumes. Often, dahl is soupy, to be ladled over rice. This dahl is thicker, but can be easily thinned by the simple addition of 1 cup (250 ml) water or broth at the end of cooking, if desired.

Serves 4 to 6 as a side dish

2 tablespoons (28 g) unsalted butter
2 medium-sized onions, one thinly sliced, the other one chopped
½ teaspoon (3 ml) cinnamon
1 tablespoon (15 ml) chopped gingerroot
1 cup (250 ml) yellow split peas or masoor dahl (red lentils)
4 cups (1 l) chicken or vegetable broth
1 bay leaf
2 small dried hot red chiles (tepín, hontaka, or cayenne), broken into small pieces (or left whole for less heat)
1½ medium- to large-sized lemons
1 jalapeño, thinly sliced
3 cloves garlic, chopped

½ teaspoon (3 ml) turmeric
½ cup (125 ml) chopped cilantro
Lemon wedges for garnish

1. In 1 tablespoon (14 g) butter sauté thinly sliced onion with cinnamon and gingerroot until onion is softened, not browned. Add yellow split peas or red lentils, broth, bay leaf, and chiles; simmer for 15 to 20 minutes.

2. Cut one lemon in half; squeeze the juice into the lentils, then drop the squeezed lemon halves in, too. Simmer until the lentils are tender, about 45 minutes. Remove lemon shells and discard.

3. Sauté the remaining onion with the jalapeño, garlic, and turmeric in the remaining butter until the onion is softened. Add these to the lentil mixture along with the juice from the remaining lemon half and the cilantro. Serve immediately, garnished with lemon wedges.

ADVANCE PREPARATION: Store tightly covered in refrigerator for up to 4 days. It is more delicious each day.

VARIATION: Increase liquid to 6 cups (1.5 l) for a soupy consistency instead of the thicker one. Serve in bowls, topped with 1 or 2 slices of lemon and a scattering of cilantro leaves.

Southwestern Chilied Hominy

New Mexico

This rustic cuisine, which authentically is unsoftened by cream and other fancifications, is as bold as the landscape of its origins. That landscape embraces a great expanse of deserts, the majestic Sangre de Cristo Mountains, crisp, clear air, and the elegant, often primitive adobe architecture. Its distinctive cuisine makes a statement too: red or green chile, crusty breads baked in adobe ovens, flat tortillas, pink beans simmered with a few herbs, such as mint and thyme.

Hominy is a southwestern food eaten by Native Americans long before the European settlers arrived. Left to soak in a lye solution, the kernels of corn swell up and shed their skins. Its flavor is bland and rich, its texture different from that of other corn preparations. The first time I ate hominy I was not sure I liked it, but by the second time I was almost addicted to the earthy quality and slightly chewy texture.

Ground into a coarse meal it is known as grits, a staple of the American South.

This version of hominy celebrates the long, happy marriage of Native American and Mexican culinary cultures.

Serves 4

1 medium-sized onion, chopped
3 cloves garlic, chopped
1 tablespoon (15 ml) vegetable oil
3 Anaheim chiles, roasted and peeled
2 tablespoons (30 ml) ancho or New Mexico chile powder
1 tablespoon (15 ml) paprika
1 teaspoon (5 ml) cumin
3 cups (750 ml) beef, chicken, or vegetable broth
2 tablespoons (30 ml) chopped cilantro
2 to 3 corn tortillas, finely chopped
3 cups (750 ml) cooked white or yellow hominy (see Note)
Salt and cayenne pepper to taste

NOTE: Sometimes hominy is sold frozen, usually in Latin American grocery stores. This must usually be cooked approximately 1 hour and will have exact directions on the package. Hominy is also sold dried, and must first be soaked overnight, then boiled for at least 4 hours. Although I tend to shun most products in a tin, canned hominy, once rinsed well and simmered in sauce, is delicious.

1. Sauté onion and garlic in oil until onion is softened and lightly browned. Sprinkle with chile powder, paprika, and cumin, and cook for about a minute, to cook out the raw flavor of the spices.

2. Add broth, cilantro, tortillas, and hominy. Bring to a boil; slightly reduce heat and cook over medium-high heat, uncovered, for 15 to 20 minutes or until liquid has thickened. Add salt and cayenne to taste, as desired.

ADVANCE PREPARATION: This is even better the next day. The sauce is thicker, so you may wish to thin it out with a bit of broth. Then again, it's awfully good thick.

Alecha

Sauté of Potatoes, Green Beans, and Tomatoes

Ethiopia

A homey yet unusual dish of turmeric-tinted potatoes with crisp green beans and chopped tomatoes. Sautéeing the potatoes first seals their edges, so that when you add the green beans and tomatoes, the potatoes don't disintegrate and become mashed. The richness of the dish is lightened just before serving with a squeeze of tart lime.

Ethiopian cuisine has developed a richness and depth over the centuries, much as Italian and French cuisines have. The Ethiopians use exotic, fragrant blends of spices, with much emphasis on chiles. Meats are often simmered in spice mixtures and served with large, flat sponge-like breads called *injera*.

Serve Alecha for a sunny solitary lunch to get you through the day or for supper as an accompaniment for Sarish Bata, the Indian dish of mustard-seed–spiced fish (see Index).

Serves 4 as a side dish

2 tablespoons (30 ml) olive oil
3 large baking potatoes, peeled and diced
1½ cups (375 ml) green beans cut into 1½-inch (37-mm) lengths
½ serrano, thinly sliced
2 teaspoons (10 ml) turmeric
2 to 3 cloves garlic, chopped
4 ripe medium-sized tomatoes, chopped and drained of excess liquid, or 2 cups (500 ml) canned
Salt to taste
Juice of ¼ lime (1 teaspoon [5 ml] lime juice), or as desired

1. Heat olive oil and sauté potatoes in it until lightly golden brown, about 10 minutes, turning carefully every so often, so as not to break.

2. Add green beans and sauté 1 or 2 minutes until they begin to turn bright green, then add serrano, turmeric, garlic, and tomatoes. Cook until green beans are crisp-tender, a few minutes longer.

3. Season with salt to taste and lime juice. Serve immediately.

ADVANCE PREPARATION: May be prepared ahead of time; it tastes even better at room temperature or cold, the next day.

Black Bean–Chipotle Puree

Mexico

Smoky chipotle chiles blend with earthy black beans in this smooth but *picante* puree.

Black beans are an important and beloved part of Latin American *cocina*, that is, "cooking." Their protein sustains, their starchiness satisfies, and their hearty flavor pleases the soul. In some countries black beans are simmered with a variety of meats and ladled over rice, in other countries the beans are pureed. This dish is a cross-cultural combination of El Salvadorean puree with Mexican chipotle chiles.

Serve with steamed rice and tender carnitas, or roast chicken and Chipotle Salsa (see Index).

Serves 4

¾ to 1 cup (180 to 250 ml) black beans, sorted through for any
    small pebbles
2 cups (500 ml) water
2 cups (500 ml) rich vegetable or chicken broth
1 cup (250 ml) tomato sauce
2 tablespoons (30 ml) olive oil
½ medium-sized onion, chopped
5 cloves garlic, chopped
¼ medium-sized red bell pepper, chopped
½ small-sized carrot, chopped
1½ teaspoons (8 ml) cumin
1 teaspoon (5 ml) mild chile powder
½ teaspoon (3 ml) dried oregano
    Salsa to taste
1 teaspoon (5 ml) chopped cilantro
1 to 2 chipotle chiles
2 teaspoons (10 ml) canned chipotle chile marinade
3 tablespoons (45 ml) shredded Jack, Lappi, or other white
    mild cheese
2 tablespoons (30 ml) sour cream

1. Soak beans in water overnight; or boil for 2 minutes, remove from heat, cover, and let stand for 1 hour.

2. Add broth and tomato sauce to beans and soaking liquid. Simmer, covered, until beans are tender, about 1 to 1½ hours. (Some beans are tougher and take longer.) Add more water or broth if beans seem dry.

3. Heat olive oil in skillet and sauté onion, garlic, red bell pepper, and

carrot, until onions are limp. Sprinkle on cumin, chile powder, oregano, and salsa, then add to beans and continue to simmer for 30 to 45 minutes. Boil over high heat for a few minutes, if necessary, to reduce liquid, then add cilantro.

4. Puree beans with chipotle chile and chipotle chile marinade until smooth. Arrange in baking pan, top with cheese, and broil to melt cheese.

5. Serve immediately, topped with sour cream, if desired.

VARIATION 1: Huaraches

A bowl of this puree is wonderful to have in the refrigerator to spread on soft pita, to blanket grilled lamb, and to fill thick, homemade tortillas (these are called huaraches).

VARIATION 2: Huevos Motuleños

To make this delicious Yucatecan egg dish, spread a few tablespoons of spicy tomato sauce on a plate, top with a layer of puree, then a lightly browned tortilla. Layer this with 2 sunny-side up eggs, another tortilla, top with more tomato sauce, a few slices of fried plantain or bananas, and a sprinkling of peas and diced ham. Serve additional puree on the side and enjoy for brunch or supper.

Ful Midammis

Simmered Brown Beans with Olive Oil, Lemon, and Seasonings

Egypt

Ful is an ancient Egyptian staple, hearty simmered beans eaten in the days of the Pharaohs and sold at food stalls on the streets of Cairo today. You find it in luxury restaurants, as well as at the humblest table. It is the breakfast for nearly everyone.

This dish is served in an almost ritualistic manner, with a cruet of olive oil, wedges of lemon or lime, chopped onions, hot pepper, and a hard-cooked egg to crumble into each bowl of seasoned beans.

Ful midammis is deeply satisfying. The finished dish transcends the humble ingredients to create a meal that is exceedingly good.

Serves 4

Beans:

    1 cup (250 ml) ful misri (small, dried, brown fava beans, either imported from the Middle East or California-grown; as a last resort use canned, spiced with a little cumin)

1 heaping tablespoon (15 ml) masoor dahl (red lentils) or yellow split peas
2 teaspoons (10 ml) cumin
¼ teaspoon (1.5 ml) salt or to taste

Garnishes:
⅓ cup (85 ml) extra-virgin olive oil
3 tablespoons (45 ml) lemon or lime juice, or 1½ lemons or limes, cut into wedges
5 green onions, thinly sliced
2 tablespoons (30 ml) chopped parsley or cilantro
4 cloves garlic, chopped
2 freshly cooked hard-boiled eggs, peeled and diced
Cayenne pepper to taste

1. Cover fava beans in water and soak in a covered pot overnight.
2. Drain, then add 4 cups (1 l) fresh water. Bring to a boil, add red lentils or yellow split peas, reduce heat to very low, and simmer until beans are tender. Check occasionally to be sure that the beans remain moist. If dry, add ¼ cup (60 ml) water. When done, nearly all the liquid should be absorbed. This may take as long as 5 hours. The lentils are traditionally placed in a slow oven and cooked overnight. Then add cumin and salt to taste. (If preparing canned ful misri, just heat in its liquid and season with cumin.)
3. Serve immediately in shallow soup bowls, accompanied with olive oil, lemon or lime juice, green onions, parsley or cilantro, garlic, eggs, and cayenne pepper. Each portion may be served with these garnishes, instead of offering them at the table.

ADVANCE PREPARATION: Beans may be cooked up to several days ahead and reheated. Store, covered, in refrigerator.

VARIATION 1: Beans may be tucked into a pita bread, doused with tahini sauce, and seasoned with raw chopped onion, and cayenne pepper, Tabasco, or other hot seasoning. Chopped tomato and cucumber is a delicious addition.

Variation 2: Ful midammis may also be pureed with garlic, olive oil, and lemon juice and served as a dip for pita bread, garnished with hot pepper seasoning, and so on.

Indonesian Asparagus and Tofu with Curried Steamed Noodles

Indonesia

This is a rich simmer of bright, fresh asparagus and meaty tofu in a sauce of tomatoes and coconut milk, ladled over fresh, steamed curry-spiced noodles. It's a wonderful mélange of flavors and fragrances, color and textures.

As with many Southeast Asian curries, this one begins by slowly frying onion, garlic, chile, and turmeric, which gives a deep rich flavor, important especially when meat is not included. The curried steamed noodles, my idea, is a variation of a Chinese steamed rice noodle or a Sri Lankan rôti, made with a flour and coconut-milk batter, steamed, and topped with a sprinkling of curry spices.

Serves 4

Noodles:
- 2 cups (500 ml) cake flour
- ¼ cup (60 ml) cornstarch
- 1 teaspoon (5 ml) salt
- ⅓ cup (85 ml) vegetable oil, plus a few tablespoons more for oiling the pans
- 2⅔ cups (670 ml) water, or 1⅔ cups (420 ml) water and 1 cup (250 ml) coconut milk (see Aromatics and Special Ingredients)
- 2 teaspoons to 1 tablespoon (10 to 15 ml) homemade Curry Powder (see Index)

Vegetable Curry:
- 1 block firm tofu, approximately 3 by 5 inches (75 by 125 mm), cut into 1- by ½-inch (25- by 12-mm) cubes
- 1 cup (250 ml) vegetable oil, for frying
- 1 medium-sized onion, thinly sliced
- 3 cloves garlic, chopped
- 5 small dried red chiles, broken in half (see Note)
- 1 tablespoon (15 ml) vegetable oil
- 1 teaspoon (5 ml) turmeric
- 3 medium-sized tomatoes, chopped (canned is fine)
- ¼ cup (60 ml) coconut milk (see Aromatics and Special Ingredients)
- 1 pound (450 g) asparagus, trimmed and cut into 2-inch (50-mm) lengths

Salt to taste
Juice of ½ lemon (1 tablespoon [15 ml])
½ cup (125 ml) dry roasted peanuts

NOTE: For a milder dish leave chiles whole; for a hotter one, break into small pieces.

1. To prepare noodles: Combine cake flour with cornstarch, salt, oil, and water or water and coconut milk. It will be a thin batter; stir well to remove any lumps.

2. Place 1 or 2 teaspoons (5 or 10 ml) of oil in a 9-inch (225-mm) pie tin, then ladle in about ¼ cup (60 ml) batter. Sprinkle with ⅛ teaspoon (.5 ml) Curry Powder, then place in steamer. Steam 5 minutes until noodles no longer look opaque and liquidy, but become translucent and firm.

3. Remove from steamer and carefully slide out of pan onto plate. Repeat until batter is used up. It is easiest to use 2 pie tins: as one is steaming the other may be filled. Stack up and set aside.

4. When ready to serve, cut into slices ¾-inch (18-mm) wide and heat in a tiny bit of oil over medium heat.

5. To prepare curry: Fry tofu in oil over high heat until lightly browned, about 5 to 10 minutes. Drain on paper towels and set aside. Discard all but 1 tablespoon (15 ml) of the oil.

6. Over low-medium heat stir-fry the onion, garlic, and chiles in 1 tablespoon (15 ml) vegetable oil until onion is softened. Sprinkle with turmeric and cook about 5 minutes.

7. Add tomatoes and coconut milk, increase heat, and bring to boil. Add asparagus and cook 1 or 2 minutes, only until asparagus is bright green; salt to taste, and squeeze lemon juice over all.

8. Top with peanuts and serve over curried noodles.

ADVANCE PREPARATION: The batter may be prepared ahead of time, and so may the noodles. Stack on a plate, cover with plastic wrap, and store up to 2 days in the refrigerator. The noodles may be used as wrappers for a stir-fry or curry, or cut into strips and warmed with a curry-spiced stew.

PASTA AND GRAINS

From the Middle and Far East, from the Mediterranean to the balmy Caribbean and the wide, wide Pacific, grain dishes are the staff of life.

The tender noodles splashed with cinnamon-scented tomato sauce in a Greek Island *taverna*, or the platter of good, honest spaghetti the Italian mama places before her family; the bowl of rice topped with spicy fish stews eaten in bamboo huts; and the couscous partaken of in walled, ancient North African medinas—this is the food that fuels much of the world.

Here we have many very traditional dishes, such as Lasagne alla Veneziana or Pasta al Funghi, and many new dishes based on traditional flavors but with unexpectedly bright tastes. Try pasta topped with watercress and tarragon, combined with herb cream and chicken; or tender ravioli filled with pungent, rich Gorgonzola on a bed of sautéed radicchio. Gnocchi happily collided with ancho chile in my kitchen, and the result is a delicious variation of the Italian classic. Sample, too, the ancient Venetian dish of tender fettucine with a bit of duck confit or the cool and spicy noodles from Phõ Bò.

Pasta al Funghi

Pasta with Porcini

Italy

Italy's art treasures, history, and architecture are significant reasons to visit that country, but to me fresh porcini season is no less significant a reason. Since these mushrooms are wild, not planted, one really does not know when or where they will pop up; they're like a whimsical gift from nature. Unfortunately, you cannot plan a visit during porcini season; it follows rain and moist, warm weather. During the season, the large woodsy fungi are displayed in restaurant windows, piled up against the mounds of fresh pasta, whole legs of prosciutto, and other specialties of the house. The mushrooms are served in soups or salads, with veal or chicken, simmered in stews, or—my favorite!—with tender, silken pasta. Their earthy perfume accompanied almost every meal I ate for 3 weeks.

Here we must make do with dried porcini. Though expensive, they are delicious; they keep for long periods of time, and they may be combined with fresh cultivated mushrooms to add texture.

Serves 4

    4 ounces (112 g) dried porcini (see Note)
    1 cup (250 ml) very hot, but not boiling, water
    2 tablespoons (28 g) unsalted butter
    5 shallots, minced
    2 cloves garlic, chopped
    2 tablespoons (30 ml) brandy
    2 cups (500 ml) whipping cream
    ¼ teaspoon (1.5 ml) freshly grated nutmeg
      Salt and pepper to taste
    1 pound (450 g) fresh fettucine or papardelle, or 12 ounces
      (336 g) imported Italian fettucine
    ½ cup (126 ml) freshly grated Parmesan or to taste

NOTE: It is difficult to measure dried mushrooms except by weight. You can use any amount of porcini from 2 to 4 ounces (56 to 112 g). The more porcini, the more flavor. Any amount of porcini will flavor the sauce deliciously so if you have only 2 ounces (56 g), this is fine.

1. Place porcini in a bowl and cover with hot water. Soak for 20 minutes or so. Remove porcini from liquid (strain and reserve liquid for another use—it's great in onion soup). Slice soaked porcini into ½-inch (12-mm) strips.

2. Gently heat 1 tablespoon (14 g) butter and lightly sauté shallots, garlic, and porcini. Do not let brown, merely sweat in the warm butter.

3. Add brandy, raise heat, and cook until liquid is almost evaporated. Add cream and nutmeg and heat through. Salt and pepper to taste.

4. Cook pasta until just tender. Drain and serve pasta immediately, tossed with remaining butter, then topped with sauce and accompanied by freshly grated Parmesan.

Pastitsatha

Macaroni with a Grecian Lamb-Tomato Sauce

Greece

When I first visited Greece, I was surprised that the Greeks are so fond of pasta—I expected a pale imitation of Italian dishes. Instead, I discovered wonderful pastas full of the flavors of Greece: leg of lamb, roasted with tomatoes and olive oil, served with the small rice-shaped pasta called orzo; or pastitsio, a casserole of meat sauce and pasta covered with a cheese custard and baked golden. Greek spaghetti sauce is cinnamon-scented and topped with either crumbled feta or a Parmesan-like kefalotiri or kasseri.

This dish is earthy and robust: sturdy macaroni or penne, topped with a lusty tomato-and-lamb sauce, spiced with cinnamon and cloves. It's a variation of a dish I enjoyed on the Greek isle of Corfu, and may be prepared with beef instead of lamb.

Serve with crusty bread, of course, and a salad of cold, cooked spinach dressed with extra-virgin olive oil and lemon juice.

Serves 4

    1 medium-sized onion, chopped
    3 cloves garlic, chopped
    3 tablespoons (45 ml) extra-virgin olive oil
    1 pound (450 g) lamb shoulder, cut into 1-inch (25-mm) cubes
       (keep the bones, too; they add flavor to the sauce)
    1 teaspoon (5 ml) cinnamon
  ¼ teaspoon (1.5 ml) ground cloves
    1 cup (250 ml) sturdy dry red-wine, such as zinfandel
    1 teaspoon (5 ml) sugar
    2 medium-sized tomatoes, chopped (canned is fine)
1½ cups (375 ml) tomato sauce
    3 tablespoons (45 ml) tomato paste

¾ **pound (336 g) macaroni such as penne**
¼ **pound (112 g) feta cheese, crumbled**

1. Sauté onion and garlic in 1 tablespoon (15 ml) olive oil until onion is softened, about 5 minutes. Add meat, cinnamon, and cloves and sauté with onion-garlic mixture for about 5 minutes.
2. Pour in wine, sugar, tomatoes, tomato sauce, and tomato paste, and simmer over low heat until sauce is rich and flavorful, about 30 minutes.
3. Cook pasta al dente; drain and toss with remaining olive oil, then with half the feta cheese.
4. Top each portion of pasta with some of the lamb and sauce, and serve immediately. Pass additional feta cheese around the table.

ADVANCE PREPARATION: Like all stew-like dishes, this one is even better the next day. Store tightly covered in the refrigerator. When ready to use, remove any fat that might have accumulated at the top of the sauce. Heat the sauce and cook the macaroni just before serving.

VARIATION 1: Instead of feta, sometimes a hard, grated Parmesan-like cheese, kefalotiri, is used, or a combination of both. Or, try tossing the pasta with feta and offering the kefalotiri or Parmesan at the table.

VARIATION 2: Vegetarian Sauce
   Instead of lamb, use 1 cubed eggplant, adding extra olive oil during the sautéeing if needed. Proceed according to the basic recipe.

Pasta Printemps

The Mediterranean
Tender fettucine with morsels of chicken breast, swathed in an herb-cream sauce, complemented by the salty tang of coarsely shredded Parmesan and the peppery freshness of watercress leaves, create a pasta dish unlike any I've tasted.
   The flavors are Mediterranean, both Italian and French, hence the bilingual title. The watercress and herbs create a spring-like flavor, so I have given it a French name, *printemps,* or "springtime," much like the Italian dish of pasta and vegetables called pasta primavera.
   Serve separately, as its own course, so that nothing will detract from its uniqueness.

Serves 4

2 cloves garlic, chopped

½ cup (125 ml) fresh rosemary leaves, lightly crushed, or 2 tablespoons (30 ml) dried rosemary

2 tablespoons (28 g) unsalted butter

1½ cups (375 ml) whipping cream

⅔ cup (170 ml) chicken or vegetable broth

8 ounces (224 g) boned chicken breast, diced into 1-inch (25-mm) cubes

1 tablespoon (15 ml) fresh tarragon, or 1 teaspoon (5 ml) dried tarragon

1 pound (450 g) delicate fresh fettucine, or 12 ounces (336 g) good-quality, dried noodles ¼-inch (6-mm) wide

1 cup (250 ml) coarsely grated Parmesan or dry Jack cheese

⅔ cup (170 ml) watercress leaves

1. Lightly sauté half the garlic with the rosemary in 1 tablespoon (14 g) butter. Pour in cream and broth, and raise heat to high, cooking until reduced to half the volume, about 10 minutes. Strain and reserve the liquid, discarding the rosemary leaves.

2. Lightly sauté chicken breast cubes with remaining garlic in remaining butter, adding more butter if necessary, for about 5 minutes, until opaque. Add to cream-broth liquid, along with tarragon. Set aside.

3. Cook fettucine in boiling water until just tender. Time will vary depending on what type of pasta you choose; follow package directions. Drain, then toss with cream-and-chicken mixture.

4. Toss with the shredded cheese, and garnish with the watercress leaves. Serve immediately.

ADVANCE PREPARATION: Garlic-rosemary cream may be prepared up to a day ahead of time, but the rest of the dish should be made just prior to serving.

VARIATION: For a vegetarian dish, simply omit the meat. The herb sauce and pasta alone will be delicious.

Penne con Ricotta

Pasta Tubes with Tomato Sauce and Ricotta Cheese

Italy

With all the recent popularity of fresh pasta we seem to have forgotten all about *pasta asciutta,* dried pasta such as spaghetti, vermicelli, bucatini, macaroni, and penne. Good quality pasta—that usually means imported from Italy—can be delicious and has the body to stand up to heartier, more assertive sauces. Cooked al dente and blanketed in sauce, it is satisfying indeed.

The creamy addition of ricotta to tomato-sauce spaghetti is a favorite in the south of Italy. Serve with a salad of mixed greens and herbs tossed in extra-virgin olive oil with the barest touch of good wine vinegar, and for dessert, oranges marinated in red wine and sugar, with tiny almond macaroons.

Serves 4

4 to 6 cloves garlic, chopped
1 small-sized carrot, chopped
1 small-sized stalk celery, with leaves, chopped
2 tablespoons (30 ml) extra-virgin olive oil
1½ teaspoons (8 ml) fennel seeds
1 teaspoon (5 ml) fresh thyme leaves, or ½ teaspoon (3 ml) dried thyme, crumbled
Generous pinch fresh rosemary leaves, lightly crushed
¼ teaspoon (1.5 ml) dried marjoram, crumbled (optional)
1 cup (250 ml) dry red wine
3 cups (750 ml) tomato sauce
Pinch sugar
¾ pound (336 g) penne
¾ pound (336 g) fresh whole-milk ricotta cheese
Freshly grated Parmesan, as desired

1. Sauté garlic, carrots, and celery in olive oil until fragrant and vegetables become soft. Add fennel seeds, thyme and rosemary, and marjoram, if desired.

2. Pour wine into vegetable mixture, raise heat, and boil until liquid is reduced by half. Stir in tomato sauce and pinch sugar, and continue cooking over low heat, uncovered, simmering while you cook the spaghetti.

3. Cook the spaghetti in boiling water until barely tender, but with bite —al dente. Drain and serve topped with tomato sauce and dollops of ricotta cheese. Sprinkle with Parmesan as desired.

Cold Chinese Noodles
with Salad and Peanut Sauce

China

At first glance this does not appear to be a remarkable dish, but it is. Smooth noodle, crunchy salad, and a hauntingly complex peanut sauce combine to make outstandingly good cold noodles. The addition of cold, cooked chicken breast, cut into strips would be good, as would be strips of Chinese roast pork or ham.

Despite the fabulous flavor and long list of ingredients in the sauce this dish is extremely easy to prepare. Adding brewed tea to a sauce is unusual for Western palates, but the flavorful liquid acts much like broth does. The flavor of tea enhances the flavor of the Szechuan peppercorns. Catsup is an authentic part of the sauce; do not be tempted to eliminate it as it adds a slightly sweet, fruity flavor. The word *catsup* is of Malaysian origin, and, surprisingly, you'll find this all-too-familiar red condiment in exotic Far Eastern sauces such as pad thai, mee krob, and many others.

Serves 4 to 6

Noodles:
1 pound (450 g) thin Chinese egg noodles
2 tablespoons (30 ml) sesame oil
2 tablespoons (30 ml) soy sauce

Sauce:
1 teaspoon (5 ml) Szechuan peppercorns
6 to 8 cloves garlic, chopped
2 teaspoons (10 ml) chopped gingerroot
⅓ cup (85 ml) smooth unsweetened peanut butter
¼ cup (60 ml) tahini (see Aromatics and Special Ingredients)
⅓ cup (85 ml) strong brewed tea
¼ cup (60 ml) soy sauce
2 tablespoons (30 ml) catsup
2 tablespoons (30 ml) dry sherry or Chinese rice wine
2 tablespoons (30 ml) sesame oil
1½ tablespoons (23 ml) wine vinegar
¼ cup (60 ml) sugar
1 teaspoon (5 ml) chile oil

Salad:
1 to 2 medium-sized cucumbers, peeled and cut into julienne or diced
4 green onions, thinly sliced

1 medium-sized carrot, shredded coarsely
⅓ to ½ pound (150 to 225 g) bean sprouts, blanched and rinsed
  in cold water
3 tablespoons (45 ml) chopped cilantro
¼ pound (112 g) green beans, cut into 2-inch (50-mm) lengths,
  steamed until green and crisp-tender

1. Boil noodles until just tender; rinse and drain well. Toss with sesame oil and soy sauce. Set aside.

2. To make sauce: Crush Szechuan peppercorns coarsely, either with a mortar and pestle or a bottle and cutting board, rolling the bottle along the peppercorns, crushing them as you roll.

3. In processor or blender combine with the remaining ingredients and mix until very well blended.

4. Place noodles on a platter and arrange piles of cucumber, green onions, carrots, bean sprouts, cilantro, and green beans on top. Spoon peanut sauce as desired over vegetables and noodles or let each person help him or herself.

ADVANCE PREPARATION: A great prepare-ahead dish! The noodles may be boiled and tossed with the soy sauce and sesame oil the day before, and stored tightly covered in the refrigerator. The vegetables may be cut the day before, wrapped separately, and refrigerated.

Lasagne alla Veneziana

Baked Lasagne with Two Sauces and Peas

Italy

The canals steamed in the shimmering Venetian heat. I longed for romance, but got a great recipe instead. Maybe it's better this way—pasta will never break my heart. This lasagne is tender in its delicate béchamel, savory tomato sauce, and fresh flurry of peas. It is a lovely classic dish.

Peas are a hallmark of dishes labeled Venetian, much in the same way that spinach dishes are called Florentine. Beautiful peas grow around Venice, and you'll find them in many local dishes, stewed with veal or fish chunks, simmered with rice, or tossed in pasta.

Of course, Jack cheese would not be used in Italy, but there are so many good Jack cheeses made locally that this is my choice; your choice can be the traditional mozzarella, if you prefer.

Yields 1 large pan; serves 8 to 10

Béchamel Sauce:
- 3 tablespoons (42 g) unsalted butter
- 3 tablespoons (45 ml) flour
- 3 cups (750 ml) milk
- Pinch freshly grated nutmeg
- Salt and pepper to taste

Tomato Sauce:
- 1 medium-sized onion, chopped
- 3 cloves garlic, chopped
- 1 medium-sized carrot, chopped
- 2 tablespoons (30 ml) chopped parsley
- 2 tablespoons (30 ml) extra-virgin olive oil
- ½ to 1 teaspoon (3 to 5 ml) fennel seeds
- ½ teaspoon (3 ml) dried thyme, crumbled, more if desired
- 4 cups (1000 ml) chopped tomatoes (canned is fine)
- ¼ cup (60 ml) tomato paste
- ½ teaspoon (3 ml) sugar, if needed to counter the tomatoes' acidity
- Salt and pepper to taste

To Assemble and Cook:
- 3 pounds (1350 g) fresh spinach pasta in wide sheets, or cut to lasagne size; or 1½ pounds (675 g) dried lasagne noodles, cooked al dente
- 2 cups (500 ml) peas (see Note)
- 1½ to 2 cups (375 to 500 ml) freshly grated Parmesan
- 12 ounces (336 g) Jack or mozzarella cheese
- 2 tablespoons (30 ml) extra-virgin olive oil
- ½ teaspoon (3 ml) dried thyme or oregano leaves, crushed between fingers

NOTE: If using peas that are fresh and tender, simply add raw; if peas are older and starchier, precook for a few minutes; if using frozen, use as is.

1. Make béchamel sauce: Melt butter in heavy saucepan over medium heat and when melted, sprinkle in flour. Cook over medium-low heat, stirring, to make a roux. Do not let burn or brown.

2. Remove from the heat and add the milk all at once, stirring well or whisking to smooth the sauce. Add nutmeg and salt and pepper. Return to the heat and cook over medium-high heat, stirring until it comes to a boil.

3. Reduce the heat to low and let simmer for about 20 minutes, stirring every so often to be sure the flour is not on the bottom. With all the other ingredients in the dish, a few lumps in the sauce won't be noticed. Sauce should have thickened considerably. Set aside.

4. To make tomato sauce: Sauté onion, garlic, carrots, and parsley in olive oil for a few minutes, until onion is softened. Add fennel seeds, thyme, tomatoes, tomato paste, sugar, and salt and pepper, and simmer 10 minutes or until sauce is well flavored.

5. Assemble lasagne: Into a 13-by-9-by-3-inch (325-by-225-by-75-mm) baking pan, ladle several tablespoons of tomato sauce. Place a layer of lasagne noodles in bottom of pan, slightly rising up the sides. Next, 1 cup (250 ml) of béchamel sauce, 1 cup (250 ml) peas, and about ⅔ cup (170 ml) Parmesan.

6. Top with another layer of pasta, several cups of tomato sauce, and half of the Jack cheese. Another layer of pasta, the rest of the béchamel, peas, and ⅔ cups (170 ml) Parmesan. Top with a final layer of pasta, the rest of the tomato sauce and Jack cheese. Sprinkle with the remaining Parmesan, drizzle with olive oil, and sprinkle thyme or oregano over the top.

7. Cover tightly with foil and bake at 375° F. for about 15 minutes, then uncover and bake another 10 to 15 minutes, until cheese is bubbly and lightly browned. Serve immediately.

ADVANCE PREPARATION: Both béchamel and tomato sauces may be prepared up to 2 days ahead of time and kept refrigerated. They could also be frozen. Lasagne may be assembled several hours ahead of time and refrigerated, but should be served shortly after baking.

Lamb, Pork, and Chipotle-Filled Tamales

Mexico

Can anyone who has ever eaten good, homemade tamales not be passionate about them forever after? When I was a child, our Mexican neighbors would periodically deliver a pot of them, looking lopsided and lumpy, nothing like the huge, perfectly round ones from the supermarket. One bite made me forget appearances, though. They were earthy and delicious, tasting of corn, filled with tender stewed meat and chiles.

The following tamales are unlike any you'll find elsewhere: filled with a chipotle-spiced meat mixture. The bland corn taste of the masa dough is enhanced by the chipotle's smokiness, and the corn returns the favor. And Chipotle Salsa (see Index) echoes that distinctive taste and fragrance.

Yields about 10 tamales

20 dried corn husks

Masa Dough:
⅔ cup (150 g) unsalted butter, at room temperature
2 cups (500 ml) masa harina (see Aromatics and Special Ingredients)
1 teaspoon (5 ml) baking powder
½ teaspoon (3 ml) salt
1⅓ cups (335 ml) warm beef broth

Filling:
2 large dried mild red chiles (New Mexico or California)
4½ cups (1125 ml) hot, but not boiling, beef broth
6 to 8 ounces (168 to 224 g) pork shoulder chop, boneless and cut into ½-inch (12-mm) pieces
6 to 8 ounces (168 to 224 g) lamb shoulder chop, boneless and cut into ½-inch (12-mm) pieces
1 medium-sized onion, chopped
2 cloves garlic, chopped
2 chipotle chiles, mashed with a fork
½ cup (125 ml) chopped tomatoes, peeled and seeded (canned is fine)
1 tablespoon (15 ml) masa harina

1. Soak corn husks in warm water to cover for at least an hour.
2. Whip butter until fluffy; mix masa harina with baking powder, salt, and warm broth, then add to butter and beat together until well combined. Chill until ready to use.
3. Toast dried red chiles by holding over flame for only a few moments on each side or by broiling under high heat for a few seconds on each side. Break up and add to hot broth. Cover and steep for 30 minutes to an hour. Puree in processor or blender and strain through sieve or strainer.
4. Place this chile sauce in saucepan and add pork, lamb, onion, garlic, chipotle chiles, tomatoes, and masa harina. Bring to boil, then reduce heat and simmer gently over low heat until meat is tender, 40 to 60 minutes. Let cool.
5. Remove a corn husk from the water; pat dry on both sides. Repeat with a second corn husk and lay over the first, overlapping by about ½ inch (12 mm). Spread with several tablespoons of the masa mixture, leaving a ¾-inch (18-mm) border around the edges. Top with a tablespoon (15 ml) of the filling. Fold each side of the corn husk over, one on top of the other, then fold the ends, making a neat package. Repeat until masa or filling is

used up. Place each tamale in a steamer or pie pan, fitting them tightly together.

6. Cook in steamer with a tight-fitting lid for 45 minutes, or until masa dough is cooked through.

7. Serve hot, accompanied by Chipotle Salsa (see Index).

ADVANCE PREPARATION: Tamales are at their best when freshly made, but the filling and masa dough may be prepared up to a day ahead, and stored tightly covered in the refrigerator.

VARIATION: Shredded Zucchini Tamales Filled with Black Beans

Though it seems unusual, vegetable-filled tamales are enjoyed in many parts of Mexico. The mild zucchini blends with the masa dough, lightening it a bit, and the black beans fill the tamales with rich earthy flavor and substance.

Reduce liquid in masa dough to 1½ cups (125 ml) and add 1 grated zucchini; work in well. For filling use the recipe for Black Bean–Chipotle Puree. Canned are okay, but be sure they do not have too much liquid or the tamales will be gummy. Use several tablespoons of beans to fill each tamale, and wrap and steam according to previous recipe.

Serve hot, accompanied by Chipotle Salsa.

Ancho Gnocchi in Corn Cream

Gnocchi are Italian dumplings—solid and satisfying as all dumplings are, but everything Italian has a certain flair, and dumplings Italian-style are special indeed. Sometimes prepared from semolina, other times from a spinach-and-ricotta or cream puff paste, gnocchi most often appear as tender nuggets, kneaded from potato dough. When good, they are sublime, and when bad, they can weigh leadenly in your stomach and on your spirit.

The following cross-cultural recipe came about as a result of a delicate tomato-tinted gnocchi I sampled in Orvieto. Recreating them in my California kitchen, my eyes strayed to the spice shelf, landing on the ancho chile powder. It was a fluke idea, and I fully expected it not to work—especially when the dough took on an odd and not very pleasant shade of brown. But when those brown dumplings emerged from their hot-water bath and were splashed with cream and corn, the result was delicious and exciting, with the surprise combination of flavor and texture. The ancho powder I used was quite *picante;* if your ancho is particularly mild, add a good shake of cayenne pepper.

Serve followed by Vitello con Peperoni e Olives (see Index).

Serves 4

1½ cups (375 ml) freshly cooked and mashed baking potatoes, no butter or milk added (see Note)
1 cup (250 ml) flour
1 teaspoon (5 ml) salt
2 teaspoons (10 ml) olive oil
1 egg
¼ cup (60 ml) ancho chile powder
¼ cup (60 ml) tomato paste
1 teaspoon (5 ml) cumin
½ teaspoon (3 ml) dried oregano leaves
2 cups (500 ml) whipping cream
1 cup (250 ml) corn kernels, scraped off the cob (frozen is okay, but fresh is preferable)
¼ cup (60 ml) freshly grated Parmesan, more as desired, to pass at the table

NOTE: Although it is considered heretical amongst gnocchi purists, I have used leftover mashed potatoes, the kind with butter and milk, and the result was just fine.

1. Place mashed potatoes in bowl and add flour, salt, olive oil, egg, ancho chile powder, tomato paste, cumin, and oregano. Knead until well mixed and slightly elastic.

2. Bring pot of water to boil. Shape the gnocchi by rolling into a "snake" shape, about ½- to ¾-inch (12- to 18-mm) thick (the length is not important, as you will be cutting it). Cut into 1½-inch (37-mm) lengths.

3. Cook by dripping the formed dough into boiling water. They will sink at first, then rise to top. After they've risen to the top, reduce heat and cook in the slowly boiling water for 5 more minutes. Remove with a slotted spoon and set aside while you prepare the sauce. Unless your pot is quite large, cook the gnocchi in several batches.

4. Heat cream with corn and boil for 1 or 2 minutes. Pour half the corn cream into a casserole, then half the cheese. Add the gnocchi, then cover with the rest of the corn cream and cheese. Bake in a hot (425° F.) oven or broil, just long enough to heat it all through. An alternate way would be to toss the gnocchi into the sauce and cheese, and heat it on the stove top, taking great care not to break up the gnocchi with the spoon as you toss them all together.

Pasta al Basilico

Pasta with Blue Cheese, Cream, and Basil

Italy

If you've ever sampled that decadent concoction known as Torta Basilica, then you'll recognize the flavors in this creamy pasta dish.

Because it is rich, I wouldn't serve it as a main course, but a small portion is great as a first course, Italian style, followed by thin, boned chicken breasts, marinated in olive oil, thyme, and lemon, then grilled.

Serves 4

- 8 ounces (224 g) blue cheese, crumbled
- ⅓ cup (85 ml) whipping cream
- 2 to 3 tablespoons (30 to 45 ml) pesto, or 2 to 3 tablespoons (30 to 45 ml) finely chopped basil (see Note)
- ¼ cup (60 ml) pine nuts
- 1 pound (450 g) tender fresh pasta, or 8 ounces (224 g) very good-quality dried pasta

NOTE: As one who loves basil in all guises, I prepare large batches of pesto and freeze it for year-round use. That way, when I wish to add its fragrant accent to a sauce, stew, or soup. I just pop out a tiny container. Use your favorite pesto recipe or substitute finely chopped basil. Commercial pesto is also good in this dish.

1. Mix blue cheese with cream and pesto or basil.
2. Toast pine nuts until lightly browned.
3. Cook pasta in boiling water until just tender. (Different brands and types of pasta will take different cooking times, so follow directions, slightly undercooking.) Drain and toss with the cheese mixture and the pine nuts. Garnish with basil sprigs, if desired.

Porcini Pasta

Italy

It was while walking in Venice that I spotted a pasta shop window filled with baskets of the most intriguing pastas. There were the usual piles of green spinach and herb pastas, the pink tomato-tinted ones, as well as a basket filled with inky-gray colored fettucine, made from cuttlefish ink. There was a pasta strongly flavored with fresh rosemary ("a specialty of

Siena," the proprietor informed me, "served with garlic-rosemary-flavored olive oil and freshly grated pecorino cheese"). But the most unusual pasta was nut-brown in color, flavored with pureed porcini.

Because porcini are expensive, this may seem a bit extravagant, but the mushroom flavor in the tender delicate pasta is extravagant, too.

Serve generously powdered with freshly grated Parmesan; the cheese helps bring out the taste of the mushrooms.

Serves 4 to 6

2 ounces (56 g) dried porcini
1½ cups (375 ml) hot water
½ teaspoon (3 ml) salt
2 large eggs
2 to 3 cups (500 to 750 ml) unbleached flour
3 tablespoons (42 g) unsalted butter
1 cup (250 ml) whipping cream
Pinch freshly grated nutmeg
¼ cup (60 ml) freshly grated Parmesan, plus extra for sprinkling

1. Soak dried porcini in hot water and let stand for 20 minutes until they soften. The gritty bits will fall to the bottom of the water. Remove mushrooms from soaking water and puree in processor or blender, scraping the sides down several times. Add 2 to 3 tablespoons (30 to 45 ml) of the soaking water, then puree until it becomes a somewhat smooth paste. (Strain the soaking liquid and reserve for sauces, soups, and so on.)

2. If using a processor, add the eggs and combine with the mushroom puree. Slowly add 2 cups (500 ml) flour and blend until it has a consistency somewhat like peas, but forms a dough when pressed together.

3. If doing by hand, beat eggs together with mushroom puree, make a well of the flour and place the egg-mushroom mixture in it. Slowly incorporate small amounts of flour as you work, until it forms a dough and all the flour is incorporated. When it becomes too difficult to use a fork, use your hands.

4. Cover dough and set aside for at least ½ hour; if letting it rest for longer, refrigerate.

5. Using a hand-rolling pasta machine, break off a walnut-sized piece of dough and put through the rollers starting at the widest, folding over, and putting it through again several times to knead the dough, then put it through the rollers on successively thinner widths until you have a noodle. Continue until all the dough is used up. Cut to fettucine width, about ¼ inch (6 mm), either by hand or in the machine.

6. Bring a large pot of water to a boil. Cook the fettucine for only 2 minutes, or until just tender. This is delicate pasta and overcooking will

result in a mushy, gummy mess. Drain, and gently toss with the butter, cream, and a few spoonfuls of the soaking liquid from the mushrooms, nutmeg, and cheese. Serve immediately. Since neither salt nor pepper are in the dish, offer them at the table.

ADVANCE PREPARATION: Dough may be prepared up to 2 days ahead of time, refrigerated, and rolled out the day you wish to cook it. It may also be prepared and rolled out that day, and tossed with a little extra flour to keep it from sticking together.

VARIATION: Leftover dough may be stored in the refrigerator for this homey pasta dish. Take the lump of cold dough and grate it over the large holes of a hand grater. It will make tiny dumpling-like noodles. Boil until tender and serve with sautéed mushrooms (domestic or wild), a grating of cheese, and a splash of cream.

Ravioli di Gorgonzola con Radicchio

Gorgonzola-Stuffed Ravioli on a Bed of Sautéed Radicchio

Italy

Delicate pasta encases rich yet pungent Gorgonzola, bursting with creamy flavor as you bite into it. On a bed of slightly bitter sautéed radicchio it is perfect.

I first enjoyed this dish in the Venetian sun on a terrace surrounded by colorful flowers. I was charmed by its simple yet uncommon flavor, having only eaten radicchio before as a salad ingredient. Bright red with white or green veins when raw, radicchio turns a purple-brown when cooked, and contrasts elegantly with the richness of the ravioli.

This "red lettuce of Treviso" is indigenous to the area around Venice. It is eaten in salads, and less often, grilled, or sautéed. Its slightly bitter, fresh taste, reminiscent of Belgian endive, pairs remarkably well with other, richer ingredients. Radicchio is delicious tossed into salads of any sort—I think it is especially good with sweet basil and fennel.

Serve as a first course, Italian style, or enjoy as I did recently, following a homey, honest bowl of broth made from simmered turkey bones and vegetables.

Serves 4

About 10 egg-roll wrappers, cut in half to form 20 rectangles, about 6 inches (150 mm) long by 3 inches (75 mm) wide, or

cut to same size rectangles of your favorite homemade pasta
dough
8 to 10 ounces (224 to 280g) Gorgonzola or other blue cheese
(see Note)
4 cloves garlic, chopped
3 tablespoons (45 ml) extra-virgin olive oil
3 cups (750 ml) thinly sliced radicchio
Salt and freshly ground pepper to taste
½ to ⅔ cup (125 to 170 ml) whipping cream
½ to ⅔ cup (125 to 170 ml) freshly grated Parmesan

NOTE: You may stuff these ravioli with whatever blue cheese you desire,
Gorgonzola being rich and creamy, a maytag blue being sharper and more
pungent.

1. Lay each pasta rectangle flat and place 1 to 2 teaspoons (5 to 10 ml)
blue cheese on one side, leaving enough room to seal the edges. Wet the
edges with a brush dipped in water, then fold over, press together, and
seal.
2. Heat garlic in olive oil and briefly sauté radicchio for about 1 to 2
minutes, until radicchio wilts and darkens. Salt and pepper to taste.
3. Bring a large pot of water to boiling. Cook the ravioli for only 2 to 3
minutes. They cook extremely quickly.
4. Place several spoonfuls of radicchio on each plate and top with 4 or
5 ravioli. Spoon 2 tablespoons (30 ml) of cream over this and sprinkle with
about 1½ tablespoons (23 ml) Parmesan. Serve immediately.

ADVANCE PREPARATION: Ravioli may be assembled up to a day ahead
and kept in the refrigerator arranged in a single layer on a plate and
tightly wrapped. When ready to use, prepare radicchio as in recipe, and
cook ravioli, allowing a few extra minutes for the ravioli to cook, as they
will be cold from the refrigerator.

VARIATION: Instead of the sautéed radicchio, serve the Gorgonzola-
stuffed ravioli with your favorite pesto. The pungent cheese stuffing is
splendid with the fragrant sweet basil.

Aashak

Lamb-Stuffed Noodles with Minted Yogurt and Fried Garlic

Middle East

Though it is often explained that pasta was brought to the Western World by Marco Polo, the Arabs and Indians were eating various pasta dishes at least 50 years before Marco Polo's travels. I have a hunch the Italians were, too. The following meat-stuffed noodle dish is probably very similar to what was eaten then, with the exception of the small amount of tomato sauce, which of course is a New World food.

The topping of golden fried garlic is scattered on many dishes throughout the Middle East and even in parts of the Far East. You may find fried garlic blanketing a pilaf or, as in this dish, a platter of delicate yogurt-sauce-stuffed noodles. The garlic bits become crunchy from frying, without the hot bite of raw garlic.

The lamb filling is spicy and intriguingly seasoned much like the North African merguez sausage, with curry spices and lavender. Though not essential, it adds a subtle, elusive floral quality. Wrapped in the tender noodle, tossed with crunchy garlic, and cooled with minted yogurt, this is as unusual as it is delicious.

Serves 4

Dumplings:
- 4 cloves garlic, chopped
- 1 tablespoon (15 ml) chopped gingerroot
- ½ cup (125 ml) coarsely chopped cilantro, more if desired
- 1 pound (450 g) lean ground lamb
- 2 teaspoons (10 ml) homemade Curry Powder
- 1 teaspoon (5 ml) lavender buds, lightly crushed (see Aromatics and Special Ingredients), or 1½ (8 ml) teaspoons rose water
- ½ cup (125 ml) tomato sauce
- 2 teaspoons (10 ml) salsa, either commercial or Roasted Tomato Salsa (see Index), or favorite homemade medium-hot salsa
- Salt to taste
- 1 tablespoon (15 ml) paprika

Dumplings:
- 6 ounces (168 g) wonton wrappers, or 6 ounces (168 g) fresh noodle dough cut into 4-to-5-inch (100-to-125-mm) rectangles

Fried Garlic Sauce:
10 cloves garlic, peeled and sliced
½ cup (125 ml) olive oil

Minted Yogurt Sauce:
 2 cups (500 ml) yogurt
 2 teaspoons (10 ml) dried mint, crumbled

1. To prepare filling: Combine chopped garlic with gingerroot, cilantro, ground lamb, curry powder, lavender, tomato sauce, salsa, salt, and paprika. Mix to a somewhat smooth consistency. I do this in a processor, though you could do it by hand; the consistency will not, however, be as smooth.

2. To prepare dumplings: Onto each wonton wrapper or piece of noodle, place 1 tablespoon (15 ml) of filling. Brush the edges of the noodle with a little water and top with another noodle. Pinch the edges together, set aside on a plate, and proceed to the next dumpling. (This makes quite large stuffed noodles; if you wish smaller ones, simply reduce the size of the noodle.) Continue until all the filling is used up. Set plate of dumplings aside while you prepare the sauces.

3. To prepare Fried Garlic Sauce: Sauté garlic in olive oil until it is golden. Be careful to only lightly brown it. If the garlic burns or even browns too deeply, it will taste acrid and bitter. Set aside to cool.

4. To prepare Minted-Yogurt Sauce: Combine yogurt with dried mint, crumbling mint between your fingers as you add it. Set aside.

5. Bring a large pot of water to a boil. Add dumplings and cook them until filling is cooked through. Take one out after 2 minutes and taste for doneness, repeating again at 3 minutes. Wonton wrappers cook very quickly, but other noodles will take a little longer. Do not overcook.

6. When dumplings are tender, drain carefully and place on platter.

7. Pour fried garlic sauce over dumplings, and serve immediately, each portion topped with a spoonful of minted yogurt.

ADVANCE PREPARATION: Stuffed noodles may be prepared and stored uncooked, tightly covered in the refrigerator, for up to one day. The minted yogurt may be made up to 3 days ahead and kept covered in the refrigerator, and the garlic oil may be made the day before and kept, tightly covered, at room temperature. The dumplings should be cooked and assembled just before serving.

VARIATION: An American vegetarian version traditionally uses a filling made of leeks, but I like to use curried spinach and chick peas.

1 onion, chopped
2 cloves garlic, chopped
½ teaspoon (3 ml) turmeric
½ teaspoon (3 ml) homemade Curry Powder (see Index)
1 teaspoon (5 ml) chopped gingerroot
2 teaspoons (10 ml) olive oil
2 cups (500 ml) cooked, squeeze-dried, and chopped spinach,
    mustard greens, or your favorite combination of greens
2 tablespoons (30 ml) bread crumbs
1 tablespoon (15 ml) yogurt
1 tablespoon (15 ml) chopped cilantro
1 egg
1 cup (250 ml) cooked chick peas, partially mashed
    Salt to taste

1. Sauté onion and garlic gently with turmeric, curry powder, and gingerroot in olive oil, until onion is softened.

2. Add spinach or other cooked greens and cook 1 or 2 minutes to combine flavors.

3. Remove from heat and add the rest of the ingredients. Let cool, then proceed with steps 2 through 7 described above.

Meat-Filled Dumplings on a Bed of Stir-Fried Greens with Ginger Sauce

China

The variety of Chinese dumplings in existence is dizzying. All sorts of ingredients are used for the fillings: fish, meat, vegetables, seafood. They may be bland, spicy, or even sweet. Sometimes, fillings are wrapped in noodle dough, other times in bread dough. They may be steamed, boiled, fried, or baked.

I have fun at home experimenting with different types of dumplings. These started as a variation on the standard shu mai, usually filled with pork, shrimp, or a combination of the two. I like the more unusual filling of beef. Placed on a bed of greens, the dumplings gently steam to tenderness and are then splashed with a sauce bold with fresh gingerroot. Traditionally, shu mai are left open at the top; I've also made them with a large, egg-roll-wrapper-sized noodle, gathered together like a string purse, then steamed. The chewy topknot makes an attractive presentation.

Serve as either a first course or a main course, but do serve it on its own, unaccompanied by other dishes that would detract from its distinctive charm.

Serves 4

Filling:
2 teaspoons (10 ml) chopped gingerroot
2 teaspoons (10 ml) chopped salted turnip greens (see Aromatics and Special Ingredients)
2 tablespoons (30 ml) chopped cilantro
½ cup (125 ml) coarsely chopped water chestnuts (canned is fine)
2 teaspoons (10 ml) cornstarch
2 teaspoons (10 ml) soy sauce
2 teaspoons (10 ml) sesame oil
1 pound (450 g) lean ground beef

Dumplings:
6 ounces (168 g) wonton wrappers, egg-roll wrappers, or your favorite noodle dough, cut into 3- to 4-inch (75- to 100-mm) rectangles

Ginger Sauce:
1½ tablespoons (23 ml) chopped gingerroot
2 green onions, chopped
¼ cup (60 ml) sesame oil
¼ cup (60 ml) soy sauce
⅔ cup (170 ml) coarsely chopped cilantro
1 tablespoon (15 ml) red-wine vinegar
2 teaspoons (10 ml) chile oil
1 teaspoon (5 ml) sugar

Greens:
3 tablespoons (45 ml) vegetable oil
3 green onions, coarsely chopped
1 bunch, about 1 pound (450 g), fresh kale or mustard greens, washed and torn into large pieces (use only fresh greens)
⅔ cup (170 ml) water

1. To prepare filling: Combine all the filling ingredients and mix well. For a smoother consistency use a food processor. I prefer it smoother, but either way is fine.
2. To prepare dumplings: Place 1 tablespoon (15 ml) of filling in the

center of each square wrapper. Wet the edges, then bring the sides up, gathering together like a string purse. Pinch the edges together on top to form a topknot. Set the plate of dumplings aside.

3. To prepare ginger sauce: In blender or processor combine all the sauce ingredients. Mix to form a smooth, green-speckled sauce. Set aside.

4. In wok or heavy skillet, heat oil and briefly stir-fry green onions and kale. Place dumplings on top of the bed of kale. Pour water around dumplings, then cover tightly and steam over medium-high heat until done, 5 to 10 minutes depending on how large the dumplings are. They are done when noodle dough is translucent and meat is no longer pink.

5. Transfer to a serving platter and pour ginger sauce over the dumplings. Serve immediately.

ADVANCE PREPARATION: The dumplings could be stuffed and the ginger sauce prepared several hours ahead of time, but be sure to refrigerate the dumplings. When ready to cook the dumplings, add 2 or 3 more minutes cooking time to time given above, as dumplings will be cold.

VARIATION: Spicy eggplant makes a wonderful vegetarian filling.

> 1 tablespoon (15 ml) fermented black beans
> 3 tablespoons (45 ml) vegetable oil
> 3 cloves garlic, chopped
> 1 teaspoon (5 ml) chopped gingerroot
> ½ teaspoon (3 ml) red pepper flakes
> 1 medium-sized eggplant, or 4 Oriental eggplants, long and narrow, coarsely chopped
> 3 tablespoons (45 ml) soy sauce
> 2 tablespoons (30 ml) sesame oil
> 1 tablespoon (15 ml) chopped cilantro
> 1 green onion, thinly sliced

1. Place fermented black beans in a bowl and cover with water. Let soak about 5 minutes while you prepare other ingredients.

2. Heat 1 tablespoon (15 ml) oil in wok and briefly stir-fry garlic, gingerroot, and red pepper flakes. Do not let garlic brown. Remove and set aside.

3. In remaining 2 tablespoons (30 ml) oil, stir-fry eggplant, then when tender add reserved garlic-gingerroot-red pepper mixture. Drain black beans, mash a bit with a fork, then add to eggplant along with soy sauce, sesame oil, cilantro, and green onions.

4. Let cool, then proceed with steps 2 through 7 in basic recipe.

Hameen

Sephardic Yellow Rice with Chicken

Israel

Traditionally, this dish is prepared with a whole chicken and put to bake in an oven at a low temperature for a long time, to be eaten on Friday night when the family returns from synagogue prayers. The yellow color comes from turmeric, which together with cardamom is typically found in the cooking of the Sephardic, or Eastern Jews.

Serve with Salata, a relish made from chopped tomatoes, fresh mint, green onions, and lemon. The tart, fresh accent of Salata is astonishingly good paired with the richer, spice-redolent yellow rice.

> 1 pound (450 g) chicken drummettes (the meaty part of the wing, with the other half cut off)
> 2 small- to medium-sized carrots, finely diced
> 3 cloves garlic, chopped
> 2 tablespoons (30 ml) olive oil
> 1 teaspoon (5 ml) turmeric
> Seeds from 10 cardamom pods
> 2 cups (500 ml) white rice
> 1 cup (250 ml) chopped tomatoes
> 3 cups (750 ml) chicken broth

1. Sauté chicken drummettes with carrots and garlic in olive oil until chicken is lightly browned. Sprinkle turmeric over chicken mixture, add turmeric and cardamom, then stir in rice, letting it sauté in the olive oil for 1 or 2 minutes.

2. Add tomatoes and chicken broth, cover, and bring to a boil. Reduce heat and simmer until rice is tender, about 15 to 20 minutes.

3. Serve immediately, accompanied by Salata (recipe follows).

> *Salata:*
> 3 medium-sized ripe tomatoes, diced
> 1 cup (250 ml) fresh mint leaves, pressed down, coarsely chopped
> ⅔ cup (170 ml) thinly sliced green onions
> Juice of 2 lemons (¼ cup [60 ml])
> Salt to taste

Combine all ingredients. Salata is delicious accompanying many kinds of foods such as grilled meats and fish, or tucked into a melted fontina cheese and Kalamata or Niçoise olive paste sandwich in a pita bread.

ADVANCE PREPARATION: Sauté chicken with carrots, garlic, and spices up to a day ahead. Heat this mixture and proceed with the rest of the recipe when ready to prepare the dish. Fully prepared, Hameen can be kept warm at a low setting in the oven for about an hour.

VARIATION 1: For a delicious vegetarian variation, substitute 1 cup (250 ml) of cooked, drained chick peas for the chicken, and vegetable broth for the chicken broth.

VARIATION 2: Koppe Bhaat
   This is a typical rice presentation from the lush tropical island of Sri Lanka. At the southern tip of India, in the azure Indian Ocean, lies Sri Lanka, formerly known as Ceylon. Its climate simmers in sweltering heat, and the cuisine favors rice and spicy flavors.
   Here, a favorite dish is Koppe Bhaat, a cup of yellow spiced rice molded around a bit of hot condiment and half a hard-cooked egg. It is often served for breakfast by itself or accompanied by small bowls of various spicy and incendiary curries. Koppe Bhaat is also sold to-go from tiny restaurants, where it is wrapped with newspaper into a tidy parcel.
   1. Prepare Hameen according to recipe, but omit chicken or chick peas. Substitute half coconut milk and half water for the broth and tomatoes.
   2. Line individual buttered custard cups with a few spoonfuls of the spiced cooked rice. Place half a teaspoon (3 ml) hot condiment, such as Tamatar Chatni (see Index) or a fresh salsa based on chiles, tomatoes, and cilantro, in the center and top with a half-peeled hard-cooked egg. Top with rice to the top of the cup, press down tightly, cover with foil and keep warm until ready to serve.
   3. Serve accompanying a saucy curry, such as Indonesian Asparagus and Tofu (without the steamed noodles) (see Index).

Risotto Giardino e Mare

Risotto with Asparagus and Shrimp

Italy

Risotto is that creamy dish of rice cooked in flavorful broth, stirred slowly until the kernels are al dente.
   It may contain almost any bit of vegetable or seafood. In Milan, the classic osso buco, braised veal shanks, is served with a saffron-scented risotto, while on the coasts you'll find a wonderful risotto cooked with a potful of shellfish and an occasional tomato. In Venice, I tasted a dark gray-hued risotto, colored with the ink of squid.

Peas have a special affinity to this rice dish, as does almost anything from the garden, including the ubiquitous salad green, arugula.

Enjoy as a first course, followed by Rôti de Porc Provençal, or as a main course, accompanied by Salade Auvergne (see Index for both).

Serves 4 as a first course, 2 as a main course

2 tablespoons (30 ml) extra-virgin olive oil or (28 g) unsalted butter
2 tablespoons (30 ml) chopped shallots
3 cloves garlic, chopped
1⅓ cups (335 ml) Arborio rice (see Note)
¼ cup (60 ml) dry white wine
3 to 4 cups (750 to 1000 ml) chicken or vegetable broth, preferably unsalted
Salt to taste
5 to 6 spears of asparagus, cut into 1½-inch (37-mm) lengths
¼ pound (112 g) shrimp, peeled and cleaned
¼ cup (60 ml) freshly grated Parmesan
2 tablespoons (30 ml) chopped fresh basil leaves

NOTE: Italian Arborio rice must be used in this dish, as these plump grains have the ability to stand up to the long cooking and keep their firmness, while at the same time making a creamy sauce as they cook. I also think that this particular rice imparts a distinctive, subtle flavor and aroma not present in other types of rice. Do not overcook the rice. Add the stock in several batches, cooking each as the rice swells to absorb it, before adding more.

1. Heat oil or butter, and gently sauté shallots and garlic until just softened; do not brown. Stir in rice and cook for 1 or 2 minutes.

2. Add the wine, 1 cup (250 ml) of broth, and salt. Cook the rice over low-medium heat, stirring frequently, until the liquid is almost absorbed. Then pour in another cup (250 ml) of stock and cook until that is nearly absorbed. The grains will swell, and the liquid will become creamy as it cooks. Repeat, adding the stock and stirring until the grains of rice are tender but firm. This will take about 35 to 40 minutes total. Unlike other types of rice, a risotto is not covered during the cooking.

3. About 5 minutes before rice is finished, add the asparagus and cook for 2 minutes. Then add the shrimp and cook a few minutes longer, until shrimp are pink and opaque, and asparagus green and tender. Do not overcook.

4. Stir in Parmesan and serve immediately, garnished with a scattering of fresh basil.

ADVANCE PREPARATION: Risotto is, alas, not a dish to be prepared ahead.

VARIATION 1: I'm particularly fond of risotto with artichokes and sun-dried tomatoes. Use about ⅔ to 1 cup (170 to 250 ml) sliced or quartered pre-cooked artichoke hearts (not marinated), and about 5 to 8 plump, marinated, sun-dried tomatoes, thinly sliced. I prefer not to use the dried unmarinated kind, since they are too chewy for this dish; besides, the marinade adds to the flavor of the dish. Add both the artichokes and sun-dried tomatoes to the risotto about 5 minutes before the rice is ready.

VARIATION 2: The delicate sun-yellow squash blossoms are cherished at the Italian table. Often deep-fried or stuffed, they're also very good added to a risotto. They fleck the soupy-rice dish with their bits of bright color and fresh flavor.
   Omit the asparagus, shrimp and basil from the basic recipe. Stir in about 10 squash blossoms, coarsely diced, 5 to 10 minutes before rice is done. If desired, 2 to 3 ounces (56 to 84 g) of diced prosciutto may be added.

VARIATION 3: Omit the asparagus, then cook according to the basic recipe. When rice is just tender, toss in a lavish amount of finely chopped basil, fresh rosemary, sage, and any other fresh herbs you like.

Some Simple Pasta Dishes

Pasticchio   Cook ricotta ravioli al dente; toss with a very flavorful tomato sauce and layer with Italian fontina cheese, cubed, and a generous amount of fresh rosemary leaves. Sprinkle cheese on the top and bake in a very hot 450° F. oven, until top is browned and sauce is bubbly.

Spaghetti alla Norma   Sauté thin slices of eggplant in olive oil and serve alongside al dente spaghetti covered with a simple tomato sauce. Strew the whole platter with fresh parsley, marjoram, basil, and other fresh herbs.

Pasta Solatia   Sauté several chopped cloves garlic, and add a handful of green beans and fresh chopped tomatoes. Cook quickly until green beans are tender but not overcooked and tomatoes are saucy. Sprinkle with pitted black Mediterranean-style olives and lots of coarsely chopped fresh basil. Serve with spaghetti al dente.

Farfalle Portofino Cook butterfly-shaped pasta al dente and serve topped with Confiture de Tomates (see Index), crumbled blue cheese, and coarsely shredded Parmesan. Delicious at room temperature, too.

POULTRY

Truly one of nature's generous gifts, the chicken is easy to raise, nourishing, and sustaining to eat. Even in the poorest of villages the world over, you will see a few scrawny chickens scratching and pecking at bits of corn.

It is a versatile fowl, its flavor at home with humble turnip and elegant truffle as well. The delicate taste and lightness of chicken lends itself to vibrant flavoring—simmer it with herbs and wine, grill it with spicy marinades, stuff it with vegetables and aromatics.

But to be delicious and of a sun-drenched land was not enough to deserve a recipe in this book. So many superlative dishes fit into that category, and I wanted to include only those you're unlikely to find elsewhere. Chicken Shacutti was inspired by a dish Indian friends served to me in London; Pollo Pibil was so succulently delicious in the Yucatan that I had to devise a recipe to prepare it at home. The national dish of Guatemala was scribbled in Spanish on a scrap of paper and pressed into my hand by a new emigrant from that country, translated with the help of Latin American friends. The Thai Grilled Chicken with Peanut Sauce was a spur-of-the-moment creation, and Poulet le Midi sings with the flavors of Provence yet is an original dish. And speaking of Provençal flavors, be sure to try the Provençal Chicken Salad, made with aïoli, green beans, and olives.

Duck, too, lends itself well to bright spicing—roasted with red wine it is savory and sublime. Simmered into a big pot of Gumbo Ya-Ya it is a complex mix of flavors. In southwestern France and parts of Italy, duck and goose are both slowly cooked in their own fat to preserve them. I've included a lively rendition of this preserved meat, a traditional ingredient for cassoulet and Venetian-style pasta.

Try also simple roasted duck or chicken accompanied by a salsa or condiment; or baste the bird with soy sauce and ginger, then serve it with steamed rice and Atjar Lobak. Marinate boned chicken breasts in yogurt and curry spices, grill, and serve with Tamatar Chatni or Podina Chatni. Also try marinating duck or chicken in red chile powder and citrus juice, grill over an open fire, and serve with smoky Chipotle Salsa or fruity X-Nipek.

Poulet le Midi

Roast Chicken with Garlic, Artichokes, Olives, and Sun-Dried Tomatoes

France and Italy

What finer flavors of summer could there be? Artichokes, olives, sun-dried tomatoes—those strong, savory tastes marry well with the mild flavor of chicken. A well-roasted chicken, skin crisp, flesh juicy, is always welcome on my plate. Artichokes contain a certain chemical that sweetens the flavor of foods that follow it, especially chicken. Though many say that artichokes destroy the wine accompanying the meal, I'd enjoy this with a cool Chardonnay.

While I've named this dish after the Provence region of France, the sun-dried tomatoes provide a lusty, southern Italian accent. You could start the meal with Warm Peppers Stuffed with Two Cheeses on a Bed of Greens, accompany with crusty bread, and end with Watermelon Ice and small slices of Mandalorta (see Index for each).

Serves 4

1 whole chicken, 2½ to 3 pounds
½ medium-sized lemon
    Salt and pepper to taste (go easy on the salt, sun-dried tomatoes and olives are salty)
20 cloves garlic, whole and unpeeled

1 cup (250 ml) dry white wine
4 artichokes (frozen artichoke hearts are okay)
15 Italian- or Greek-style black olives, pitted
5 to 10 sun-dried tomatoes, quartered (see Aromatics and Special Ingredients)
½ cup (125 ml) chicken broth

1. Preheat oven to 325° F. Rub chicken with lemon; when finished stick the lemon inside the chicken. Place in roasting pan.

2. Sprinkle with salt and pepper to taste. Strew the garlic cloves around the chicken, including a few inside the cavity. Pour white wine into pan and roast for 45 minutes or until chicken is almost done. Skim any fat from the surface of pan drippings.

3. While chicken is roasting, prepare artichokes: Pull back their leaves and snap them off. Stop when you reach the tender small leaves. With a paring knife, trim the bottom of the artichoke of any rough edges. Quarter the artichokes, with small knife remove the inside prickly thistle, and cut the artichoke quarters into slices ½- to ¾-inch (12- to 18-mm) thick. Parboil the artichoke slices for 3 or 4 minutes, then drain.

4. Add cooked artichoke slices, olives, sun-dried tomatoes, and broth to pan around chicken. Return to oven for another 15 to 20 minutes.

5. Serve immediately, each portion of chicken garnished with some of the garlic, artichoke, olives, sun-dried tomato bits, and pan juices. The whole garlics are luscious—use your fork to squeeze out the tender, almost sweet, garlic flesh.

VARIATION: Poulet Mistral (Roast Chicken with Pureed Artichoke and Pepper Sauce)

Reduce amount of garlic cloves to 10 and peel them. Instead of sun-dried tomatoes and olives add 2 red bell peppers, coarsely diced. When chicken is cooked through and ready to serve, spoon off the fat, and puree the artichokes, peppers, and whole roasted garlic cloves along with the defatted pan juices for a delicious unusual sauce.

Poulet au Vinaigre

Chicken Cooked with Raspberry Vinegar

France

The vinegar in this French country sauté evaporates and its sour harshness is replaced by a slightly tart, flavorful essence, perfect for accentuating the flavor of the chicken.

The process is the same as that of deglazing with wine, but using a well-flavored vinegar instead—in this case, raspberry vinegar. Raspberry vinegar dates back to the Renaissance. Not too long ago it enjoyed a wild spate of popularity and was splashed thoughtlessly onto nearly everything. Now it seems like a forgotten sweetheart. I still like it, but if you prefer, a good red-wine vinegar would work as well.

For a sun-splashed menu, enjoy this Poulet au Vinaigre after Minestra alla Zingara (pureed red pepper soup with lemon cream) and accompanied by Insalata alla Giovanni, a toss of fennel, radicchio, and sweet orange (see Index for both).

Serves 4

6 chicken breasts (about 1½ pounds [675 g]), bones removed but skin left on
1½ teaspoons (8 ml) fresh thyme, or 1 teaspoon (5 ml) dried thyme
1 clove garlic, finely chopped
½ stick unsalted butter
½ cup (125 ml) raspberry vinegar
Salt and pepper to taste

1. Sprinkle chicken breasts with thyme and sauté until lightly golden in garlic and half the butter, turning once or twice. Cook longer on the side with the skin, since the skin serves to hold in moisture and to keep the meat from toughening. Do not overcook.

2. Remove chicken breasts from pan and set aside while you prepare the sauce.

3. Pour off excess fat from pan, and over high heat add vinegar, stirring to dissolve the brownish bits stuck on the bottom from the sautéeing. Cook over high heat until vinegar is reduced by half and darkened in color. It should not have a sour taste any longer, just a slight piquancy. Salt and pepper to taste.

4. Remove from heat. Using a whisk, beat the remaining butter into the reduced vinegar; it should thicken slightly. Pour sauce—there will only be a tiny amount—over chicken and serve immediately.

Petti di Pollo alla Sorpresa

Prosciutto-Stuffed Chicken Breasts in Yellow Pepper Chèvre Puree

Italy

In Italian, *sorpresa* means "surprise," and this dish has two surprises. Cut into the succulent chicken breasts, and you find a savory stuffing of prosciutto, garlic, and tangy goat cheese. That is the first surprise. The second comes in the smooth canary-yellow sauce made from only yellow peppers and thickened with a nugget of goat cheese. It is at once creamy and complex, yet easy to prepare. Topped with a generous shower of fresh basil leaves, it is a voluptuous dish indeed.

Try it on a bed of tender fettucine tossed with a tiny bit of cream or sweet butter. Follow with a salad of mixed lettuce leaves and arugula, tossed with olive oil and a splash of good wine vinegar. For dessert: Poached Peaches in Strawberry Sauce (see Index).

Serves 4

> 4 chicken breasts (about 1½ pounds [675 g]), bones removed but skin left on
> 4 to 8 thin slices prosciutto (about 3 ounces [84 g])
> 4 cloves garlic, chopped (see Note)
> 1 teaspoon (5 ml) fresh thyme leaves, or ½ teaspoon (3 ml) dried thyme
> 8 ounces (224 g) Montrachet cheese (chive- or herb-flavored)
> 3 tablespoons (42 g) unsalted butter
> 4 medium-sized yellow bell peppers, diced
> 1 cup (250 ml) chicken broth
> 2 cups (500 ml) fresh sweet basil leaves, whole or coarsely cut

NOTE: I sometimes use regular garlic for the sauce, and thinly sliced elephant garlic for the stuffing. It is milder, but huge. You will need only one, and then you may not use the entire clove.

1. Holding each chicken breast skin-side down cut a pocket from side to side, leaving one side attached. Stuff each with 1 or 2 slices of prosciutto, a pinch of the garlic (or several slices of elephant garlic), a pinch of thyme, and approximately 1 tablespoon (14 g) of the Montrachet cheese. Close up tightly either by tying with a string or skewering to close with a bamboo skewer from side to side and up to down.

2. In a wide, deep frying pan melt half the butter. When foamy, sauté chicken parcels, skin side down first, then turn when lightly browned. Add remaining garlic and peppers and sauté for 1 or 2 minutes. Pour broth into

pan, reduce heat, and simmer 5 minutes, or until peppers are tender and chicken flesh is not pink inside.

3. To prepare the sauce: Place peppers and broth in blender or processor. Puree until smooth, then add the remaining Montrachet cheese and puree a minute longer.

5. Serve the hot chicken immediately, with the sauce poured around it and the whole scattered with the leaves of fresh basil.

ADVANCE PREPARATION: The chicken breasts may be stuffed up to 4 hours ahead of time and kept, tightly wrapped, in the refrigerator.

VARIATION: Red bell peppers could also be used in this dish for a vivid scarlet color and sweet flavor, or a combination of the red and yellow could be used as well.

Panthé Kaukswé

Chicken Curry with Cellophane Noodles and Condiments

Burma

Many Burmese meals consist of a saucy stew served with a bland starch such as rice or noodles. They are surrounded by an assortment of condiments, each to contrast with another and complement the meal. In this way each diner is able to season the meal to his or her taste. The condiments include wedges of lime and hot, fresh, sliced chiles or powdered cayenne pepper. Onion, both green and white, gives freshness, as do leaves of cilantro. Two more unusual additions are toasted chick-pea flour and toasted lentils or split peas, both popular seasonings and snacks in Burma with a nutty, earthy flavor. The variety of condiments makes these meals a visual delight and a curious adventure. It's fun to decide where to put that squeeze of lemon or that sprinkle of chile, and no two bites are the same.

This chicken curry is rich from stewing in coconut milk and redolent with spices, with mysterious overtones from the cardamom. As in many curries, it has a long list of ingredients but is simple to prepare. Enjoy a lush platter of fresh fruit for dessert.

Serves 4

3 medium-sized onions, chopped
6 to 8 cloves garlic, chopped
1½ tablespoons (23 ml) chopped gingerroot

1 teaspoon (5 ml) turmeric

4 to 6 pods of cardamom, hulls removed

1 medium-sized stalk lemongrass, peeled and cut into 2-inch (50-mm) lengths, lightly crushed, or ½ teaspoon (3 ml) sereh (see Aromatics and Special Ingredients)

2 tablespoons (30 ml) vegetable oil

1 tablespoon (15 ml) sesame oil (see Aromatics and Special Ingredients)

1 chicken, about 3 to 3½ pounds, cut into serving pieces

2 to 3 tablespoons (30 to 45 ml) toasted sesame seeds (optional)

2 to 4 small hot dried red chiles (see Note)

2 tablespoons (30 ml) chick-pea flour (see Aromatics and Special Ingredients)

3 to 4 cups (750 to 1000 ml) coconut milk (see Aromatics and Special Ingredients), or a combination of coconut milk and chicken broth

8 ounces (224 g) cellophane noodles (see Aromatics and Special Ingredients)

Condiments:

¼ cup chick-pea flour, lightly fried in a tiny bit of oil

Fish sauce to taste (see Aromatics and Special Ingredients)

Hot chile oil to taste (see Aromatics and Special Ingredients)

¼ cup (60 ml) chopped cilantro

2 lemons or limes, cut into wedges

⅔ cup (170 ml) toasted split peas

3 hard-cooked eggs, diced

2 to 4 serranos or jalapeños, thinly sliced

½ cup (125 ml) chopped shallots, yellow onion, or green onion

10 to 15 garlic cloves, sliced and lightly fried to golden, not browned to bitterness

¼ cup (60 ml) dried shrimp, crushed into a powder (optional; see Aromatics and Special Ingredients)

1. In skillet or wok, sauté onions, garlic, gingerroot, turmeric, cardamoms, and lemongrass or sereh in the vegetable and sesame oils. Cover and cook over a medium-low heat until onions and spices lightly brown and yield much of their liquid, the oil beginning to pull away from the cooking onions and spices. This should take 15 to 20 minutes and is a typically Burmese way of preparing a dish.

2. Uncover, add chicken pieces and sesame seeds, and sauté in this mixture. When cooked to a golden color, both from the spices and the sautéeing, sprinkle in the chick-pea flour and pour in the coconut milk or coconut milk and broth. Simmer, uncovered, until chicken is cooked

through and gravy thickened, 30 to 45 minutes. If sauce becomes too thick, or starts to separate, add a little more water.

3. Soak cellophane noodles in cold water to cover until they soften, about 10 to 15 minutes. Place on stove over high heat. As soon as water is hot, before it boils, the noodles will be tender; do not let them become mushy. They will be translucent and jelly-like in consistency. Rinse with cold water and drain.

4. To arrange condiments: Place the chile oil, fish sauce, and chick-pea flour in small bowls, the other condiments on a platter.

5. Serve curried chicken on another platter, alongside a bowl of the cellophane noodles. Let everyone help themselves to the noodles, chicken curry, and condiments as desired.

ADVANCE PREPARATION: The chicken curry is delicious the next day. Assemble the condiments and prepare the cellophane noodles just before serving, however.

Pollo Asado con Tres Clases de Chiles
Roast Chicken with Three Kinds of Chiles

Mexico

This unorthodox dish combines three different types of chiles to produce a complex blend of flavors and heat. The dried ancho gives a rich, mild taste, while the poblano adds freshness. The final kick comes from the jalapeños en escabeche, with their fiery brine flavor.

Enjoy with a crunchy, spicy salad of diced radish, tomato, and green onion, with raw serrano or jalapeño slices and a little chopped cilantro, and French bread to dip in the pan juices. Accompany with extra jalapeños en escabeche. To drink? How about a Riesling or Chenin Blanc.

Serves 4

4 cloves garlic, coarsely chopped
½ cup (125 ml) coarsely chopped cilantro
2 anchos, 1 left whole and 1 torn into small pieces
2 poblanos, 1 left whole and 1 sliced into ½-inch (12-mm) strips
(though poblanos should generally be roasted and peeled before using, in this dish I don't think it's necessary)
½ medium-sized lemon
2 medium-sized onions, cut into quarters or wedges

1 whole chicken, approximately 2½ pounds (1125 g)
2 teaspoons (10 ml) cumin
½ cup (125 ml) tomato sauce
½ cup (125 ml) chicken broth
2 jalapeños en escabeche (see Aromatics and Special Ingredients), thinly sliced, plus 1 tablespoon (15 ml) of marinade
Salt to taste

1. Combine half the garlic and cilantro, the whole anchos and poblanos, lemon half, and 1 of the cut-up onions. Place chicken in roasting pan and stuff with chile-onion mixture.

2. Mix the rest of the garlic, cilantro, onion, and ancho and poblano pieces, and strew on and around the chicken. Sprinkle with cumin, then pour tomato sauce over the top. Pour the chicken broth into the pan around the chicken and top with the jalapeños en escabeche.

3. Roast in a 350° F. oven, basting occasionally, for about an hour or until juices run clear when deeply pricked with a fork.

4. Serve immediately, spooning some of the savory pan juices onto each serving, and passing around extra jalapeños en escabeche.

Pollo a la Chilindrón

Chicken Braised with Peppers, Ham, and Olives

Spain

A la Chilindrón is a style of cooking in which an abundance of sweet peppers, a little ham, a tomato or two, and perhaps a handful of olives are used. In addition to chicken, veal, rabbit, and lamb are all popular meats to cook *a la Chilindrón.* Though other wines may be used as the braising liquid, I find the nuttiness of sherry just right to bring out the rich olive flavor.

This dish is popular throughout Aragon and Navarre. Serve with a simple green salad tossed with fresh tarragon or herb of your choice, and chunks of crusty bread to dip into the sauce.

Serves 4

1 chicken, about 3 to 3½ pounds (1350 to 1575 g), cut into serving pieces
¾ cup (180 ml) flour
3 tablespoons (45 ml) extra-virgin olive oil

1 medium-sized onion, chopped
4 to 8 cloves garlic, chopped
2 medium-sized red bell peppers, cut into 1- to 2-inch (25- to 50-mm) pieces
2 medium-sized green peppers, cut into 1- to 2-inch (25- to 50-mm) pieces
4 to 6 ounces (112 to 168 g) good-quality ham
15 green olives (see Note)
15 black Greek-style olives (see Note)
1 cup (250 ml) tomato sauce or puree
Fresh thyme to taste, or ½ teaspoon (3 ml) dried thyme
1½ cups (375 ml) dry sherry
Pinch sugar
½ cup (125 ml) coarsely chopped cilantro
Several generous dashes hot pepper sauce, such as Tabasco

NOTE: Authentically, the olives would not be pitted; when pitted they tend to fall apart. If using unpitted olives, however, warn your guests of the pits.

1. Toss chicken in flour; sauté in 2 tablespoons (30 ml) olive oil until lightly browned. Remove chicken to a platter while you sauté the onions and garlic over medium heat until they turn golden, not brown. Add peppers to the onions and raise the heat a little, cooking the peppers until they are tender but not mushy. Remove to platter with chicken, then sauté ham.

2. Combine chicken with onion-pepper mixture and ham, then add both green and black olives, tomato sauce or puree, thyme, sherry, pinch of sugar, cilantro, and red pepper sauce or Tabasco.

3. Simmer, covered, on top of the stove over low heat for 35 to 45 minutes, or until chicken is tender. This may also be baked in the oven, covered, at 350° F. for 45 minutes to 1 hour.

VARIATION: For a vegetarian dish, substitute chunks of eggplant for the chicken and eliminate the ham.

Pollo en Jacón

Guatemalan Chicken in Tomatillo Sauce

Guatemala

Pollo en jacón is the national dish of Guatemala. It is chicken cooked in a tomatillo (or *miltomatoes* as they are called in Guatemala) and cilantro sauce, thickened with bread and tortillas, and fired with jalapeños. As with most national dishes there are endless versions, some with large amounts of green onions, others with garlic or leek.

Since the sauce should be rather *picante,* I like a spoonful of sour cream for a topping. The tart creaminess rounds out the spiciness of the sauce.

Serve with a simple rice pilaf cooked in chicken broth or plain steamed rice and puréed black beans topped with cheese and heated to melting.

Serves 4

1 medium-sized onion, chopped
4 to 5 green onions, thinly sliced
1 medium-sized green bell pepper, diced
3 to 4 jalapeños, thinly sliced
2 teaspoons (10 ml) cumin
3 tablespoons (45 ml) vegetable oil
2 French rolls (total 3 to 4 ounces [84 to 112 g] of bread), broken up
6 corn tortillas, torn or cut up into small pieces
About 20 tomatillos, quartered fresh, or 2 cans (13 ounces [364 g] each, drained) (see Aromatics and Special Ingredients)
3 cups (750 ml) chicken broth
1 chicken, about 3½ pounds (1575 g), cut into serving pieces (see Note)
2 bunches cilantro, coarsely chopped
Juice of ½ lemon or lime (1 tablespoon [15 ml])
Salt and pepper to taste
1 cup (250 ml) sour cream

NOTE: As an option you may remove the skin of the chicken. This lets the flavor permeate the meat better and also leaves the sauce less fatty.

1. Sauté onion, green onions, bell pepper, and jalapeños with the cumin in vegetable oil until onion is softened. Add the bread and tortillas and cook together over medium heat, stirring for a few minutes so that the

bread and tortillas do not burn. Add the tomatillos and broth and reduce heat. Let simmer for 10 to 15 minutes, uncovered, or until tomatillos are tender. If using canned tomatillos, cook for only 5 minutes.

2. Add the chicken pieces and cilantro and continue cooking, covered over low heat, until chicken is tender, about 40 minutes. Season with lemon juice, and salt and pepper to taste.

3. Serve immediately, topped with spoonfuls of cool sour cream.

ADVANCE PREPARATION: The stew may be prepared several hours to a day ahead of time, and even frozen. Garnish with sour cream just before serving.

VARIATION: Tomatillo sauce is delicious on fried eggs, roast fish, or chicken—even as a topping for enchiladas.

Petti di Pollo Allesandro

Chicken Breasts and Peas in Lemon Sauce

Italy

I enjoyed this pleasing dish of tender chicken in creamy lemon sauce in northern Italy long ago, and over the years I have prepared it in countless ways. Sometimes I make the sauce very lemony, like a Greek avgolemono. Other times I eliminate the Marsala and add a touch of cinnamon and North African spices. I've cut the chicken into bite-sized pieces for party buffets, and have even prepared the dish with lamb instead of chicken. The hint of fennel adds just the right touch, even for those who are not usually fond of its flavor.

Serve accompanied by buttered rice or crusty bread to soak up the sauce and peas. You could start with a soup such as Soupe de la Nuit des Noces, and for dessert, ripe sun-sugared nectarines sliced over vanilla ice cream and splashed with blackberry brandy or Fraises de Bois (see Index for each).

Serves 4

2 whole chicken breasts, each boned and halved, about 1½
   pounds (675 g)
¼ to ½ cup (60 to 125 ml) flour
1 medium-sized onion, chopped
1 tablespoon chopped parsley

1½ teaspoons (8 ml) fennel seeds
2 tablespoons (30 ml) extra-virgin olive oil
¼ cup (60 ml) Marsala
½ cup (125 ml) chicken broth
1½ cups (375 ml) shelled peas, or 1 pound (450 g) unshelled peas (frozen is fine)
Juice of 1 lemon (2 tablespoons [30 ml])
1 egg, beaten

1. Dust each of the 4 chicken breasts with flour; shake off excess.

2. Lightly sauté onion, parsley, and fennel in 1 tablespoon (15 ml) olive oil until onion softens. Remove from pan and set aside.

3. In remaining oil, sauté chicken breasts until lightly browned, about 4 to 5 minutes on each side. Remove from pan and set aside with the onion mixture.

4. Deglaze pan by pouring in Marsala and cooking it down over high heat to about 2 tablespoons (30 ml). Pour in broth, peas, reserved onion mixture, and chicken breasts. Simmer over low heat while you prepare egg-lemon mixture.

5. Beat lemon juice together with egg. Slowly add about a half cup (125 ml) of the hot liquid from the chicken and peas, stirring well to combine. Return this egg-lemon mixture to the pan with the chicken and peas. Cook over a low heat, stirring until slightly thickened and creamy in color and consistency. Be careful not to let it curdle.

6. Serve immediately, sprinkled with a little extra parsley if desired.

ADVANCE PREPARATION: May be prepared up to a day ahead of time to the point that you are simmering the chicken breasts with peas and sauce. To reheat, bring to a boil, adding a little broth if it seems too thick, and add egg-lemon mixture according to the recipe.

VARIATION: Sauté with unsalted butter instead of olive oil and thicken sauce with 2 egg yolks instead of 1 whole egg, reducing amount of lemon juice to 1 tablespoon (15 ml). When you add the peas and broth, add also 2 to 3 chicken livers, diced, to simmer in the sauce.

Chicken Shacutti

Chicken Breast Simmered in Coconut Curry Topped with Popadums

India

Tender boned breasts of chicken simmer in a rich russet-hued sauce, thickened with lots of chopped onions, and enriched with coconut milk. Here is a rich-flavored sauce that permeates the meat of the chicken. Served with crisp Indian breads called popadums, made from ground lentils and spices.

The list of spices is long, as in most curries, but the preparation is simple. The curry is excellent even without the popadums. You could serve it with steamed rice, flour tortillas, or soft pita bread.

Serves 4

3 medium-sized onions, chopped
4 cloves garlic, chopped
½ to 1 jalapeño, chopped
2 tablespoons (28 g) unsalted butter
1 teaspoon (5 ml) turmeric
1 teaspoon (5 ml) coriander
1 teaspoon (5 ml) fennel seeds
1 teaspoon (5 ml) paprika
½ teaspoon (3 ml) cayenne pepper
1 teaspoon (5 ml) homemade Curry Powder (see Index)
½ teaspoon (3 ml) cinnamon
¼ teaspoon (1.5 ml) nutmeg
1 cup (250 ml) coconut milk (see Aromatic and Special Ingredients)
¼ cup (60 ml) chicken broth
4 chicken breasts, about 2 pounds (900 g) chicken meat, bones and skin removed and each breast cut into 2 or 3 chunks
6 to 8 popadums (see Aromatics and Special Ingredients), any flavor as well as plain
1 cup (250 ml) vegetable oil for frying popadums
Juice of ½ lemon (1 tablespoon [15 ml])
Salt to taste

1. Sauté onions, garlic, and jalapeño in butter lightly until just softened; add turmeric, coriander, fennel seeds, paprika, cayenne pepper, curry powder, cinnamon, and nutmeg and sauté for 1 or 2 minutes.

2. Pour in coconut milk and broth and simmer for 10 minutes, or until sauce is deep and rich. Add chicken breast chunks to sauce and let gently simmer until firm and opaque, about 5 to 10 minutes.

3. Meanwhile, cook the popadums. Frying makes them crisp and light but they may be broiled or held over an open flame as well. To fry, heat oil in deep frying pan or wok and when quite hot, fry popadums one at a time, adding more oil if needed. They cook very quickly, only a few seconds on each side. They will puff up and brown almost at once if the oil is hot enough. Do not let them overcook or they will have a burnt taste. They should be golden brown, not darker. If broiling or baking, turn the heat up as high as possible and bake or broil popadums first on one side, then the other, or hold over flame on top of stove for a few seconds, evenly toasting the popadum.

4. Season chicken and sauce with lemon juice and salt to taste. Break popadums over each portion of the chicken and curry sauce, and serve.

ADVANCE PREPARATION: This is even more delicious when prepared the day before: The spices and flavorings have a chance to permeate the meat, and the sauce becomes smoother.

Pollo Pibil

Marinated Chicken Baked in Banana Leaves

Mexico

Marinating meats and poultry in bright red achiote-seed seasoning paste, then wrapping the meat in banana leaves and slowly roasting is a beloved cooking method in the Yucatan Peninsula of Mexico. The achiote flavors in much the same way that saffron does, imparting a subtle and elusive quality, while the wrapping of banana leaves keeps the chicken moist as it gently perfumes. It comes to the table as an exotic parcel wrapped in grayish green leaves and when unwrapped releases a fragrant steam. The chicken itself is meltingly tender.

When making the seasoning paste, you must allow time to soak the achiote seeds. They are rock hard when purchased and must be soaked and simmered before they are soft enough to grind.

In the Yucatan, this would be baked in a special oven called a pib; hence the name of the dish, pibil. Serve accompanied by warm, fresh corn tortillas or steamed rice with black beans and a coarsely chopped salad of radish, green onion, and cilantro. Offer a hot condiment such as Chipotle Salsa or X-Nipek (see Index for both).

This dish is equally delicious served cold the next day.

Serves 4

Seasoning Paste:

3 tablespoons (45 ml) achiote seeds
2 cups (500 ml) water
3 mild chiles, such as New Mexico, California, pasilla, or ancho
3 cloves garlic, chopped
1 to 2 jalapeños, chopped
2 tablespoons (30 ml) paprika
2 teaspoons (10 ml) cumin
½ teaspoon (3 ml) oregano leaves
1 teaspoon (5 ml) salt
3 tablespoons to ¼ cup (45 to 60 ml) chopped cilantro
1½ teaspoons (8 ml) chopped fresh orange rind, or ¼ teaspoon (1.5 ml) dried orange rind
Juice of 1 orange (¼ cup [60 ml])
Juice of 1 lemon (2 tablespoons [30 ml])
Juice of 1 lime (1½ to 2 tablespoons [23 to 30 ml])

Cooking and Serving:

1 package banana leaves (see Note)
1 whole chicken, about 3½ pounds (1575 g)
3 to 4 green onions, whole
3 to 4 slices bacon
2 limes, cut into wedges, for garnish (optional)
¼ cup (60 ml) whole cilantro leaves

NOTE: Purchase banana leaves dried or frozen in Latin American or Asian grocery stores. They are slightly unwieldy to fold, with a tendency to crack, but lightly heating them over the stove makes them pliable and easy to handle. Hold each leaf over a gas flame or directly on top of a hot electric element for only a few seconds, until the color changes slightly. Use each leaf immediately, and when ready for a new one, simply heat another leaf and proceed. While there is no substitute for the banana-leaf flavor, this chicken is delicious prepared in a clay pot, and could be prepared wrapped tightly in foil as well.

1. To make seasoning paste: Combine achiote seeds with 1 cup (250 ml) water and bring to a boil. Reduce heat and simmer over low heat for 5 minutes, then cover and let soak for at least 2 hours, better overnight.

2. Half an hour to an hour before you are to grind the achiote seeds, prepare the chiles. Lightly toast each chile by holding over an open flame or in an ungreased skillet. Tear into pieces and cover with remaining cup of hot water. Cover and let soak for 30 minutes to 1 hour.

3. Puree achiote seeds and chiles together with the soaking liquid in blender or processor. The bright coloring of the achiote seeds will, alas, stain the plastic container of the processor or blender, but will fade and disappear within several days of using and washing. The color is harmless.

4. When pureed as smoothly as you can (it will still have texture), put through strainer, pushing against the strainer to extract all the goodness of the ingredients, leaving behind the skins and other hard bits (discard them).

5. Combine strained achiote-chile paste with the garlic, jalapeños, paprika, cumin, oregano, salt, cilantro, orange rind, and juices of orange, lemon, and lime.

6. Rub this mixture all over the chicken, both inside and out. Heating each leaf briefly over the flame to soften, wrap chicken in about 2 thicknesses of banana leaves. Place wrapped chicken in baking dish, cover with foil, and marinate overnight.

7. Remove from refrigerator; partially unwrap chicken, insert green onions into cavity, and top chicken with bacon slices. Rewrap with banana leaves, then foil, and bake at 350° F. for 2 to 2½ hours.

8. Unwrap leaves and remove chicken to serving platter. Garnish with lime wedges, if desired, and cilantro leaves.

ADVANCE PREPARATION: Achiote seasoning paste may be frozen and kept almost indefinitely in the freezer.

VARIATION: Puerco Pibil

Pork is also prepared in the same way. Prepare according to basic recipe, but increase cooking time for pork accordingly. Choose a boned loin or shoulder cut, and cut into chunks about 2 inches (50 mm) in size. Allow about 45 minutes per pound cooking time.

Thai Grilled Chicken
with Peanut Sauce

Southeast Asia

Tender and juicy, coated with a torrid Thai curry paste of chiles and cilantro, then broiled to perfection. The peanut sauce echoes the flavors of Thai Green Curry Paste (see Index) and adds its own smooth nuttiness. Serve sizzling chicken breasts and creamy sauce over gentle rice to cool your tongue, and garnish with the freshness of chilled cucumber chunks and sweet shredded carrot.

Serves 4

1 pound (450 g) chicken breasts, bones removed but skin left on
2 tablespoons (30 ml) Thai Green Curry Paste, or to taste
3 tablespoons (45 ml) smooth peanut butter
1 tablespoon (15 ml) sugar
1 tablespoon (15 ml) chopped cilantro
1 teaspoon (5 ml) soy sauce
1 teaspoon (5 ml) lemon juice
⅛ teaspoon (.5 ml) finely chopped lemon rind (do not include any white pith)
2 tablespoons (30 ml) water
Salt to taste
3 cups (750 ml) freshly cooked white or brown rice
1 medium-sized carrot, shredded
1 medium-sized cucumber, peeled and cut into ¾-inch (18-mm) chunks

1. Coat chicken breast in 1½ tablespoons (23 ml) Thai Green Curry Paste; let marinate while you prepare the rest of the dish, about 10 minutes.

2. Stir 1½ (8 ml) teaspoons Thai Green Curry Paste into the peanut butter, then add sugar, cilantro, soy sauce, lemon juice, and lemon peel, and mix until smooth. Slowly add water to thin it to a creamy consistency. Salt to taste.

3. Grill chicken breasts over hot coals or broil marinated, until just cooked through. Because boned chicken breasts cook very quickly, take care they do not overcook.

4. Serve grilled chicken breasts over a bed of rice, topped with a few spoonfuls of peanut sauce per breast, a sprinkling of carrot, and a cool garnish of cucumber.

ADVANCE PREPARATION: The curry paste can be prepared ahead of time and frozen. The peanut sauce may also be prepared ahead of time, up to 2 days, and stored tightly covered in the refrigerator. It takes just a few minutes to put this meal together once these ingredients are assembled.

Canard aux Olives et Vin Rouge

Roast Duckling with Olives and Red Wine

The Mediterranean

Duck roasted with olives and wine is prepared throughout much of the Mediterranean. In the Camargue region of Provence, the olives may be black and the duck scented with brandy. In other parts of Provence, a red Côte-du-Rhone will be poured over the bird, and the olives may be a combination of both black and green. In Andalusia, a dry nutty sherry or Madeira is the wine used.

In the following recipe any rustic dry red wine will do, but I particularly like the uniquely Californian zinfandel. Serve this roasted duck accompanied by Puree de Pommes de Terre à l'Ail and crusty herbed bread to dip into the delicious sauce of the duck. End with a small, leafy green salad and a plate of varied cheeses.

Serves 4

> 2 whole dressed ducklings, 4 to 5 pounds (1800 to 2250 g) each
> 1 tablespoon (15 ml) flour
> 1 cup (250 ml) beef broth
> 1½ cups (375 ml) zinfandel, or other robust red wine
> 1 medium-sized carrot, coarsely chopped
> ½ to ¾ cup (125 to 180 ml) pimento-stuffed green olives
> 6 cloves garlic, chopped
> ½ teaspoon (3 ml) Herbes de Provence, or ½ teaspoon (3 ml) thyme
> ½ cup (125 ml) tomato sauce
> 2 tablespoons (30 ml) chopped fresh parsley
> Salt and pepper to taste (go easy on the salt as the olives are salty)

1. Preheat oven to 400° F. Place ducks in large roasting pan and prick them all over with the tines of a fork; this helps the fat escape. Roast for 40 minutes. Remove from oven and pour off fat, being sure not to lose the flavorful drippings from the bottom of the pan.

2. Reduce heat to 325° F. Dissolve flour in 3 tablespoons (45 ml) broth, stirring until smooth. Add this along with all the rest of the ingredients to the pan to make olive sauce, return ducks to the oven, and continue baking until duck is tender, about 40 minutes.

3. Serve the duck surrounded with the olive sauce and carve at the table.

VARIATION: Flambé the duck just before serving. Gently heat ¼ cup (60 ml) brandy in a ladle or small pan, then pour it over the duck. Carefully light quickly with a match, and the whole thing will burst into lovely blue flames. Soon these will die down, leaving behind a subtly delicious flavor.

Gumbo Ya-Ya

Duck and Sausage Gumbo

United States

Deep and rich with layers of flavors revealed in each bite, this is what gumbo should be.

Because it is based on broth, a gumbo is only as good as the broth it is made from. This is made from duck broth, which I make whenever I prepare Confit of Duck (see following recipe) and keep in the freezer. It is dark and gamey and makes this gumbo special, but a good double chicken or beef broth could be used instead. Another flavor that gives gumbo its distinction is that nut brown mixture of cooked flour and oil, roux. The secret to a good roux is to get it dark enough to develop the deep, rich flavor but not to let it blacken and burn.

There are two kinds of gumbo: that which is made from okra (actually *gumbo* is an African word for "okra") and that which is made with filé powder, the crushed leaves of dried sassafras. Each has a slightly different quality, but since they both have the ability to give a bit of viscosity, the two are never used together.

Serve in bowl, as it will have a soup-like consistency, and top with a spoonful of steamed rice and a sprinkling of chopped green onions.

Serves 4

   1 medium-sized onion, chopped
  ½ medium-sized green pepper, chopped
   1 stalk celery, leaves included, chopped
   3 cloves garlic, chopped
   6 to 8 ounces (168 to 224 g) firm smoked beef or pork sausage, cut into ¼-inch (6-mm) slices
   2 tablespoons (30 ml) vegetable oil
   3 cups (750 ml) rich duck broth, or a combination of beef and chicken broth
1½ tablespoons (23 ml) flour
  ½ teaspoon (3 ml) dried thyme leaves

  2 small hot dried red chiles, or as desired (depending upon the
    spiciness of the sausage)
  ½ medium-sized red bell pepper, diced
  3 medium-sized tomatoes, chopped (canned is fine)
  ½ cup (125 ml) tomato juice
  ¼ teaspoon (1.5 ml) coarsely ground black pepper, or as desired
  ½ to 1 cup (125 to 250 ml) leftover duck or chicken meat
  2 teaspoons (10 ml) filé powder (see Aromatics and Special
    Ingredients)
  3 cups (750 ml) freshly cooked steamed rice
  6 to 8 green onions, chopped

1. Sauté onion, green pepper, celery, garlic, and sausage in 2 teaspoons
(10 ml) oil until the onions are softened and bits of both onion and sausage
are lightly browned. Add broth and let simmer while you prepare the
roux.

2. To make the roux: Heat remaining oil over medium-low heat. When
hot, sprinkle in flour and stir the roux constantly as it gradually takes on
color, going from white to beige, to caramel, then to a nice nut brown.
Immediately remove from heat as the next color is black, and the roux
would be ruined.

3. Add roux to simmering broth mixture, along with thyme, chiles, red
bell pepper, tomatoes, tomato juice, and black pepper. Simmer for 15
minutes, to blend flavors and lightly thicken the mixture. Add duck or
chicken meat and filé powder and simmer a few minutes longer.

4. Serve, accompanied with a spoonful of rice and a sprinkle of chopped
green onions. Do not be tempted to omit the green onions, for they add
great freshness and bright contrast to the richness of the gumbo.

ADVANCE PREPARATION: Delicious the next day. Store well covered
in the refrigerator. When chilled, the fat will solidify at the top and may
be easily removed before reheating.

VARIATION: Instead of, or in addition to, the duck or chicken, try 1 cup
(250 ml) raw shrimp and heat just long enough for shrimp to turn pink and
opaque.

Confit of Duck

France and Italy

Flocks of plump geese and ducks waddle across the fields of southwest France happily oblivious to their place in the rich cuisine of the area. These flavorful birds are roasted, stewed, and put up for confit—a method of preserving the meat by first salting, then slowly simmering in its own fat. When no freezers existed, this was the practical way of preserving the meat, not only in France, but also in parts of Italy, where it was a part of the Venetian diet for centuries. Now, we prepare confit for its tasty flavor.

How to describe the flavor of a confit? Mellow . . . rich . . . rustic . . . dense, but tender. Confit is indispensable in a good cassoulet, such as Spicy Casoulet (see Index). It's a delicious addition to the hearty Basque soup Garbure (see Index) with potatoes cooked in the confit fat, or with sautéed wild mushrooms. In Italy you might enjoy a bit of the meat and fat tossed with delicate fresh pasta. These and other ideas appear in Suggestions for Confit following this recipe.

My version of confit of duck is actually a combination of two dishes— whole garlic cloves from the south of France and fresh herbs from Venice. This is an aromatic confit, and it will enliven anything you add it to.

Yields a two-duck confit

> 2 whole ducks, cut into serving pieces (see Note)
> ½ cup (125 ml) water
> ¼ cup (60 ml) coarse salt
> ½ teaspoon (3 ml) freshly ground black pepper
> 8 cloves garlic, chopped
> 1 cup (250 ml) fresh rosemary leaves
> 4 bay leaves
> 2 heads of garlic, peeled and broken into cloves
> 2 cups (500 ml) extra-virgin olive oil, or to cover

NOTE: The legs and thighs make the best confit, for the breasts have a tendency to become stringy if cooked over too high a heat. The breasts, however, are splendid for use in other recipes—for instance, grilled dishes or Gumbo Ya-Ya (see Index). If you should serve a meal of grilled duck breasts, use the leftover legs, thighs, and wings instead of 2 whole ducks to make confit.

When cutting the duck for confit, you will have the neck and backbone left over. Save the bones to make a rich duck broth, adding 1 or 2 onions and a handful of garlic cloves. It makes the most wonderful stock for Gumbo Ya-Ya.

1. Trim the skin and excess fat from the carcass and neck of the duck, and cut it into ¼- to ½-inch (6- to 12-mm) pieces. Place in a double boiler or heavy saucepan along with water and cover. Render over very low heat for about 2 hours, or until the skin pieces turn light brown. Strain pieces of skin from fat to use as cracklings, and reserve fat for preparation of confit.

2. Combine duck pieces with salt, pepper, chopped garlic, chopped rosemary leaves, and bay leaves, and toss to mix well. Place in glass or other noncorrosive container and refrigerate at least 12 hours, but no longer than 24 hours.

3. Rinse pieces of duck to remove the salt, and dry well with paper towels. Place duck pieces in pan and cover completely with the rendered fat, adding olive oil if the fat does not cover. Add whole garlic cloves. Slowly bring to a boil, then reduce heat to very, very low and simmer as low as possible for 1½ to 2 hours, or until the meat is very tender and soft.

4. Pour a layer of olive oil over the top of the confit the day after you have prepared it and leave undisturbed until ready to eat. Confit will keep as long as 2 months, tightly sealed with fat and kept in the refrigerator. Once the protective seal of fat is broken, the confit should be eaten within a week. I generally make batches of confit to last for 1 week, which may be stored in any sort of glass container or crock. If it is to be kept longer than a week, be sure that you do not include any of the perishable juices when you are ladling the meat and fat in, as they could sour and ruin the confit.

Suggestions for Confit

Cracklings Place drained pieces of skin and fat (from the rendering of the fat) onto a heavy ungreased skillet and brown over low-to-medium heat until crispy and golden. Serve lightly salted as a rather extravagant snack, or in salads or omelets.

Pasta con Sugo de Anitra Conservato Cut the meat away from the bones of several pieces of confit. Dice. Heat with several tablespoons of its fat, plus 1 to 2 cloves of garlic, chopped. Toss this with about 12 ounces (336 g) freshly cooked, tender fettucine, and 1 tablespoon (15 ml) each of chopped parsley and coarsely grated Parmesan. Season with coarsely ground black pepper. Serves 4.

Simple Garbure Prepare a vegetable soup using carrots, turnips, leeks, cooked red or white beans, red and green peppers, potatoes, cabbage, and thyme. Add some sliced garlic sausage or kielbasa and a piece of confit, the meat removed from the bone and diced. Serve each bowlful with 2 ounces (62 ml) of red wine added and a piece of toasted French bread rubbed with garlic.

Cook with Potatoes Fry potatoes until golden in a small amount of confit fat; heat the pieces of confit in a pan with only the tiniest bit of its own fat until the skin browns.

Some Simple Ideas for Poultry

Leftover duck may be shredded and tossed with cooked waxy new potatoes, pitted Greek-style black or green olives, and garlic vinaigrette. Serve on a bed of greens and herbs, and strew with a little chopped parsley and a spoonful of capers.

Poulet Arlesienne Roast a chicken with 1 red and 1 yellow pepper, cut into bite-sized pieces, at least 20 cloves of garlic unpeeled, 8 to 12 Kalamata olives, a generous amount of thyme, and a cup of white wine. Bake until chicken is golden brown and peppers are soft and tender.

Mousakhan Arabian chicken baked in a loaf of bread. Marinate a cut-up chicken in olive oil, lemon, herbs or favorite spices, and/or dried red chiles for several hours or overnight. Prepare a yeast dough, flatten it onto a cookie sheet, and top with marinated chicken, lots of thinly sliced onions, whole, peeled cloves of garlic, and a sprinkling of olive oil. Bake at 375° F. until both bread and chicken are tender and lightly browned and garlic soft and sweet. Break or cut into serving pieces, making sure each person gets some of the savory bread to go with the chicken.

Pollo en Escalibada Grill marinated chicken halves or pieces with peppers and eggplant. Serve with garlicky aïoli.

FISH AND SEAFOOD

Throughout the sun-drenched lands the fruits of the sea are cherished. They're grilled with little fuss, doused with olive oil or spicy sauces, or tossed into a great cauldron of broth to be ladled out generously. They're eaten at any and all meals, with a bowl of rice and pungent condiments for breakfast in the Far East, or as herring with raw vegetables and sour cream or yogurt cheese in Israel.

Often the fish dishes are the simplest of all, too simple to write a recipe for: Choose fresh fish, brush with olive oil, grill. Or dip pieces of calamari in your favorite batter and fry until brittle-crisp. Eat at once with a wedge of lemon. Try stuffing tiny sardines with garlic-spicy mashed potatoes, then frying the stuffed sardines until crisp-tender for a marvelous Spanish tapa. I remember arriving in Italy for the first time via a lonely mountain road. We stopped at the first village to purchase provisions, then hiked down to the beach at dusk. We prepared a fire, grilled the tiny fresh fish with a splash of olive oil and a dash of lemon, and made a big salad of fennel, red peppers, and olives. To this day whenever I taste fennel in olive oil or fry tiny sardines, I can smell the sea air. It was, of course, one of the best meals of my life.

Sea Bass with Lime-Ginger Cream

California

I'm not sure what gave me the idea for this dish—it isn't based on any particular ethnic flavoring—but the result is blissful.

The piquant fish bathes in a complex sea of flavors, sublimely sauced with cream, perfumed with shallots, zesty lime, and exotic fresh ginger-root. It is ethereal.

Serve this spectacular fish with butter-steamed potatoes, tender green asparagus, and dill-sautéed carrots simple classic accompaniments to show off this fantastic dish.

Serves 4

1½ pounds (675 g) sea bass, cut into 3-inch (75-mm) pieces
Juice of 1 lime (1½ tablespoons [23 ml])
1 cup (250 ml) dry white wine
9 to 10 shallots
Rind of 1 lime, finely chopped (include no white pith)
1 teaspoon (5 ml) chopped fresh gingerroot
2 tablespoons (28 g) unsalted butter
1 cup (250 ml) whipping cream

1. Marinate fish in lime juice and ½ cup (125 ml) wine for 1 hour.

2. Sauté shallots, lime rind, and gingerroot in butter until shallots have softened, about 5 minutes; do not brown. Add marinade from fish to pan, then the rest of the wine.

3. Simmer fish in this mixture until they are opaque and cooked through. Do not overcook. Remove fish from pan and boil remaining liquid until reduced to a concentrated, almost syrupy shallot mixture. Stir in the cream and gently toss with fish. Serve immediately.

Salmon with Watercress-Tarragon Sauce

France

An elegant, small portion of pale pink salmon contrasting with emerald-colored sauce beneath it—this dish tastes as lovely as it looks.

The watercress-tarragon sauce is deliciously easy and can be prepared several hours ahead of time. Try it also on shellfish, as a dressing for chicken and potato salad, or offer it in a bowl alongside a whole grilled salmon.

This is an impressive beginning to any dinner party. Follow with Poulet le Midi (see Index).

Serves 4 as a first course, 2 as a main course

12 to 16 ounces (336 to 450 g) salmon steak
Water to cover
1 medium-sized lemon, cut into halves
1 clove garlic
½ cup (125 ml) watercress, tough stems removed
½ teaspoon (3 ml) dried tarragon
½ cup (125 ml) mayonnaise
2 tablespoons (28 g) unsalted butter, melted
Salt to taste

1. Cut salmon into bite-sized chunks, free of bones and fat. Place salmon chunks (along with the bones and fat for added flavor) in a shallow saucepan. Cover with water and add half the lemon. Bring to a boil and remove from heat. Let cool in the water, and when cool remove to a plate and cover. Chill in refrigerator at least 30 minutes.

2. In a blender or food processor finely chop garlic. Add watercress and chop until it becomes a fine puree. Add tarragon, mayonnaise, melted butter, the juice of the reserved lemon half, and salt to taste, then whirl it all together, making a creamy sauce. Remove to a bowl, cover, and refrigerate for at least an hour to mellow the flavors.

3. When ready to serve, place 1 to 2 tablespoons (15 to 30 ml) of the watercress sauce on each plate. Top with several bite-sized pieces of salmon, and serve immediately.

ADVANCE PREPARATION: Because both sauce and salmon must be prepared ahead, this dish is excellent for advance preparation. Sauce may be made 2 days ahead of time, and salmon may be prepared several hours to a day in advance.

VARIATION: Oeufs Cressonière
A typical French countryside first course that substitutes a hard-cooked egg for the salmon. Cut egg into quarters and arrange attractively on the sauce-covered plate. Allow 1 to 2 eggs per person, and garnish, if desired, with a sprig of watercress.

Pescado con Aceitunas

Fish with Olives

Spain

Spain's magnificent coastline yields a rich harvest of seafood, unrivaled elsewhere. And rarely do you find such joyous appreciation of the fruits of the sea as you do in Spain. Fish and seafood appear in nearly every course from the baby squid at a tapas bar to a simmering casserole of a peasant's paella. It is eaten enthusiastically in sophisticated guises in 3-star restaurants and grilled over open fires by shepherds.

The following is from Andalusia, an unusual dish of marinated tuna or mahi mahi, dipped in flour and sautéed, then sauced with its own marinade plus a generous amount of pimento-stuffed green olives. The tart-salty olives combined with the marinade give each bite of fish a piquancy that is delightful.

Serve with crusty bread, of course, and perhaps Warm Peppers Stuffed with Two Cheeses on a Bed of Greens. Accompany with a glass of icy-cold dry vermouth.

Serves 4

4 steaks of fresh tuna or mahi mahi (1¾ to 2 pounds [786 to 900 g])
⅓ cup (85 ml) extra-virgin olive oil
3½ tablespoons (53 ml) red-wine vinegar
1 teaspoon (5 ml) fresh thyme leaves, or ½ teaspoon (3 ml) dried thyme
1 bay leaf
½ cup (125 ml) dry white wine
¼ cup (60 ml) flour
½ cup (125 ml) pimento-stuffed green olives, sliced

1. Marinate fish in olive oil, red-wine vinegar, thyme, bay leaf, and wine. Marinate for at least an hour, no longer than 2 hours.

2. Remove from marinade and toss lightly with flour.

3. Heat a few spoonfuls of the olive oil from the top of the marinade and sauté the floured fish in this, over medium heat. When fish turns opaque, pour in the rest of the marinade and olives, and cook for 1 to 2 minutes, until sauce is thickened and fish tender. If sauce gets too thick, while fish is cooking add ¼ cup (60 ml) water.

4. Serve immediately.

Sarish Bata

Mustard-Seed Fish Fillets

India

In spring, the countryside comes alive with yellow fields of mustard flowers, throughout India as well as across California's rolling hills. What a marvelous plant this is! Condiments prepared from its ground seeds find their way to kitchen shelves around the world. Smooth, speckled with whole seeds, yellow, brown, or tinted with vegetable essences, mild, tart, sweet, or very hot—all of these mustards start with the basic little yellow or brown seed.

Mustard seeds are also pressed into an oil favored in several parts of India. Hot in its raw state, it takes on a mellow, almost sweet flavor as it cooks. Even the mustard plant is useful; gathered in the springtime, it tastes like a strong, piquant spinach or broccoli de rabe and can be simply boiled and dressed with olive oil and vinegar as a salad, or added to a hearty soup such as minestrone.

In the following dish both the mustard seeds and oil are used. Although the amount of seeds specified in the recipe may seem generous, when eaten whole and fried to pop a little, they have none of the taste we associate with mustard, and they blend so harmoniously with the mustard oil.

Enjoy with buttered rice, curried spinach, and a fresh chutney or Atjar Lobak (see Index).

Serves 4

2 jalapeños, chopped
1 medium-sized onion, chopped
6 to 8 cloves garlic, chopped
1 teaspoon (5 ml) turmeric
2 tablespoons (30 ml) mustard oil, more if needed
1 to 1½ pounds (450 to 675 g) fillets of fish, such as red snapper
3 tablespoons (45 ml) yellow mustard seeds
Juice of 1 lemon or 1½ limes (about 2 tablespoons [30 ml])
Salt to taste

1. Combine jalapeños, onion, garlic, and turmeric with 1 tablespoon (15 ml) mustard oil. Mix with fish pieces and let stand for at least 15 minutes.

2. Heat mustard seeds in remaining oil until they begin to sputter and pop. Immediately add the fish, reduce the heat, and cook over low heat for 5 to 8 minutes, turning carefully so as not to break up the fish too much.

3. When fish is just cooked through, squeeze on the lemon or lime juice, season with salt, and serve immediately.

VARIATION 1: In Aturi, another Indian dish, a whole fish is used, and it is coated with the onion-spice-mustard-oil mixture. Bake at 350° F. until cooked through, about 30 minutes for a 3-pound (1350-g) fish. Squeeze lemon or lime juice over fish and serve immediately.

VARIATION 2: Baked fish fillets
   Coat with spice mixture and bake at 350° F. for 10 to 15 minutes or until fish flakes when prodded with a fork.

Otak-Otak

Chopped Fish with Curry Spices Wrapped in Banana Leaves

Indonesia

From the lush tropical islands of Indonesia comes this dish of chopped fish seasoned with bright spices, wrapped in banana leaves, and steamed to tenderness—something akin to a Far Eastern fish tamale. Wrapping foods in banana leaves imparts a subtle, indefinable scent, and the drama of unwrapping these parcels adds to the charm. When the leaves are unwrapped the exquisite aroma of spicy fish is released, and the steamed fish patties in their jackets of large green leaves look rather exotic. If you have no access to banana leaves (see Aromatics and Special Ingredients), foil is a fine substitute—although it doesn't look as pretty or contribute to the fragrance.

   Serve with wedges of lime to squeeze over fish, and a hot condiment such as Atjar Lobak or Tabasco. Serve a small portion as a first course, or a larger one as a main course, accompanied by steamed rice and Gulai Malabar or Thai Cauliflower and Beef Stir-Fry (see Index for each).

Serves 4 to 6

1 stalk lemongrass, peeled and chopped, or 1 teaspoon (5 ml) sereh (see Aromatics and Special Ingredients)
1 teaspoon (5 ml) laos powder (see Aromatics and Special Ingredients)
4 cloves garlic, chopped
8 shallots, chopped

2 jalapeños, chopped
2 tablespoons (30 ml) coriander
2 teaspoons (10 ml) cumin
2 teaspoons (10 ml) fennel seeds
1 teaspoon (5 ml) coarsely ground black pepper
2 teaspoons (10 ml) turmeric
½ cup (125 ml) coconut milk (see Aromatics and Special Ingredients)
1 pound (450 g) fillet of fish, such as tuna, swordfish, or any strong-flavored fish, cut into several pieces
¼ cup (60 ml) coarsely chopped toasted cashew nuts
12 banana leaves, 10-by-6-inch (250-by-150-mm) rectangles, or more if needed (see Note)
1 lime, cut into wedges

NOTE: To make banana leaves easier to handle, cut out their central stalk. Lightly heat over flame on top of stove or in ungreased pan to make pliable.

1. Finely chop lemongrass in processor or blender. Add laos, garlic, shallots, jalapeños, coriander, cumin, fennel seeds, black pepper, turmeric, and coconut milk and process to a paste.
2. Add fish pieces and process or blend until fish is finely chopped and blended with the spice-coconut-milk mixture. Add cashew nuts.
3. Take each banana leaf, lightly heat over flame or ungreased pan, and place several tablespoons of the fish filling onto each leaf, one at a time. Fold up the ends, then repeat with the other leaves, completely enclosing the fish mixture. Place leaf-wrapped parcels tightly next to one another in steamer and steam over high heat for about 15 minutes (test one to see if fish is cooked through).
4. Serve immediately, accompanied by wedges of lime.

Thisra Dum Masala
Curry-Spiced Mussels or Clams

India

I love mussels and clams. They take on the flavor you cook them with, and are especially good with spicy savory flavors, whether Indian, Latin American, or Mediterranean.

The spicing in this dish is bursting with gingerroot and topped with fresh cilantro and tart lemon. Preparation is extremely simple, and the clams are exotic, yet earthy and satisfying. Serve in a bowl accompanied by soft and chewy, warm flour tortillas.

Serves 4 to 6

1½ pounds (675 ml) mussels or clams, scrubbed clean of any clinging debris
2 medium-sized onions, chopped
6 cloves garlic, chopped
1 tablespoon (15 ml) chopped gingerroot
3 tablespoons (42 g) unsalted butter
3 jalapeños, chopped (a combination of red and green if available)
1 teaspoon (5 ml) turmeric
2 teaspoons (10 ml) coriander
1 teaspoon (5 ml) cumin
1 cup (250 ml) chicken broth or clam juice
1 tablespoon (15 ml) lemon juice
3 tablespoons (45 ml) chopped cilantro
1 lemon, cut into wedges

1. Soak mussels or clams in cold water for 15 to 30 minutes to release any trapped sand bits. Drain.

2. Lightly sauté onion, garlic, and gingerroot in butter with jalapeños, turmeric, coriander, and cumin, until onion is softened; add a little more butter if needed.

3. Add broth or clam juice, and mussels or clams. Cover and cook over medium heat for 10 to 15 minutes, or until shells open up. Discard any that do not pop open.

4. Squeeze lemon juice and gravy over mussels or clams, sprinkle with cilantro, and serve immediately with lemon wedges.

VARIATION: From Goa comes the following variation, which includes spicy pork sausage. Indian Goa was once ruled by Portugal, and many of its culinary influences have remained. Here you will find sausages and bacon combining with the curry flavors of India. Here also you will find sweets with a Portuguese flavor made of egg yolks.

Add 4 to 6 ounces (112 to 168 g) of diced spicy sausage, such as kielbasa, to the onion-garlic-gingerroot mixture before you add the curry spices.

Lone Star Mussels

Texas

From Texas comes an intriguing type of seafood dish: mussels poached in a spicy beer broth and served with fresh cilantro, wedges of lemon or lime, and a touch of Tabasco or hot salsa. This dish is equally good with clams or shrimp in their shells.

Serve with crusty bread or tortillas, and enjoy as a first course, followed by Pinchitos (Moroccan kabobs).

Serves 4

> 2 medium-sized onions, chopped
> 6 cloves garlic, chopped
> 2 tablespoons (30 ml) olive oil
> 2 teaspoons (10 ml) cumin
> ¼ teaspoon (1.5 ml) Tabasco, or to taste
> 2 12-ounce (372-ml) bottles dark beer
> 2 pounds (900 g) mussels, scrubbed clean of any clinging debris
> 3 tablespoons (45 ml) chopped cilantro
> 1 tablespoon (15 ml) lemon juice
> Salsa of choice or Tabasco to taste
> 1 lemon or lime, cut into wedges

1. Lightly sauté onion and garlic in olive oil until onion softens. Sprinkle in cumin and cook 1 minute over medium heat.

2. Add Tabasco and beer and bring to a boil. Add mussels, cover, and cook over medium heat until mussels open up, about 10 minutes. Discard any that do not open.

3. Serve mussels with just a tiny bit of the cooking liquid, sprinkled with cilantro, splashed with lemon juice, and seasoned with Tabasco or salsa, as desired. Serve with lemon or lime wedges.

Sopa de Mariscos

Shrimp and Clam Soup

Brazil

Bahia is what comes to mind when I think of Brazil—the colorful contradictions of traditional religion and black magic, the huge expanse of pale sandy beaches, and palm trees dancing in the sultry breezes. Imagine the scent of tropical flowers in the air, and all around you the pulsing beat of the samba.

With its idyllic seacoast, it is no wonder that Brazilians, Bahians in particular, enjoy a huge variety of fragrant fish dishes. This soup is pale yellow colored, accented with the blushing pink of shrimp and the sand hues of clam shells. It is a harmony of strange flavors blending perfectly, each taste a transport to exotic locales. Though rich in flavor, it is light, and you might like to have it as a first course, followed by something savory and substantial such as black beans and rice or Hameen (see Index).

Serves 4

 2 medium-sized onions, chopped
 4 cloves garlic, chopped
 1 to 2 jalapeños, chopped
 2 tablespoons (30 ml) olive oil
 ½ teaspoon (3 ml) turmeric
 1 to 1½ pounds (450 to 675 g) clams in shells, washed and scrubbed
 1 cup (250 ml) clam juice
 1 bay leaf
 ½ pound (225 g) small shrimp in shells
 1 cup (250 ml) coconut milk
 1 tablespoon (15 ml) lemon juice
   Salt and cayenne pepper to taste

1. Lightly sauté onion, garlic, and jalapeños in olive oil until softened; sprinkle with turmeric and add clams, clam juice, and bay leaf. Simmer for 5 to 10 minutes or until clams begin to open up. Discard any clams that do not open.

2. Add shrimp and coconut milk and simmer 2 to 3 minutes until shrimp turn pink and opaque. Do not overcook shrimp. Stir in lemon juice, season with salt and cayenne pepper, and serve immediately.

ADVANCE PREPARATION: May be prepared up to a day ahead of time and kept tightly covered in the refrigerator. When reheating, take care not to overcook the seafood.

Garlic-Saffron Scallops

France

Tender scallops poached in yellow-tinted saffron and fragrant garlic cream; it's almost like a chowder.

Ah, but what a chowder—smooth and suave, cloaking fleshy sea scallops. The poaching sauce is delicious with other types of seafood as well: shiny black mussels—their shells opened to expose plump pink flesh—or sand-colored clams, or salmon-colored shrimp. The sauce is even delicious for cooking halibut.

Serve small portions in soup bowls and follow with something less rich —perhaps Poulet au Vinaigre (see Index).

Serves 4

2 cloves garlic, chopped
1 tablespoon (15 ml) extra-virgin olive oil
1 cup (250 ml) whipping cream
1 cup (250 ml) milk
  Generous pinch saffron
1 pound (450 g) sea scallops, sliced or halved
2 teaspoons (10 ml) finely chopped parsley

1. Gently sauté garlic in olive oil for 1 minute; do not let brown. Pour in cream and milk, add saffron and simmer a minute, until saffron dissolves and mixture becomes yellowish in color.

2. Add scallops, cover, and poach in this cream mixture over low heat, until scallops are just cooked through, about 5 minutes. Do not overcook or they will become tough.

3. Serve immediately, garnished with chopped parsley.

VARIATION: Cook an assortment of shellfish in the cream, starting with those that take the longest cooking time, gradually adding those that take less time.

Buckwheat Pasta with Crab, Peas, and Cream

California

Buckwheat pasta, also called soba, is popular in Japanese and Korean cuisines. In the summer, the simmered buckwheat noodles are eaten cold, in chilled soup, or topped with all sorts of spicy condiments such as wasabi (green horseradish paste), strips of fresh hot chile, soy sauce, chile oil, chopped green onion, and so on. In addition to the traditional ways of enjoying soba, I'm fond of preparing it in the following very Western way.

This dish involves an Italian butter-cream-cheese sauce, combined with fresh San Francisco crab and buckwheat pasta. It's an old favorite of mine.

Serve a small portion as a first course and follow with Pollo Asado con Tres Clases de Chiles (see Index).

Serves 4

8 ounces (224 g) buckwheat pasta
4 tablespoons (56 g) unsalted butter
2 cloves garlic, finely chopped
½ to ¾ pound (225 to 336 g) crab meat, cooked
2 cups (500 ml) petite-sized peas, precooked (frozen is okay; thawed)
1 cup (250 ml) whipping cream
1 cup (250 ml) freshly grated Parmesan
Salt and pepper to taste

1. Cook buckwheat pasta in boiling water until just tender. Drain.
2. Melt butter with garlic, then add crab and warm together. Add peas and cream, and heat until bubbles form around edge of pan.
3. Toss hot, drained pasta with crab-cream mixture, then toss with Parmesan and salt and pepper to taste. Serve immediately.

Some Simple Grilled Fish Ideas

Trout in Vine Leaves   Wrap trout individually in several fresh or bottled vine leaves, drizzle with olive oil, then grill. Discard the vine leaves after cooking, as they become brittle and have already perfumed the dish. Dress with olive oil and lemon or serve with tahini.

Coat scallops or fat shrimp with Thai Green Curry Paste (see Index). (If using fresh shellfish, prepare on the mild side using fewer chiles. If it has been frozen, it will be milder.) Skewer curry-coated shellfish and grill. Serve with lemon wedges.

When grilling fish, throw a branch or two of dry fennel on the fire to make an aromatic smoke that will permeate the fish. Echo that flavor by stuffing the inside of the fish with fennel stalks as well as a little parsley, salt, and pepper.

Almost any type of fish or shellfish benefits from a Greek-style marinade: 1 cup (250 ml) olive oil, ¼ cup (60 ml) ouzo, 1 tablespoon (15 ml) crushed herbs, such as oregano or thyme, 2 tablespoons (30 ml) lemon juice, and salt and pepper to taste. Marinate at least ½ hour, then grill over hot coals. Serve with a green country salad of ripe tomatoes, red onion slices, and feta cheese, and accompany with a bowl of rice pilaf and yogurt.

Indian-Flavor Fish   Rub the juice of 3 lemons or limes over a whole cleaned fish, about 2½ pounds (1125 g), then rub with several table-spoons curry powder (homemade only), 3 or 4 cloves garlic chopped, ½ cup (125 ml) vegetable oil, and 3 tablespoons (45 ml) chopped cilantro (optional). Grill over hot coals or bake, wrapped in foil, until inside flakes and outside is roasted.

Emparedado de Mejillones   In Galicia, Spain, thickly sliced crusty bread is brushed with olive oil, then made into a sandwich filled with cold, cooked mussels and several rings of onion, then doused with alli-oli, a garlic sauce much like aïoli.

Atun Fresco con Escalibada   Fresh tuna, with its meaty taste and texture, requires robust flavoring. Marinate in olive oil, garlic, and lemon juice for at least an hour, then grill along with a selection of vegeta-bles: red and green peppers, long oriental eggplant, whole heads of garlic, ripe but firm tomatoes. Baste with marinade as it grills, and serve with a big bowl of aïoli to slather on.

MEAT

Meat dishes from the sun-drenched lands are prepared with simplicity. Where the meats available are often tough and less than abundant, they are cut into small pieces and stir-fried with vegetables or simmered slowly with biting spices and aromatic herbs. They may be ground and formed into patties, crisply fried and generously spiced, or slowly simmered in rich tomato sauce.

Sometimes the meats are roasted in big chunks and seasoned with only lemon, wild strong herbs, or garlic and cumin. The roasted meats may be drenched with chile-based sauces.

Surprisingly, in this chapter, too, there are many dishes that lend themselves easily to vegetarian variations—ways of preparing the dishes without any meat: a Korean stir-fry of tofu and mushrooms in hot bean sauce, or a peanut butter curry from Cameroon, brown rice-stuffed cabbage leaves in lemon sauce, and a most delicious meatless cassoulet. Try these vegetarian variations even if you are a confirmed meat eater.

Boeuf Hâché avec Fromage Roquefort

Chopped Sirloin Patties Stuffed with Roquefort Cheese

France

I first tasted this dish in a small restaurant not far from the Roquefort region of France. What may at first appear to be nothing more than a glorified hamburger is, in fact, an outstanding dish worthy of the most elegant occasion. The cheese stuffing retains its salty creaminess, and just enough melts into the sauce to give it distinction.

Serve with a simple green salad—with fresh herbs, parsley, and chopped green onion or chives—and lots of crusty French bread to help you get every last bit of the rich, savory sauce. For dessert serve fresh raspberries, if they are in season, along with peach or pear sorbet.

Serves 4 to 6

> 1½ pounds (675 g) very lean chopped sirloin
> 8 to 12 shallots, chopped
> 5 ounces (140 g) Roquefort or other strong blue cheese, cut into 6 slices as best as you can (it will crumble)
> Freshly ground coarse black pepper to taste
> 3 tablespoons (42 g) unsalted butter
> ¼ cup (60 ml) brandy
> ½ cup (125 ml) red wine, such as zinfandel
> ½ cup (125 ml) beef broth
> 1 cup (250 ml) whipping cream
> 1 tablespoon (15 ml) finely chopped parsley, for garnish

1. Mix sirloin with half the shallots. Form into 12 thin patties.

2. Place a slice or several chunks of cheese on a patty. Cover with another patty and press the two together, sandwich style. Season generously with freshly ground pepper. Repeat until all the meat and cheese is used up.

3. In skillet, melt half the butter and sauté the stuffed patties over medium-high heat until browned on both sides, but still rare on the inside. Be careful not to burn the butter. Remove to hot platter and place in warm oven.

4. Pour off fat. Add remaining butter and sauté remaining shallots until soft. Remove from heat, add brandy, then return to stove and cook over high heat until liquid is almost evaporated. Add wine and broth and boil sauce to about ¼ cup (60 ml) in volume. It will be almost syrupy.

5. Stir in cream, heat through, and return patties to sauce for 1 or 2

minutes to warm through. Serve immediately, garnished with a little chopped parsley.

Pinchitos

Lamb Kabobs with Lemon-Spice-Olive Sauce on French Bread with Tomatoes

Morocco

The heady aroma of spicy roasting meats emanates from Moroccan street stalls and permeates the air as you wander about the souk, or Arab market-place. The Moroccans are fond of grilled meats and often serve a kabob or two with no other seasoning than a mixture of salt and ground cumin. Many different meats are grilled: beef, lamb, and camel—and not just muscle cuts, but liver, kidney, and heart, as well. Often, Moroccan grilled meats will be tucked into a pita bread and sauced with a fiery condiment of small dried chiles called *harissa.*

This dish is a variation of Moroccan-style grilled meat, the lamb kabobs served on French bread, the sauce containing hot chiles, but made gentler with the unexpected flavor of salty, tangy olives, cilantro, garlic, and lots of lemon, including half a chopped lemon, peel and all. Although spicy, it is not for fire-breathers only. It is so pleasingly unusual I generally make more sauce than I need and enjoy it in Diced Eggplant in Spicy-Tart Sauce (see Index), as well as on everything from feta cheese omelets to canned tuna served with roasted peppers, fresh sliced tomatoes, and a wedge of lime.

Serve Pinchitos preceded by Karnabit bi Tahini (Arabian Cauliflower Tahini Salad; see Index) and accompanied by slices of grilled eggplant.

Serves 4 to 6

Lemon-Spice-Olive Sauce:
½ cup (125 ml) boiling water
3 small hot dried red chiles, such as cayenne, tepín, or hontaka, crumbled
2 teaspoons (10 ml) cumin
2 teaspoons (10 ml) paprika
5 cloves garlic, finely chopped
¼ cup (60 ml) lemon juice
2 tablespoons (30 ml) extra-virgin olive oil
3 tablespoons (45 ml) chopped cilantro
½ lemon or lime, peel and all, finely chopped (I do this in the processor)

8 Mediterranean green olives, pitted and coarsely chopped
8 Mediterranean black olives, pitted and coarsely chopped

Lamb Kabobs:

2½ pounds (1125 g) lamb shoulder or leg, cut into slices ½-inch (12-mm) thick
   Salt and pepper to taste
1 teaspoon (5 ml) fresh thyme leaves, or ½ teaspoon (3 ml) dried thyme
2 to 3 medium-sized tomatoes, sliced
8 to 10 thick slices of crusty French bread, about ½- to ¾-inch (12- to 18-mm) thick (if using baguettes, the long, narrow French bread, allow 12 to 15 slices of bread)

1. To prepare the sauce: Pour boiling water over crumbled chiles; let stand until it reaches room temperature. Puree in blender or processor.

2. Combine cumin, paprika, and garlic with lemon juice. Stir in olive oil, cilantro, lemon or lime, and both green and black olives.

3. Add pureed chile to the spice-lemon-olive mixture and set sauce aside while you prepare the meat.

4. To prepare the kabobs: Sprinkle meat with salt, pepper, and thyme, then either sauté or thread onto skewers and grill, until medium rare. When halfway cooked, spoon a little of the sauce onto the meat.

5. Serve meat on slices of French bread, topped with a tomato slice and a spoonful of sauce.

ADVANCE PREPARATION: Sauce will keep about 2 weeks, covered tightly in refrigerator.

VARIATION: Use swordfish instead of lamb.

Rôti de Porc Provençal

Pork Roasted with Orange Peel, Tarragon, Bay Leaf, and Garlic

France

Spiced so differently from other pork roasts, with sweet orange peel, piquant tarragon, and deep-flavored bay leaf, Rôti de Porc Provençal exudes the flavor and aroma of that wind-swept fragrant land of Provence.

Incisions are made all over the roast, and these are stuffed with pieces of orange rind, tarragon, bay leaf, and cloves of garlic. It's slowly roasted until tender, and until your house smells wonderful. Fresh orange rind is essential to this dish (dried orange peel is harsh and doesn't have the same fresh sweetness). When cutting orange rind, use a small, sharp paring knife and remove only the zest, not the pith, as that has a bitter taste.

I like to serve this delightful roast with spaghetti cooked al dente and tossed with a little butter and chopped parsley to spoon the meat juices over, French style. End the meal with a salad of lettuces mixed with fresh rosemary or watercress leaves and tossed in good olive oil with a dash of wine vinegar. Follow with a plate of several cheeses and fresh fruit, sweet and juicy.

Serves 4 to 6, with leftovers for next-day sandwiches

> 1 pork roast, either butt or boned rib, about 4 pounds (1800 g)
>   Rind of ¼ orange, cut into strips ¼-inch (6-mm) wide and ¾- to 1-inch (18- to 25-mm) long
> 1½ teaspoons (8 ml) fresh or dried tarragon
> 3 to 4 bay leaves, broken into quarters
> 6 to 8 cloves of garlic, each cut in half lengthwise
> 3 cups (750 ml) white wine, such as Sauvignon Blanc
> ¼ cup (60 ml) extra-virgin olive oil, if needed (most pork these days is quite lean; if fatty, omit olive oil)
> 1 teaspoon (5 ml) coarse salt
> ½ teaspoon (3 ml) coarsely ground black pepper
> 3 tablespoons (45 ml) brandy
> 1 clove garlic, chopped (optional)
> 3 tablespoons (45 ml) finely chopped parsley

1. Place meat in roasting pan. Cut incisions all over roast, 6 to 8 on each side, about 1½ to 2 inches (37 to 50 mm) deep.

2. Into each incision, stuff a piece of orange rind, dipped in the tarragon leaves. Then add a piece of bay leaf to the incision, then half a garlic clove. This combination will perfume the roast from the inside as it cooks.

3. Pour two cups white wine over the roast, then 2 tablespoons (30 mm) of the olive oil. Salt and pepper the roast, then place in a 325° F. oven for 2½ hours or until flesh is no longer pink. I recommend using a meat thermometer so you can more accurately gauge the doneness and enjoy it juicy, not overcooked. Baste several times as it cooks, with the pan juices and the remaining olive oil.

4. Remove the roast to a platter and keep warm. Pour off fat from pan juices, then add remaining wine and brandy, stirring to incorporate all the drippings. Pour into saucepan and cook over high heat to reduce to half its volume. (I like to add a chopped garlic clove at this point; it's optional.)

5. Slice the meat and pour hot sauce over the slices. Sprinkle with finely chopped parsley and serve immediately.

VARIATION: Leftover pork makes wonderful sandwiches. Scrape off all the solid fat (the fat will solidify when cold). Slice the pork and generously layer it into a baguette that has been sliced in half lengthwise and spread with aïoli or basil aïoli. Sprinkle with capers and add a few tomato slices. Close up and press together, and let stand at least an hour before eating.

Thai Cauliflower and Beef Stir-Fry

Thailand

Delicate and spicy at the same time, this Thai stir-fry gets its distinctive flavor from the fragrant and fiery puree of chiles and cilantro known as Thai Green Curry Paste. After stir-frying the meat and cauliflower, the sauce is given a slightly creamy consistency with the addition of coconut milk.

Serve with plain steamed rice or buttered rice tossed with a little lemon juice, green curry paste, and seedless grapes. Its flavor is evocative of bamboo mats and thatched roofs and a life-style far simpler than my own. The fruity-flavor rice is sublime with the savory sauce of the meat and cauliflower. While cauliflower is not usually thought of as the world's most exciting vegetable it is a perfect complement for the exquisite hot spice and rich meat. And the florets are very pretty, too.

Serves 2 as a main course, 4 as a side dish

8 to 10 ounces (224 to 280 g) sirloin steak, cut into thin strips along the grain
1 clove garlic, chopped
1 tablespoon (15 ml) soy sauce
½ medium- to large-sized cauliflower, broken into 1½-inch (37-mm) florets
2 tablespoons (30 ml) vegetable oil
2 tablespoons (30 ml) Thai Green Curry Paste (see Index)
3 tablespoons (45 ml) coconut milk (see Aromatics and Special Ingredients)

1. Toss steak strips with garlic and soy sauce; let marinate 30 minutes.
2. Stir-fry cauliflower florets in wok or heavy skillet in 1 tablespoon (15 ml) oil over high heat until lightly browned but still crunchy. Remove and set aside. Be sure not to overcook.
3. Reduce heat slightly and add 1 tablespoon (15 ml) oil; cook curry paste for several minutes until the oil begins to pull away from the green paste.

Add beef strips and stir-fry briefly; the meat should be cooked for only 1 minute, and should appear too rare to be eaten—it will continue cooking in the sauce. Cook meat in two or three batches so as not to overcrowd the pan, which would result in simmered rather than stir-fried meat.

4. Return cauliflower florets to wok and add coconut milk. Stir together and serve immediately.

ADVANCE PREPARATION: Meat may be tossed with soy sauce and garlic up to two hours ahead of time and set in the refrigerator, covered. The curry paste may be kept in the freezer, and the cauliflower may be cut up to 2 hours ahead of time. The stir-fry, however, must be done just before serving.

Kefta

Simmered Spiced Meatballs in Tomato Sauce with Spinach and Peas

Middle East

Known variously as keftedes, kofta, kifta, as well as kefta, depending on what country they hail from, the name means nothing more than highly seasoned meatballs. In Greece they may be fried up crisp and served with lemon wedges or cinnamon-scented tomato sauce. On Crete, my favorite keftedes were seasoned with cinnamon, cumin, and mint, then blanketed with an egg-lemon sauce. A Moroccan way is to simmer curry-flavored meatballs in a spicy tomato sauce and poach eggs alongside the meatballs. In India, the meat may be bound together with yogurt or perhaps chickpea flour, then fried, grilled, or simmered. Everywhere in the Middle East you find less-than-tender meat chopped up with spices and served as delectable spiced kabobs known as kofta, kefta, and so on.

This version originates from either Morocco or Iraq—I had it for the first time in Israel. The addition of spinach and peas simmering in the saffron-scented sauce is what makes it special. Serve with Hameen (prepared without the chicken; see Index), and a simple salad of greens, watercress, Belgian endive, shredded carrot, and Kalamata olives dressed in extra-virgin olive oil and red-wine vinegar.

Do not be put off by the long list of ingredients; most of them are spices or other flavoring ingredients. The dish is really simple to prepare, and involves no more than frying meatballs, then simmering them in tomato sauce with vegetables.

Serves 6

1½ pounds (675 g) lean ground beef or lamb
10 cloves garlic, chopped
2 to 3 slices whole-wheat bread, soaked in water to cover for a minute, then squeezed dry
1 egg
½ jalapeño, chopped (or substitute 1 to 2 teaspoons [5 to 10 ml] hot salsa)
1 teaspoon (5 ml) cinnamon
1 teaspoon (5 ml) turmeric
2 tablespoons (30 ml) yogurt
1 teaspoon (5 ml) homemade Curry Powder (see Index)
¼ cup (60 ml) chopped cilantro or parsley
Salt and coarsely ground black pepper to taste
1 tablespoon (15 ml) cumin
2 medium-sized onions, chopped
1 tablespoon (14 g) unsalted butter
¼ teaspoon (1.5 ml) allspice
1 teaspoon (5 ml) whole cardamom pods (½ teaspoon [5 ml] of the small black hulled seeds, or ¼ teaspoon [1.5 ml] ground)
½ teaspoon (3 ml) powdered saffron, or to taste
2 cups (500 ml) tomatoes, chopped (canned is fine)
2 cups (500 ml) tomato sauce
1 cup (250 ml) beef broth
2 bunches spinach leaves, cleaned and coarsely cut up, or 1 package frozen spinach leaves
2 cups (500 ml) peas (frozen is fine)
Juice of 1 lemon or lime (2 tablespoons [30 ml])
Salt to taste

1. Mix ground meat with half the garlic, the soaked bread, egg, jalapeño or salsa, ½ teaspoon (3 ml) cinnamon, ½ teaspoon (3 ml) each of turmeric, yogurt, curry powder, and 2 tablespoons (30 ml) cilantro or parsley. Add salt and pepper to taste.

2. Form into 2- to 3-inch (50- to 75-mm) meatballs. Fry in heavy skillet until browned but not cooked through. (There is no extra oil indicated for frying, since most ground meats will have enough; if there isn't, however, and you find the meatballs sticking to your skillet, add a few tablespoons olive oil.)

3. As the meatballs fry, sprinkle with cumin, which will develop a roasted flavor. Do not let them burn. Remove fried meatballs from the pan and set aside. In same pan, pour off any accumulated fat and sauté onions

in 1 tablespoon (14 g) butter until onions are softened. Add allspice, cardamom, saffron, and remaining cinnamon and turmeric. Cook a few minutes longer over low heat to cook out any raw flavor of the spices, then add tomatoes, tomato sauce, and broth. Cook until thickened and flavorful, about 15 minutes.

4. Return meatballs to pan with sauce. Add spinach and peas. Simmer until meatballs are cooked through and spinach is tender but still brightly colored green. Season with lemon or lime juice, salt to taste, and garnish with remaining cilantro or lemon.

ADVANCE PREPARATION: May be prepared 2 to 3 days ahead of time. When reheating, add more broth if sauce seems too thick.

VARIATION: Eggs may be poached in the simmering tomato sauce alongside the meatballs, with or without the spinach or peas.

Weta Ki

Curry-Baked Lemon Pork

Burma

Savory and spicy, this Burmese dry curry echoes exotic flavors of cardamom and coconut, tart lemon and tomato, baked into its tender meat.

While most Burmese curries start out, as this one does, with a slow stir-fry of onion, garlic, ginger, and chile, here the meat is not stir-fried but combined with the onion and spice mixture, then placed in the oven for a slow bake. It emerges tender and permeated with flavor.

Serve with Curried Steamed Noodle (see Indonesian Asparagus and Tofu in Index) or steamed rice, and a salad of crunchy raw vegetables such as Southeast Asian Vegetable Salad with Cucumber Dressing (see Index). Accompany with a sambal or other hot relish.

Serves 4

1 medium-sized onion, chopped
6 cloves garlic, chopped
2 tablespoons (30 ml) chopped gingerroot
3 jalapeños, thinly sliced
2 tablespoons (30 ml) vegetable oil
1 teaspoon (5 ml) turmeric
2½ teaspoons (13 ml) paprika
   Seeds from 10 to 12 pods of cardamom

> 1½ pounds (675 g) pork shoulder, cut into 2-inch (50-mm) chunks; include any bones as well, for they flavor the whole dish
> 3 medium-sized tomatoes, chopped (canned is fine)
> ½ lemon, cut into 4 pieces
> ¼ cup (60 ml) coconut milk (see Aromatics and Special Ingredients)
> Juice of 1 lemon (2 tablespoons [30 ml])
> Salt to taste

1. Over low-medium heat, slowly stir-fry onion, garlic, gingerroot, and jalapeños in vegetable oil; sprinkle with turmeric and cook until onion is softened and lightly golden brown. Place in a blender or processor and puree until smooth.

2. Combine pureed onion mixture with paprika and cardamom, then add pork cubes, tossing well to coat. Add tomatoes, lemon chunks, coconut milk, lemon juice, salt to taste, and place in 350° F. oven. Bake until meat is tender and cooked through, about 1½ hours.

3. Serve immediately, accompanied by steamed rice and a hot condiment.

ADVANCE PREPARATION: May be prepared a day ahead of time and reheated, with a little additional water, if needed.

Cameroon Curry

Africa

This tomatoey stew of meat and curry spices smoothed with a few spoonfuls of peanut butter reflects the culinary influence of Africa's huge Indian population. While the spicing is Indian, the inclusion of peanuts is very African.

Preparation couldn't be simpler: Sauté the onion and garlic, add the meat, spices, and tomatoes, and simmer until tender. The taste is unlike other curries, with the savor of tomatoes and the creamy nuttiness of peanut butter. Serve with a platter of condiments to choose from: banana slices, diced nectarine or mango, fresh chile slices, peanuts, coconut, sliced green onions, and cilantro. Accompany with steamed rice.

Serves 4

> 1 medium-sized onion
> 5 cloves garlic, chopped

1 tablespoon (15 ml) vegetable oil
2 teaspoons (10 ml) homemade Curry Powder (see Index)
½ teaspoon (3 ml) cumin
3 small, hot dried red chiles, such as hontaka, japonés, pequín, or cayenne, broken in half
2 pounds (900 g) lamb (round bone chop, shoulder chop, leg of lamb, and the like)
1½ cups (375 ml) tomatoes, chopped (canned is fine)
1 medium-sized potato, peeled and diced
1 medium-sized sweet potato, peeled and diced
¼ cup (60 ml) golden raisins
2 tablespoons (30 ml) peanut butter (smooth or crunchy)

Condiments:
4 green onions, thinly sliced
1 banana, sliced or diced
1 nectarine or mango, diced
3 jalapeños, chopped
3 tablespoons (45 ml) chopped cilantro
½ cup (125 ml) coarsely chopped peanuts
½ cup (125 ml) fresh shredded or dried unsweetened coconut

1. Sauté onion and garlic in vegetable oil until onion is softened, not brown.

2. Sprinkle in curry powder, cumin, and red chiles, cook for 1 minute, then add lamb. Toss together and sauté for 1 or 2 minutes, then add the tomatoes, potatoes, sweet potatoes, and raisins. Bring to a boil, then reduce heat, cover, and simmer until meat is tender, about 2 hours.

3. Stir peanut butter into stew and mix well. Keep warm while you prepare platter of fruit and condiments.

4. Arrange condiments on a platter. Serve stew accompanied by the platter of condiments and steamed rice.

ADVANCE PREPARATION: Stew may be prepared as much as 2 days in advance. In fact, it gets better each day, as do many stews. Before reheating, remove fat from the surface, and sprinkle in about an extra ½ teaspoon (3 ml) of Curry Powder.

VARIATION: For a vegetarian version, omit meat and increase amounts of potato and sweet potato to 3 each and add 1 diced eggplant. Reduce cooking time to 20 minutes, or just long enough to make the vegetables tender. Add a little powdered vegetable bouillon for a more robust flavor.

Tarragon-Veal Patties
in Red-Wine Sauce

Roumania/France

I wasn't sure if I should include this dish here; perhaps it wasn't exotic enough, maybe it didn't seem sunny enough. So I made it again. The fact is that while there is no exciting story to go along with it, it is so very, very good. The jolt of flavor comes from anise-scented tarragon and salty capers, the simple sauce is thickened with a nugget of herbed cream cheese. Its origins are Roumanian in the generous dose of chopped garlic, and French in the sautéeing and wine-cheese sauce.

Serve with Puree de Pommes de Terre à l'Ail (see Index), if you dare. Eat it with friends you like, because most likely you'll want to spend the next 3 days together, as no one else will come near. But it's worth it.

Serves 6

 2 pounds (900 g) ground veal
 10 cloves garlic, coarsely chopped
 ½ cup (125 ml) fresh bread crumbs
 2 eggs
 2 teaspoons (10 ml) capers, or more if desired
 1½ tablespoons (23 ml) fresh tarragon, or 2 teaspoons (10 ml) dried tarragon
 Salt and pepper to taste
 2 to 3 tablespoons (30 to 45 ml) olive oil, or 2 to 3 tablespoons (28 to 42 g) butter
 ½ cup (125 ml) red wine
 ½ cup (125 ml) beef broth
 2 tablespoons (30 ml) herbed cream cheese, such as Boursin

1. Mix veal with garlic, bread crumbs, eggs, capers, and tarragon. Form into patties and sprinkle with salt and pepper.

2. Sauté in olive oil or butter until browned on both sides. Patties may be quite tender, so remove carefully from pan to make sauce.

3. Discard any accumulated grease in pan, then add wine and broth. Over the highest heat boil down the wine and broth until its volume is reduced by half. Remove pan from heat and whisk in herbed cream cheese.

4. Return patties to pan, along with any accumulated juices, spoon sauce on top, and serve immediately.

ADVANCE PREPARATION: Meat mixture may be assembled and patties formed up to 2 hours ahead of time and refrigerated until cooking.

VARIATION: Garlic-Tarragon Turkey Patties
   Ground turkey may be used in place of the veal—its flavor accepts the huge amount of garlic. Eliminate the sauce, however, and broil the patties until lightly browned.

Vitello con Peperoni e Olive

Sauteed Veal with Mixed Peppers and Olives

Italy

It comes to the table ablaze with colors: red, yellow, and green strips of peppers, chunks of scarlet tomato, and dots of tiny black olives. Scattered with fresh basil leaves it evokes a summer supper in the south of Italy.

   This straightforward dish is only as good as its ingredients: the tenderness of the veal, the exuberance of the peppers, and the salty piquancy of the olives. If fresh rosemary is unavailable, do not use dried, as it has little flavor and the leaves are sharp. Instead, increase the amount of thyme and omit the rosemary.

   In the last several years multicolored peppers have become extremely popular, and where I live are available year-round. When fresh peppers are unavailable, roasted red peppers in the jar is a reasonable substitute, and the yellow could be omitted.

   Serve with a salad of raw fennel or anise, thinly sliced and dressed with extra-virgin olive oil and lemon juice. The mild licorice flavor of the fennel complements the robust tomato flavor of the sauce.

Serves 6

1 pound (450 g) veal scaloppine, thinly sliced and lightly pounded
¼ cup (60 ml) flour, for dusting
2 medium-sized red bell peppers, roasted, peeled, and thinly sliced
2 medium-sized yellow bell peppers, roasted, peeled, and thinly sliced
2 medium-sized green bell peppers, roasted, peeled, and thinly sliced
3 cloves garlic, chopped

  2 teaspoons (10 ml) fresh rosemary leaves, lightly crushed
    (omit if only dried is available and increase amount of thyme
    to 1 teaspoon [5 ml])
  ½ teaspoon (3 ml) fresh thyme leaves, or ¼ teaspoon (1.5 ml)
    dried thyme, crushed
  2 to 3 tablespoons (30 to 45 ml) olive oil
  1½ cups (375 ml) peeled and seeded ripe tomatoes, chopped
    (canned is fine)
  1 cup (250 ml) beef broth
  1 cup (250 ml) dry red wine, such as zinfandel
  ¼ cup (60 ml) Marsala
  ½ cup (125 ml) Niçoise olives (see Note)
    Juice of ½ lemon (1 tablespoon [15 ml])
  2 tablespoons (30 ml) chopped fresh basil or fresh parsley

NOTE: Niçoise olives are too small to pit, but have superb flavor. You may wish to substitute the equally good Kalamata olives, pitted and halved. (Otherwise, just warn your guests to eat carefully.)

1. Cut veal into pieces about 2 by 4 inches (50 by 100 mm). Lightly dust with flour and set aside.

2. Sauté the red, yellow, and green peppers over high heat with the garlic, rosemary, and thyme in 1½ tablespoons (23 ml) of the olive oil. Remove from pan, and in several batches quickly sauté the veal over high head in remaining olive oil until it's lightly browned. Remove from pan and set aside with the peppers.

3. Add tomatoes to pan, along with broth, red wine, and Marsala, and boil to reduce in volume while you stir to blend all the tasty brown bits left from the sautéeing. Cook to reduce volume to about 1 cup (250 ml).

4. Return peppers and meat to sauce, toss in olives, and squeeze lemon juice all over.

5. Serve immediately, topped with basil or parsley.

ADVANCE PREPARATION: Although this dish should not be cooked ahead, the peppers could be precooked, the veal cut and pounded, and the sauce prepared up to several hours ahead.

Roast Cumin Lamb

Morocco

This is the simplest of preparations, but the flavor of the dish is most distinctive. A lovely leg of lamb is stuffed with large amounts of garlic, coated with a paste of garlic, olive oil, and cumin, and slowly roasted to tenderness. The Moroccans are found of lamb, and equally fond of cumin —hence this combination. Serve with a pilaf of brown or white rice cooked with plump raisins, strewn with toasted almonds, seasoned with fried onions, and accompanied by a bowl of cool yogurt. Instead of rice, you might serve it with raisin-studded couscous, accompanied by a bowl of Harissa (see recipes in my other book, *Hot and Spicy*, also published by Jeremy P. Tarcher, Inc.).

Serves 6

  1 **leg of lamb (about 5 pounds [2250 g])**
15 **cloves garlic, peeled**
  2 **tablespoons (30 ml) olive oil**
  2 **tablespoons (30 ml) cumin**
    Salt to taste

1. With a thin, sharp knife make deep incisions all over leg of lamb.
2. Cut about 10 of the garlic cloves into halves and insert a garlic half into each incision.
3. Crush remaining garlic cloves, and mix with olive oil and cumin. Rub this mixture all over the outside of the lamb, then sprinkle with salt.
4. Roast at 325° F. until crusty brown on the outside, somewhat rare within, about an hour. Use a meat thermometer to more accurately gauge the doneness.
5. Carve into thin slices and serve immediately with pilaf, mint chutney, and yogurt.

Sangchi Ssam

Spiced Chopped Beef with Tofu

Korea

Here we have intensely flavored meat and tofu with a dab of rice, wrapped in lettuce leaves and eaten as a fresh "sandwich." Wrapping savory meat and vegetable fillings in lettuce and herbs is common everywhere in

Southeast Asia. In Korea you'll also find such condiments as kimchee, the fiery pickled cabbage, and unusual herbs, such as geranium leaves and sukkat, an herb somewhat between watercress and chervil in taste. Beef is the favored meat for this dish, sturdy enough to stand up to the Korean hot peppered food cooked in heady sesame oil.

This makes a terrific supper dish, one that is so easy to put together. Start with a light broth or seafood soup and enjoy a Coconut Rum Sorbet (see Index) for dessert.

Serves 4

2 cloves garlic, chopped
3 green onions, chopped
1 pound (450 g) lean ground beef
1 block tofu, 3 by 5 inches (75 by 125 mm) in size, cut into ½-inch (12-mm) cubes
1 tablespoon (15 ml) Chinese bean paste (see Aromatics and Special Ingredients)
½ to 1 teaspoon (3 to 5 ml) hot bean paste (or to taste, depending on how hot your brand is)
¼ teaspoon (1.5 ml) crushed Szechuan peppercorns
1 tablespoon (15 ml) sugar
2 tablespoons (30 ml) broth
1½ tablespoons (23 ml) sesame oil
¼ cup (60 ml) coarsely chopped dry-roasted peanuts, or 2 tablespoons (30 ml) toasted, lightly crushed sesame seeds
About 6 leaves of lettuce
1 cup (250 ml) freshly cooked white rice
1 tablespoon (15 ml) cilantro, watercress, or sukkat leaves (see Aromatics and Special Ingredients)
Kimchee, as desired

1. In wok or heavy skillet, stir-fry garlic, green onions, and ground beef until browned (add 1 or 2 teaspoons of vegetable oil if beef does not have enough of its own fat). Push meat to one side of wok.

2. Add tofu to empty side of wok and stir-fry for 1 to 2 minutes, then add bean paste, hot bean paste, Szechuan peppercorns, sugar, and broth and cook over high heat for 1 to 2 minutes, until a thick sauce forms. Sprinkle with sesame oil, and peanuts or sesame seeds.

3. Serve immediately, each portion on a leaf of lettuce, with a dollop of rice and a few cilantro, watercress, or sukkat leaves. Pass around kimchee, as desired.

ADVANCE PREPARATION: Each ingredient may be prepared up to a day ahead of time and reheated just before serving on lettuce leaves.

VARIATION: For a Korean vegetarian stir-fry, omit the meat, increase the tofu to double the amount, and sauté 8 to 10 large dried shiitake mushrooms (see Aromatics and Special Ingredients), sliced thinly, with the green onions and garlic.

Yemista Me Lahano

Stuffed Cabbage Leaves in Lemon Sauce

Greece

Where else would a sun-drenched version of that homey favorite, stuffed cabbage leaves come from if not Greece. There, though, the tender leaves are filled with minced lamb, fragrant with mint and cinnamon, and served with a tart lemon sauce.

I once lived above a café in a fishing village on the island of Crete. It was right on the water, and I had a hard time deciding which was most wonderful—the gentle bay outside the door or the cooking smells that wafted up the stairs from Vasili's café.

There was no menu; diners were led into the kitchen to peer into the vats of daily specials. We simply pointed to whatever looked best that day: tomatoy stews of lamb and eggplant or spinach; lemon-roasted chicken; and delicate vegetable stews of okra or artichoke. Sometimes there might be a hearty moussaka, or pastitsio of lamb and pasta, or a simmering cauldron of freshly caught seafood. I chose stuffed cabbage so often that Vasili began to bring it to me automatically as soon as I entered the café.

Enjoy this savory dish with a simple rice pilaf to spoon the lemon sauce over and a salad of ripe, sliced tomatoes and red onions, crumbled with feta cheese and dressed with olive oil and vinegar. Lovely pink taramosalata spread on bread and garnished with juicy black olives would be a nice first course, as would cold-cooked squid in a garlic-and-parsley vinaigrette.

Serves 6

> 1½ **pounds (675 g) lean ground lamb or beef**
> ½ **cup (125 ml) raw white rice, or** ½ **cup (125 ml) cooked brown rice, well drained**
> ½ **cup (125 ml) raisins**
> 1½ **teaspoons (8 ml) cinnamon**

1½ teaspoons (8 ml) cumin
3 eggs
½ cup (125 ml) chopped fresh mint, or 1 tablespoon (15 ml)
   dried mint, crumbled
3 cloves garlic, chopped
   Salt and pepper to taste
1 large whole green or white cabbage
4 cups (1 l) chicken broth
3 tablespoons (42 g) butter
3 tablespoons (45 ml) flour
   Juice of 3 lemons (⅓ cup [85 ml])

1. Mix lamb or beef with rice, raisins, cinnamon, cumin, 1 egg, mint, and garlic. Salt and pepper to taste, and mix well.

2. Blanch whole cabbage by plunging into boiling water and cooking for 5 minutes. Remove from water. When cool enough to handle, cut out the core and peel the leaves.

3. Place about 2 tablespoons (30 ml) of lamb-and-rice mixture onto each leaf. Wrap up tightly, fully enclosing each parcel. Layer in pot, seam side down, the parcels close together. Add 1 cup (250 ml) broth, cover pot tightly, and simmer until cooked through, 1 to 1½ hours.

4. Carefully drain off broth. Reserve for another use, say soup or a stew. Set cabbage rolls in a covered baking dish in a warm oven while you prepare the sauce.

5. Heat butter gently in saucepan; sprinkle in flour and gently cook a few minutes over medium-low heat. Remove from heat, stir in the remaining 3 cups (750 ml) broth, return to heat, and cook, stirring until it has thickened, about 5 minutes. Whisk it if it has any lumps.

6. Beat remaining eggs and add it to the lemon juice. Stir mixture into half a cup of thickened broth, then stir this mixture into the rest of the hot broth, stirring all the while so that it does not curdle.

7. Cook over a very low heat for 1 or 2 minutes until it thickens a bit and the egg cooks through to thicken, but does not scramble. It should be creamy.

8. Pour the egg-lemon sauce over the cabbage rolls and serve immediately.

ADVANCE PREPARATION: Cabbage rolls may be prepared and cooked up to a day ahead, but the egg-lemon sauce must be made just before serving.

VARIATION 1: For vegetarian stuffed cabbage leaves, substitute 3 cups (750 ml) cooked brown rice for the meat. Follow the recipe for the filling, but reduce amount of cinnamon to ¼ teaspoon (1.5 ml), and add 8 green onions, thinly sliced, and 2 tablespoons (30 ml) plain yogurt. A Persian variation would be to add ½ cup of cooked split peas.

VARIATION 2: This classic Greek egg-lemon sauce is delicious with roasted or simmered meats, poultry and fish as well as vegetables. I remember eating a delightful stew of artichoke hearts and new potatoes blanketed with this tangy sauce.

Spicy Cassoulet

France

I have eaten many cassoulets, some very good and some rather dismal, but none compared to the mythical cassoulet I imagined out there somewhere just waiting to be discovered, to be devoured, by me. Each cauldron of bubbling beans and sausage I tasted made me think—"Yes, this would be perfect if . . ." One summer day in southwest France—the land of confit and cassoulet, I set about creating "my cassoulet," the one I'd always wanted to eat.

Many argue about what should go into an "authentic" cassoulet, and who prepares it the best—the chefs of Castlenaudry or Toulouse. I wanted something a little less stodgy, with a zap of piquancy. I wanted the sunny flavors of tomatoes, garlic, and sweet peppers, plus the addition of assertive spices. So I threw authenticity to the wind, feeling a bit guilty in this land of tradition. But as the rain continued all afternoon, the house was filled with the sounds of French pop music on the radio and the savory aroma of simmering beans and garlic, and I proclaimed, *"Vive l'innovation!"*

Cassoulet is not a difficult dish to prepare, but it is time-consuming and the list of ingredients is long. Think of cassoulet as boiled white beans baked with an assortment of meats and flavorings. It's given a crusty bread-crumb topping at the end, which is stirred into the cassoulet to thicken it. In France you can buy one leg of confit, Moroccan sausage, saucisson à l'ail, as well as the tender white beans at the village store. Here the ingredients are difficult to get or expensive, and so we must make appropriate substitutions. Most likely you must make your own confit (or roast a duck). You could of course make your own merguez (less than traditional; I include it for its spiciness) but to do all this for one dish is more than even I am interested in: Substitute smoked beef sausage or kielbasa. If you cannot find the French garlic salami saucisson à l'ail,

substitute any garlicky salami. I find cassoulet a good dish for using my bits
of leftover meats—a tiny bit of pancetta, just enough ground lamb to make
a few meatballs, too little ham for a sandwich, and so on.

Cassoulet is rich and satisfying, with each bite containing a different
ingredient: a bit of lamb, a morsel of confit, a chunk of ham. You need only
accompany it with a simple salad of mixed greens dressed with olive oil
and tarragon vinegar. Crusty French bread is a must of course, and drink
the same red wine that you poured into the cassoulet for cooking.

Serves 4 to 6

 1 pound (450 g) white haricot or great northern beans, soaked
 overnight
 1 pound (450 g) lamb shoulder chops, include the bones for
 flavor, cut the meat into 1- to 2-inch (25- to 50-mm) chunks
 2 to 3 ounces (56 to 84 g) salt pork, or pancetta cut into small
 pieces
 8 ounces (224 g) spicy sausage, such as merguez, kielbasa, or
 smoked sausage, sliced into slices ¼-inch (6-mm) thick
 ¼ pound (112 g) ham or Canadian bacon, cut into ¾-inch
 (18-mm) chunks
 1 to 2 pieces duck confit, meat removed from bone and cut into
 chunks (include the bone for flavor; if using a wing portion
 include the whole piece); or roasted duck
 ¼ pound (112 g) saucisson à l'ail, or other garlic salami, cut into
 ¾-inch (18-mm) chunks
 1 medium-sized potato, peeled and diced
 1 medium-sized red bell pepper, diced
 1 medium-sized carrot, diced
 1 head of garlic, cloves separated and peeled, but left whole
 1 teaspoon (5 ml) Herbes de Provence, crushed
 ¼ teaspoon (1.5 ml) dried thyme leaves, crushed
 1½ cups (375 ml) dry red wine, such as a Beaujolais, Cahors, or
 zinfandel
 2 cups (500 ml) fresh tomatoes (canned is okay), chopped
 1½ cups (375 ml) rich, strong duck, chicken, or beef broth
 1 jalapeño en escabeche, chopped (add a bit more if the sausage you're using is not too spicy)
 1 cup (250 ml) bread crumbs
 3 cloves garlic, chopped
 3 tablespoons (45 ml) parsley, chopped

NOTE: This dish is great for entertaining, and may be doubled or even tripled as desired. Once the dish is in the oven you have nothing else to do except add the bread crumbs. Leftovers are delicious for 2 to 3 days.

1. Drain beans of their soaking liquid. Cover with fresh water and bring to a boil. Reduce heat to a low simmer and cook for 1½ to 2 hours or until just tender, adding extra water if it seems too dry. Drain.

2. Sauté the lamb chunks in an ungreased skillet (fat in the lamb will most likely be enough for sautéeing) until lightly browned. Set aside.

3. In earthenware casserole, layer the beans with the chunks of lamb, pieces of salt pork or pancetta, pieces of merguez, kielbasa or smoked beef sausage, ham or bacon, confit (or roasted duck), saucisson à l'ail or salami, diced vegetables, cloves of garlic, herbes de Provence, thyme, red wine, tomatoes, broth, and chopped jalapeño en escabeche.

4. Cover with tight-fitting lid and bake in a 325° F. oven for 1½ to 2 hours, checking every so often to be sure it's not too dry. Add a little more broth, if needed, to maintain a slightly soupy consistency and to keep it from burning.

5. Combine bread crumbs with garlic and parsley.

6. Remove lid from casserole and spread half the bread-crumb mixture over the cassoulet. Raise the heat to 400° F. and return cassoulet to oven. In about 15 minutes a golden crust will have formed (if your oven gets very hot, set it at 375° F.; you do not wish to burn the crumbs). With a spoon break the crust and stir into the cassoulet. Spread the remaining crumbs over the top and return to oven for another 15 minutes.

7. Serve immediately, with extra jalapeños en escabeche or pickled Italian-type peppers on the side (very untraditional, but nonetheless delicious).

ADVANCE PREPARATION: Beans must be boiled ahead of time, up to 2 days, and kept covered in the refrigerator.

VARIATION: Vegetarian Cassoulet

While the preceding cassoulet develops its layers of flavors from its variety of rich meats, this vegetarian cassoulet is delicious in a different, light way. Here, the beans are flavored with the wine, broth, vegetables, and masses of garlic, and emerge savory and fresh tasting. Simply omit the meat, and when you add the topping of bread crumbs at the end, drizzle a few teaspoons of olive oil over the top. Because there is no meat, you will have to add salt and freshly ground coarse black pepper for flavor.

Some Simple Grilled Meat Dishes

Pork Chops Veracruz   Marinate 4 pork chops, about ½-inch (12-mm) thick in 2 to 3 tablespoons (30 to 45 ml) olive oil, 3 cloves garlic, 1 teaspoon (5 ml) each of cumin and New Mexico or ancho chile powder, and 1 to 2 tablespoons (15 to 30 ml) orange juice, plus a little bit of the grated rind. Marinate at least 2 hours. Grill over hot coals until no longer pink inside then serve with X-Nipek (see Index) and sliced avocados.

Oaxaca Taco   Marinate 1 pound (450 g) of skirt or other steak in 2 cloves chopped garlic, salt and cayenne pepper to taste, and the juice of 1 lime for at least 2 hours. Grill until dark and roasted on the outside, rare and juicy within. Slice thinly and splash with the juice of 2 limes combined with ¼ teaspoon (1.5 ml) freshly grated lime rind. Spread warm corn tortillas with Black Bean–Chipotle Puree (see Index) and roll up around slices of the lime-grilled steak. Serve immediately.

Provençal Grilled Lamb   Marinate shoulder lamb chops in olive oil, garlic, lemon juice, or red-wine vinegar, and thyme, at least 2 hours, ideally, overnight. Grill and remove when medium rare. Immediately sprinkle with crumbled Montrachet or similar goat cheese and let melt in. Serve with crusty bread or tucked into pita.

Garlic-Herb Oil   To brush onto meats to be grilled: Let steep ¼ cup (60 ml) fresh chopped herbs or 2 tablespoons (30 ml) dried, with 6 cloves chopped garlic in 1 cup (250 ml) olive oil, for 1 hour. Strain if using dried herbs, or if you wish to keep longer than 2 or 3 days. Use it to brush meat, fish, or vegetables when grilling.

Throw a handful of dry bay leaves or sprigs of thyme into the flames. They will ignite and subtly perfume the grilling food.

SEASONINGS, SAUCES, AND CONDIMENTS

While the Northern climes have their distinctive condiments—horseradish spreads, myriad mustards—the sun-drenched lands have a huge array of condiments and savory sauces.

Bowls and jars filled with intensely flavored mixtures enliven almost any dish: wild herbs from the hills and pastures; olives pounded into a salty, fragrant paste; chiles chopped with vegetables or fruits; tomatoes simmered in mustard oil or olive oil until they become a thick aromatic sauce. And be sure to keep a jar of homemade Curry Powder and Herbes de Provence on your spice shelf to brighten your table.

Also, try hanging branches of thyme, marjoram, and rosemary upside down in your kitchen for a rustic, French countryside touch. When they are dried, remove the leaves from the stems and store in jars, tightly sealed.

Herbes de Provence
Provençal Herb Seasoning

France

Aromatic herbs blanket the hillsides of much of the Mediterranean and nowhere are they treasured more than in Provence. There they are gathered wild from the countryside and hung in huge bunches to dry in rustic kitchens. Nearly each household has a garden with fragrant herbs, and the marketplace provides any not found in the fields or garden.

Combinations of these herbs are blended to make the famous herbes de Provence, that aromatic mixture used to sprinkle on meats or fish for grilling, or to season a hearty stew. One whiff invokes the south of France.

In addition to the more familiar herbs, a traditional Provençal ingredient is lavender. The generous dose in this mixture adds an elusive, slightly haunting quality—a floral note among the deeper herbal ones.

Yields about 1 cup (250 ml)

2 tablespoons (30 ml) whole savory leaves
2 teaspoons (10 ml) thyme leaves
2 teaspoons (10 ml) fennel seeds
1 teaspoon (5 ml) lavender buds
1 teaspoon (5 ml) marjoram leaves
1 teaspoon (5 ml) ground coriander
2 bay leaves, ground in a coffee grinder (optional)

NOTE: All herbs are dried.

Mix all ingredients together, lightly crushing either in a mortar and pestle or in a bowl with the bottom of a small jar. You want the herbs to stay individual and separate, but you want some of their fragrances to mingle.

ADVANCE PREPARATION: Store in a tightly sealed jar, preferably away from direct light. As with other dried herbs it loses its aroma the longer it sits. Use within 4 to 6 months.

VARIATION: Herbes de Provence is a delicious classic seasoning for mustard. Add 1 teaspoon (5 ml) Herbes de Provence to ¼ cup (60 ml) French mustard, such as Maille, L'Etoile, or a mild Dijon.

Curry Powder

India

The Indian way with abundant spicing and alluring spice combinations dates all the way back to the pre-Aryan period. Of course, there were no chiles in India then; these were brought by the Portuguese explorers in the 16th century. Before then, black pepper fired up food in the East.

What we know as curry powder is a mixture of spices used to flavor Indian dishes, which we have come to call curry. Perhaps the word comes from the tamil word for stew-kari, or perhaps not. Curry powder was created when foreigners, especially the British, sent home packets of spice mixtures to recreate the exotically spiced stews they were enjoying on the huge Indian subcontinent.

One of the joys of eating Indian food is the sensuous abandon with which spices are used. If you prepared each dish with a standard curry mixture, each dish would taste the same; the subtleties would disappear. So, why have a curry powder? you may ask. Curry powders make good, basic spice mixtures to which you may wish to add other spices, to individualize each dish.

In India these mixtures are called *garam masala*, literally meaning "spicy mixture." At the marketplace you will find a masala for fish, several for vegetables, different ones for meat, and so on. Sometimes a dish may be simmered with a spice mixture for many hours, and right before serving it will be sprinkled with a bit more spice mixture to renew the flavors that have dissipated.

Since it is so useful to add a mixed spice powder to the spice rack, it's worthwhile to make it yourself. Here is a curry powder I enjoy; its exotic overtones come from the fenugreek and cardamom.

⅓ cup (85 ml) coriander
2 tablespoons (30 ml) cumin
1 tablespoon (15 ml) cloves
1 tablespoon (15 ml) cardamom
1 teaspoon (5 ml) cayenne pepper
1 tablespoon (15 ml) fenugreek
1 teaspoon (5 ml) ginger powder
2 tablespoons (30 ml) turmeric

NOTE: If using ground spices, be sure they are fresh; it makes all the difference in the world. Fresh ground spices have aroma, body, and richness. Once ground, spices begin to lose their flavor, so be sure to buy them at a store that specializes in spices and has a high turnover rate. Tasteless spices will make tasteless curry.

1. If using ground spices, simply combine and use as desired.
2. If using whole spices, place all spices—except for fenugreek, ginger, and turmeric, as these are more practical to use ground—on a cookie sheet and roast in a 200° F. oven for about 30 minutes. Grind in a coffee grinder.

ADVANCE PREPARATION: Store in a tightly closed jar, away from direct light. Since the aroma fades the longer kept, try to use within 2 to 3 months.

Thai Green Curry Paste

Thailand

This potent puree is the basis for the "green curries" of Thailand; the fresh chiles and cilantro give the green color. There are red, orange, and yellow curries as well, based on red dried chiles and spices such as paprika (red curry) or turmeric (yellow).

Because the curry paste requires so many ingredients, I find it easy to make a large batch and freeze the curry paste in small plastic bags or in ice cube trays. This way I have it at hand to add to such dishes as Thai Cauliflower and Beef Stir-Fry or Thai Grilled Chicken with Peanut Sauce (see Index for both); or season buttered rice with green curry paste, lemon juice, and grated lemon rind, then toss in seedless grapes. Indeed, use this curry paste to coat almost any kabob or to fire up a stir-fry.

Yields about 1 cup (250 ml)

    6 cloves garlic, chopped
    3 jalapeños chopped
1½ tablespoons (23 ml) chopped gingerroot
    1 tablespoon (15 ml) vegetable oil
      Rind of ¼ lemon or lime (about ⅛ teaspoon [.5 ml])
    1 teaspoon (5 ml) whole fennel seeds, or ½ teaspoon (3 ml) ground fennel
    1 teaspoon (5 ml) freshly ground cumin
1½ teaspoons (8 ml) freshly ground coriander
   ½ teaspoon (3 ml) grated nutmeg
      Pinch ground cloves
    1 teaspoon (5 ml) sereh, or 1 tablespoon (15 ml) peeled and chopped fresh lemongrass (see Aromatics and Special Ingredients)
    1 teaspoon (5 ml) freshly ground black pepper

1 teaspoon (5 ml) salt
1 cup (250 ml) chopped cilantro
½ medium-sized onion, chopped

1. In processor or blender, puree garlic along with jalapeños and ginger-root. Add oil, lemon or lime rind, fennel seeds, cumin, coriander, nutmeg, cloves, sereh or lemongrass, pepper, and salt. Puree until it becomes a thick paste (if using fennel seeds, they will remain somewhat whole, which is okay; if desired, you could crush them in a mortar and pestle beforehand, however).

2. Add cilantro and puree into a paste, then add onions and puree just long enough for onions to blend into the paste. Authentically, the onions should be pounded until very smooth, but I like the onion in little chunks for the character it adds to dishes.

ADVANCE PREPARATION: Store in small plastic bags or in ice-cube trays, tightly wrapped in plastic or foil, in the freezer; will last 6 months.

Tomatillo Guacamole

Mexico

The tart taste of tomatillo combines with rich sensuous avocado to make this a fantastic guacamole. The tomatillo's particular tanginess accents the avocado so perfectly that you may not even notice it's there. You'll only notice that this is the best guacamole you've ever tasted.

Use only the Hass avocado, rich and oily-fleshed with thick, black skin. The fuerte avocado, bright green in color with a thin skin, has a more watery consistency and does not have much flavor.

Tomatillo guacamole is delicious as a dip, spooned over black-bean enchiladas or crab-stuffed soft tacos, or as a sauce for grilled meats.

Yields 1½ to 2 cups (375 to 500 ml)

6 tomatillos (canned is fine)
3 tablespoons (45 ml) finely chopped onion
1 medium- to large-sized Hass avocado, mashed coarsely with a fork
Juice of ½ lemon (1 tablespoon [15 ml])
½ to 1 jalapeño, finely chopped, or Tabasco to taste
Salt to taste

1. Husk tomatillos, rinse briefly, and simmer in water to cover over medium-high heat until tomatillos are tender and cooked through. Drain, mash, and cool. If using canned tomatillos, simply drain and mash.

2. Combine with onion, avocado, lemon juice, jalapeño or Tabasco, and salt. Serve immediately.

ADVANCE PREPARATION: Solutions abound regarding how to keep make-ahead guacamole a nice green color; the question is, Do any of them work? The traditional one of placing the pit on top of the guacamole, covering it tightly, and refrigerating it is as good as any; besides, I like to lick the guacamole off the seed afterward. A squeeze of lemon helps, and even if the top does discolor, you just need to stir it up again before serving.

Attadindin

Sautéed Spicy Pepper Relish

Nigeria

As a devotee of hot-pepper sauces, salsas, and condiments I'm always on the lookout for a new, unusual heat fix. This one is from Nigeria, my notes say, though I'm not sure at all how it came to me. In any case, it's delicious!

The slow cooking in oil reflects an Arabic or Turkish influence. The peppers become soft and combine with the onions, yet retain their integrity, much in the same way a good ratatouille does. Enjoy Attadindin on crusty bread, especially topped with a slice of mild cheese. It's wonderful alongside a couscous, or spooned onto rice or soups.

Yields about 1½ cups (375 ml)

4 cloves garlic, sliced
1 medium-sized onion, chopped
2 medium-sized green peppers, chopped
2 to 3 jalapeños, chopped or thinly sliced
2 to 3 tablespoons (30 to 45 ml) olive oil
Salt to taste

Slowly sauté garlic, onion, peppers, and jalapeños in olive oil until soft, about 5 to 10 minutes over low heat. Season to taste with salt. When freshly made, this should be quite hot; its fire dissipates with each day.

ADVANCE PREPARATION: Store, tightly covered in the refrigerator, for 4 to 5 days. The heat will dissipate somewhat but may be spiced again accordingly.

VARIATION 1: Instead of olive oil use vegetable oil and add 1 teaspoon (5 ml) curry powder to the simmering pepper mixture.

VARIATION 2: Instead of green peppers, use red peppers or a combination of both.

X-Nipek

Fresh, Chunky Salsa with Orange, Lime, and Cilantro

Mexico

The ancient Mayans and Aztecs enjoyed a cuisine based on the chile, which itself was the foundation for much of the contemporary Mexican diet. Since the name of this salsa is Mayan, its preparation probably dates back to Mayan times.

In the Yucatan, this salsa would be made with a Seville, or bitter orange, seldom available here. I've found that using a combination of orange and lime, with a little orange rind, is, if not completely authentic, delicious nonetheless.

This chunky salsa mixture is pungent from cilantro, slightly fruity, and torrid from the chiles. It is fresh, simple to prepare, and decidedly delicious. Enjoy spooned onto thin grilled steaks splashed with lime, accompanied by Papas y Ejotes Chorreadas (see Index).

Yields about 1½ cups (375 ml)

2 medium-sized ripe tomatoes, coarsely chopped
3 jalapeños, chopped
¼ cup (60 ml) cilantro, chopped
½ medium-sized onion, chopped
Pinch salt
Pinch sugar
Juice of 1 lime (2 tablespoons [30 ml])
Juice of 1 small orange (about ¼ cup [60 ml])
Grated rind of ½ orange (¼ teaspoon [1.5 ml])

Combine all ingredients and serve as salsa or condiment.

ADVANCE PREPARATION: Best when freshly prepared; it does lose heat as it sits, but lasts for 2 to 3 days, tightly covered in the refrigerator.

Podina Chatni

Mint Chutney with Yogurt

India

Spicy hot, slightly sour, and as fragrant as a field of fresh mint, Podina Chatni shimmers pale green on the plate.

This is not a preserved chutney, sweet and hot like a spicy jam, but a fresh condiment of pounded pureed herbs. In Indian homes, at least one fresh chutney is prepared each day. They can be made from almost any-thing—coconut, cooked lentils, carrots, banana, sesame-seed paste, dried mango, even the biting, fresh horseradish; they are ground together with chiles, garlic, onion, or an herb such as cilantro. Indian cooks pound the ingredients by hand on a curry stone, much like a mortar and pestle; I find it quick and easy to use a blender or processor. The consistency should be that of a smooth to slightly chunky paste.

Mint chutney is a favorite of mine, and there are many to choose from: Some have coconut, others chopped peanuts, another just mint, garlic, chiles, and cilantro. This one is special: Cooled with yogurt, it is at once *picante,* cool, and very aromatic. For a hotter condiment increase the number of chiles to 2 or even 3. Podina Chatni is delicious dabbed on grilled lamb or chicken, or accompanying a curry dish with rice. Try also doubling the amount of yogurt and enjoy as a sauce for Aashak (lamb-stuffed noodles; see Index).

Yields about 2 cups (500 ml)

> 2 cloves garlic, chopped
> 1 jalapeño, chopped
> 2 teaspoons (10 ml) chopped gingerroot
> 1 cup (250 ml) fresh mint leaves
> ½ to ⅔ cup (125 to 170 ml) cilantro (if you dislike cilantro, substitute all mint)
> ⅓ cup (85 ml) plain yogurt
> Salt to taste

1. In a processor or blender, puree garlic with jalapeño and gingerroot; add mint and cilantro or mint, pureeing to a smooth paste.
2. Stir in yogurt and salt to taste.

ADVANCE PREPARATION: Keeps well for 3 days, tightly covered in the refrigerator. Its heat intensity dissipates each day, so you may wish to adjust the chile proportion accordingly just before serving, or add a dash of cayenne pepper.

VARIATION: When pomegranates are in season, garnish the pale green chutney with their ruby seeds.

Confiture de Tomates

France

The first time I harvested my own ripe, red, juicy crop of tomatoes was the first time I made this thick sauce, jam really, redolent of tomatoes and onion and garlic. We ate it spooned onto buttered spaghetti strewn with home-grown basil.

I've since streamlined the recipe by substituting tomato paste for half the amount of tomatoes; it cuts down on cooking time, and since the flavor of store-bought tomatoes pales beside that of homegrown, it adds a richer flavor. Serve as a sauce with pasta, green beans, black olives, and fresh basil or Ricotta al Forno (see Index).

Serves 4

> 1 medium-sized onion, coarsely chopped
> 5 to 6 cloves garlic, coarsely chopped
> 1 tablespoon (15 ml) olive oil
> 2 pounds (900 g) tomatoes (canned are not okay in this dish)
> ¼ cup (60 ml) tomato paste
> ¼ teaspoon (1.5 ml) sugar or honey
> Salt and pepper to taste

Sauté onion and garlic in olive oil until lightly browned. Add tomatoes and tomato paste, sugar or honey, and salt and pepper, and simmer over a medium heat, stirring every so often until thick and jam-like. This will take about 45 minutes.

ADVANCE PREPARATION: Freezes well, especially in small amounts that can be pulled out and popped directly into a soup or stew to enrich it with flavor. May be kept tightly covered in refrigerator for up to 4 days.

VARIATION: Sunny Tomato Butter
  This rich-flavored butter is outstanding, and belies its simple ingredi-

ents. Incredibly good with garlic-rubbed, olive-oil-brushed toasted French bread, the whole sprinkled with fresh basil.

> 4 tablespoons (56 g) unsalted butter
> 3 to 4 tablespoons (45 to 60 ml) confiture de tomates
> 1 egg yolk
> 1 tablespoon (15 ml) very hot water

1. In processor or blender whip butter until fluffy. Add confiture de tomates and whip to blend well. Scrape down sides if you need to.
2. With machine still running, add egg yolk and very hot water and let it combine. Serve immediately or chill to use as desired.

ADVANCE PREPARATION: Store tightly covered or wrapped in refrigerator for up to 3 days.

Chipotle Salsa

Salsa of Smoky-Flavored Chiles

Mexico

I first tasted chipotle chiles long ago, when I was learning to cook and beginning to expand my culinary horizons. I had prepared bean tostadas with rich, simmered beans, topped with buttery avocado, crisp radish slices, and cool dollops of sour cream. My guest brought a tiny can of richly brown-colored chiles in a mahogany sauce. Having never eaten one before, I popped one onto my tostada and took a bite. I vividly remember its wonderful smoky deep flavor and its fiery hotness. This salsa has the smoky richness, but the heat is slightly tempered by the chopped onion and tomato.

It is delicious on almost anything, especially with simple grilled foods wrapped into corn or flour tortillas, lamb and pork chipotle tamales, zucchini–black bean tamales, or, of course, bean tostadas. It is particularly good with marinated grilled duck, a pot of spicy black beans, a salad of fresh orange and avocado, and a stack of warm flour tortillas.

Yields 1 1/2 to 2 cups (375 to 500 ml)

> 1 medium-sized onion, chopped
> 2 medium-sized tomatoes, quartered
> 5 to 6 chipotle chiles, plus about 3 tablespoons (45 ml) of the marinade

2 tablespoons (30 ml) chopped cilantro
Salt to taste
Juice of ¼ to ½ lemon (½ to 1 tablespoon [8 to 15 ml])

1. In processor or blender chop onion. Add tomato and chop together.
2. Add chipotle chiles and marinade, mash with a fork or spoon, then add cilantro, salt, and lemon juice and process to desired consistency. It should still have a little texture, but the ingredients should be well blended.

ADVANCE PREPARATION: Will last 3 to 4 days tightly covered in the refrigerator.

Portuguese Olive–Sweet Basil Sauce

Portugal

Is there anything that evokes a day of sun more than the aroma of fresh-picked basil? Pulling the leaves from the stems, releasing the sweet herb fragrance, I am transported beyond my kitchen to sun-baked gardens; some I have known, others I only imagine.

Combined with pungent, salty black olives of the Mediterranean it makes a delicious sauce for grilled hamburgers, bucatini or other pasta, or as an accompaniment to a pot of simmered meats and vegetables such as pot au feu. I especially like it spooned into a steamy bowl of tomatoy vegetable soup such as minestrone, the herbal flavor mingling with the fresh vegetables.

Yields about 1½ cups (375 ml)

1 clove garlic, chopped
½ cup (125 ml) pitted Kalamata olives
⅓ cup (85 ml) olive oil
1 cup (250 ml) fresh sweet basil leaves, firmly packed

In processor, combine all ingredients and process to a smooth, slightly chunky consistency.

ADVANCE PREPARATION: Will last for up to 6 days covered in refrigerator.

VARIATION 1: Olive Sauce Provençal
Eliminate the sweet basil and use instead 1 teaspoon (5 ml) of lightly crushed fennel seeds and 1 teaspoon (5 ml) Herbes de Provence (see Index). Delicious on roast lamb or grilled fish. It has a more pronounced olive flavor and less herbiness.

VARIATION 2: To the Olive Sauce Provençal add 1 to 2 tablespoons (15 to 30 ml) fresh rosemary. Try on roast veal or hearth-roasted potatoes, or spooned over pizza.

Vambotu Pahi
Eggplant Pickles

Sri Lanka

Perhaps the only sad thing about writing cookbooks is that friends are reluctant to have you to dinner. If they do, they spend the whole time apologizing for their cooking, not realizing that the simplest of food with the best of friends is preferable to the most lavish of meals under less ideal circumstances.

A happy thing, however, about writing cookbooks is having an editor who is a great cook and invites you to dinner. This tangy eggplant dish is from my editor, Janice Gallagher. It accompanied a fennel-scented vegetable curry over spiced basmati rice, and it was so good I couldn't get enough. It is less a pickle than it is a spicy, tart eggplant dish.

This pickle is rich with spices, for the balmy island of Sri Lanka grows huge amounts of spices. Small family farms grow an incredible variety of fruits and spices—you may find an acre-sized spice garden growing black peppercorns, turmeric, gingerroot, nutmeg, allspice, lemongrass, cardamom, and vanilla beans, in addition to a huge cinnamon bark tree, many kinds of banana, 1 or 2 kinds of coconut, breadfruit, jackfruit, pineapples, and even coffee bean. Does this not sound like the Garden of Eden?

Serves 4 to 6

2 teaspoons (10 ml) turmeric
1 tablespoon (15 ml) black mustard seeds
½ cup (125 ml) cider vinegar
1 medium-sized onion, chopped
5 cloves garlic, chopped

1 tablespoon (15 ml) chopped gingerroot
1 tablespoon (15 ml) ground coriander
2 teaspoons (10 ml) ground cumin
1 teaspoon (5 ml) ground fennel
½ teaspoon (3 ml) ground cinnamon
1-inch (25-mm) square of pressed tamarind (see Aromatics and Special Ingredients)
¾ cup (180 ml) hot water
3 tablespoons (45 ml) mustard oil (see The Savory Oils)
3 serranos, thinly sliced
6 medium-sized Japanese eggplants (long and narrow), cut diagonally into 1-inch (25-mm) slices
2 teaspoons (10 ml) sugar
Salt to taste

1. Place turmeric, mustard seeds, and vinegar in blender, and blend until mustard seed is ground. A processor will not grind the mustard seed, so if you do not have a blender, grind the mustard seeds coarsely in a coffee grinder (clean it of coffee first, or course) before you add it to the turmeric and vinegar.

2. Add onion, garlic, and gingerroot to the turmeric-mustard mixture and blend until smooth.

3. Toast coriander, cumin, fennel, and cinnamon lightly in an ungreased pan, shaking or stirring until slightly darkened in color.

4. Pour hot water over tamarind and simmer for 10 minutes. Strain and discard pulp and seeds.

5. Heat the mustard oil and add serranos, onion mixture, toasted spice mixture, tamarind water, eggplant, sugar, and salt. Cover and simmer until eggplant is done, about 10 minutes. Enjoy at room temperature, accompanying any sort of curry or rice with spicy vegetables.

ADVANCE PREPARATION: Lasts for 1 to 2 weeks tightly covered in refrigerator.

Tamatar Chatni

Tomato Chutney

India

Hot and gingery, this chutney is delicious dabbed next to any curry or savory fritter. The tomato, as well as the chile are both New World vegetables adopted by the East. And while we know how beloved the chile has become in Indian food, the tomato is also used quite a bit, in sauces, curries, marinades—and in chutney, too.

Cooking the tomatoes in mustard oil imparts a distinctive tang and makes this chutney special.

Yields about 1 cup (250 ml)

2 teaspoons (10 ml) mustard oil (see The Savory Oils)
½ medium-sized onion, coarsely chopped
2 teaspoons (10 ml) chopped gingerroot
½ to 1 jalapeño, chopped
½ teaspoon (3 ml) turmeric
½ teaspoon (3 ml) coriander
4 medium-sized tomatoes, coarsely chopped (2 cups [500 ml]); (canned is okay)
½ teaspoon (3 ml) sugar
    Salt to taste

1. In mustard oil, gently sauté onion, gingerroot, and jalapeño until onion is softened. Sprinkle in turmeric and coriander, and cook 1 minute, then add tomatoes, sugar, and salt to taste.

2. Cook mixture over medium heat until it thickens and is no longer watery, about 10 minutes. Cool.

3. Serve at room temperature or chilled as a condiment with any curry or savory fritter such as Saag Pakora (see Index).

ADVANCE PREPARATION: Lasts for up to a week tightly covered in refrigerator.

SANDWICHES, BREADS,
AND SAVORY SNACKS

Sun-drenched sandwiches and snacks are hearty and full of flavor, not delicate and subtle: crusty bread spread with savory toppings, happily eaten with very little fuss . . . a paper cone filled with crisp fritters sparked with spicy sauce, eaten while wandering through a sun-baked street . . . a huge crusty roll filled with salad, olives, and tuna, and slathered with olive oil and vinegar. . . .

Anything can be a sandwich or a savory snack. Many dishes in this chapter also make fine hors d'oeuvres. There are variations throughout this book of other dishes describing sandwiches: A Spanish sandwich of mussels, for example, or cold Provençal roast pork on French bread spread with aïoli and sprinkled with capers. Try a sandwich of Imam Bayildi at room temperature, on a crusty roll or Indian-Flavor Burrito (see Index).

I've included two savory breads: one a garlic-scented flatbread, the other an olive-and-herb-studded yeast bread. They make satisfying sandwiches or accompaniments to meals, and often are the basis of the meal itself, with their sturdy textures and chewiness.

Tramezzini and Panini

Italian Sandwiches

Italy

You see selections of these sandwiches all over Italy, piled under a glass counter, covered lightly with a damp towel for protection from the hot and drying air (as well as from the flies). Almost every bar and tabac will have an array, the tramezzini prepared on thinly cut bread, the panini on small rolls. Some are no more than a roll filled with rosy prosciutto or mortadella, a slice of omelet, or tomato with fresh mozzarella and basil. Others might be more elaborate, made on focaccia, a flat, chewy pizza bread. In Milano you'll find a selection of condiments to add—mustard, pickles, olives, capers, and so on.

My favorite recipe involves a trip to Italy: Buy a prosciutto and fontina cheese sandwich from a café and tote it home, wrapped in its coarse brown paper wrapping. On the way, buy a head of garlic from an old Italian man selling it on the street. Peel a garlic clove and begin to enjoy your sandwich, alternating small bites of garlic with bites of sandwich. Peel another, and another, eating until your sandwich is gone. Do not leave your room for a day or two afterward.

Bruschetta with Prosciutto

Yields 2 open-faced sandwiches

2 thick slices of crusty country bread
1 to 2 cloves garlic, cut in half
2 teaspoons (10 ml) olive oil
2 ounces (56 g) prosciutto, thinly sliced
3 or 4 Niçoise or Kalamata olives
    A few leaves of mâche, arugula, sweet basil, or purslane

1. Toast bread under broiler on each side until golden brown. Remove from broiler and rub cut side of garlic clove over one side of toast, using two halves per toast. The rough surface of the toasted bread acts as a sort of grater and the bread becomes very garlicky.

2. Lay the toasts on a plate, garlic side up, and drizzle or brush with olive oil. Arrange prosciutto on toast, either flat or rolled up, whichever looks most attractive. Garnish with olives and small herby leaves such as mâche or basil.

VARIATION 1: Instead of olive oil, spread the garlic-rubbed toast with an ounce or so of goat cheese.

VARIATION 2: Substitute brasaeola for prosciutto; it has the same quality but is made from beef instead of pork.

Goat Cheese and Roghetta

This tramezzo is at its best when made on good-quality bread, especially a crusty one with rosemary and olive oil baked in it. The tart richness of the goats'-milk cheese, with its slight saltiness goes so beautifully with the nutty roghetta and the earthy bread. Wonderful picnic food, with a bottle of rustic red wine.

Yields 1 open-faced sandwich

1 thick slice of crusty country bread, especially one flavored with rosemary
2 ounces (56 g) goat cheese, such as Montrachet, plain or flavored with chives, Royal Provence, Caprina, or California
Several leaves of roghetta, as desired

Spread bread with goat cheese. Top with roghetta and serve immediately.

VARIATION: Make these in miniatures, using thinly sliced baguettes, with a small amount of goat cheese, and one small leaf of roghetta for each elegant, delicious hors d'oeuvre sandwich.

Crostini

The cheese topping in this dish is courtesy of cooking teacher Loni Kuhn, who passionately loves bright flavors as much as I do. While she was visiting a vineyard in Italy, the workers sat down to an alfresco snack of bread dough stuffed with the following cheese mixture, then fried in olive oil on an outdoor fire. The cheese mixture is rich, oozing pancetta and fresh rosemary, and I like it best simply spread onto baguettes and broiled until lightly browned.

This dish should be prepared with true Parmesan cheese, which comes not from Parma but from Reggiano. Dense and slightly crumbly, its rich, salty flavor little resembles the stuff that usually masquerades as Parmesan.

Yields 4

    5 to 6 cloves garlic
    ¼ pound (112 g) Parmesan, cut into ½-inch cubes
    ¼ pound (112 g) sliced pancetta
    ½ cup (60 ml) fresh rosemary leaves
    1 baguette (approximately 24 inches [600 mm] in length and 2
        inches [50 mm] in diameter), split in half lengthwise
    3 tablespoons (45 ml) olive oil

1. In processor finely chop garlic; add Parmesan, pancetta, and rosemary and puree until smooth.

2. Spread onto baguette. Drizzle with olive oil and pop under a hot broiler until golden brown and fragrant.

3. Cut into pieces about 2 inches (50 mm) long and enjoy as a snack, with a glass of wine or a stronger beverage.

Prosciutto and Olive Butter on Pita

Each bite of this voluptuous sandwich fills your mouth with the intense flavor of olives, sweet butter, salty prosciutto, and the bright accent of fresh sage or basil leaves.

Enjoy as a picnic lunch on a cliff overlooking the Pacific Ocean, on a terrace overlooking a vineyard, on a Mediterranean beach, or at your local park.

Yields 2 sandwiches

    2 to 3 cloves garlic, finely chopped
    3 tablespoons (42 g) unsalted butter, at room temperature
    1½ tablespoons (23 ml) black olive paste (see Aromatics and Spe-
        cial Ingredients) or Olive Sauce Provençal
    2 fresh pita breads, 6½ inches (162 g) in diameter, cut in half

12 to 16 leaves of fresh basil or sage, whole
3 to 4 ounces (84 to 112 g) prosciutto, thinly sliced

1. Mix garlic with butter and olive paste.
2. Spread the garlic-olive butter inside each pita half. Fill each with basil or sage leaves and prosciutto. Close up and enjoy immediately.

VARIATION: For an enticing hors d'oeuvre, make open-faced on pita bread wedges or on the miniature pitas occasionally available.

Pan Bagnat

French Roll Stuffed with Salad, Egg, Olives, and Anchovies

France

This robust sandwich is a specialty of the Côte d'Azure town of Nice. The title literally means "bathed bread" *(pain bagné)* in the patois of the area. Whether it's bathed in olive oil and vinegar or in salt water from the sea, no one is quite sure of its exact origin.

Pan bagnat is sold at little stands and kiosks throughout the city, wrapped up in paper, piled high in the morning, the pile disappearing by later in the day. The longer it sits, the more the juices from the filling soak into the bread, and the better it gets. This is the perfect sandwich to take along on a beach picnic or hike through the hillsides. Add some fresh fruit, some creamy cheese such as St. André, and a rough red wine, and you have a wonderful outdoor meal.

Serves 4

4 round French rolls, 5 inches (125 mm) in diameter
½ cup (125 ml) olive oil
¼ cup (60 ml) red-wine vinegar
1 to 2 medium-sized ripe red tomatoes, sliced
1 medium-sized green pepper, sliced
½ medium-sized red onion, thinly sliced into rings
4 leaves curly or red lettuce
3 cloves garlic, chopped
2 hard-cooked eggs, peeled and cut in halves
4 to 8 Greek-style black olives, pitted and cut into halves

4 to 8 leaves fresh basil
8 anchovies, or ¼ to ½ cup (60 to 125 ml) chunks of tuna

1. Cut rolls in halves to make a top and bottom. Remove some of the bread from inside to make more room for the filling.
2. Lay out the bread, cut side up. Drizzle with the olive oil and vinegar, saving a bit to drizzle over the vegetables.
3. On bottom halves of the rolls, layer tomato slices, pepper, onion, lettuce, and a sprinkling of the garlic. Drizzle with the rest of the oil and vinegar.
4. Top with egg halves, olives, basil, and anchovy or tuna. Place second half of rolls on top and press down. Serve immediately, or even better, wrap tightly and enjoy several hours later.

VARIATION: Instead of individual rolls, pan bagnat may be made on a long baguette sliced lengthwise; assemble sandwich, then cut into individual portions when ready to eat.

Saag Pakoras

Spinach Fritters

India

Spicy fried snacks—made from every imaginable vegetable dipped into chick-pea-and-rice-flour batters—are a beloved part of the Indian diet. They're sold from stalls in the marketplaces. They may be served as a snack, as a party hors d'oeuvre, perhaps as part of an afternoon tea.

I'm particularly fond of this fritter, or pakora, made with fresh spinach. It's delicious served with a dab of Tamatar Chatni, the gingery hot tomato flavor balancing the richness of fried chick-pea batter. The green bits of spinach in the golden brown fritter look lovely next to the red tomato chutney.

Yields about 15 fritters; serves 4 to 6

1 cup (250 ml) chick-pea flour (see Aromatics and Special Ingredients)
¼ cup (60 ml) rice flour (see Aromatics and Special Ingredients)
1½ teaspoons (8 ml) cumin
1 teaspoon (5 ml) salt

Dash hot pepper seasoning, such as cayenne pepper or
Tabasco
¾ cup (180 ml) water
1½ cups (375 ml) raw spinach, coarsely chopped
Vegetable oil for deep frying
Tamatar Chatni (see Index)

1. Mix chick-pea flour with rice flour, cumin, salt, hot pepper seasoning,
and water to make a smooth but thick batter.
2. Stir in spinach.
3. Heat oil in wok or skillet; form patties, about 2-by-3-inch (50-by-75-
mm) ovals using 2 tablespoons or your hands, and deep fry until golden
brown, approximately 2 to 4 minutes. Remove and drain on paper towels.
4. Serve immediately, accompanied by a dab of Tamatar Chatni.

ADVANCE PREPARATION: Batter may be made up to a day ahead of
time, with or without the vegetables added. Fry just before serving.

VARIATION 1: Instead of chopping the spinach leaves, they may be left
in large pieces, spread with the batter, then tightly rolled. Cover the roll
with additional batter, slice into several pinwheel slices, each about
¾-inch (18-mm) wide and deep fry.

VARIATION 2: Onion Bhajia
They're standard fare in British Indian restaurants and sold all over
India in stalls and marketplaces. They must be cooked while you wait,
because when old and reheated, they're greasy and leaden—not nice at
all. Freshly made, Onion Bhajia is crisp and fragrant and absolutely addic-
tive. Instead of spinach, use 2 (2 cups [500 ml]) onions, very thinly sliced,
and proceed as in the basic recipe.

Bhel Puri

Fried Chick-pea Noodles with
Potatoes, Yogurt, and Sweet–Sour Sauce

India

Bhel puri, called chaat in Bombay, is one of India's favorite street foods
and snacks. It consists of crispy chick-pea noodles, nuts, crisp puffed rice,
pieces of wafer-like breads, and so on. This mixture is topped with diced
potato, dressed with sweet-and-sour tamarind sauce, and piled with a

mound of chopped raw onion, cilantro, and fresh chile. It is a satisfying combination of contrasts—the sharpness of the onion and chile, the creamy softness of potato, the bright splash of sweet-and-sour, all with a background of nutty noodles.

The crunchy noodles, called *sev,* may be purchased from an Indian grocer. However, I think they're much better made at home. The batter is made from chick-pea and rice flours, available at Middle Eastern, Indian, and international grocery stores. They have distinctive textures and flavors, and are used often for many kinds of Indian snacks—Saag Pakora (see Index), Seekh Kabob, to name a few—as well as being popular in Burmese and other Southeast Asian cuisines. The sauce calls for asafoetida, an unusual spice, a resin, really, which smells unpleasant by itself, but has the ability to bring out the flavors of other ingredients.

Serves 4 to 6

Sev:
- 1½ cups (375 ml) chick-pea flour (see Aromatics and Special Ingredients)
- ¾ cup (180 ml) rice flour (see Aromatics and Special Ingredients)
- 2 teaspoons (10 ml) homemade Curry Powder (see Index)
- ½ teaspoon (3 ml) cayenne pepper
- 1½ teaspoons (8 ml) cumin
- 1½ teaspoons (8 ml) salt
- 3 tablespoons (45 ml) vegetable oil
- ⅔ to 1 cup (170 to 250 ml) water
  Vegetable oil for deep frying (about 2 cups [500 ml] if using a wok)

Sweet-and-Sour Tamarind Sauce:
- 2- inch (50 mm) square cube of pressed tamarind (see Aromatics and Special Ingredients)
- 2 cups (500 ml) water
- 1 medium-sized onion, chopped
- 2 cloves garlic, chopped
- 1 teaspoon (4½ g) unsalted butter
- 1½ teaspoons (8 ml) chopped gingerroot
- 1 teaspoon (5 ml) paprika
- 1 teaspoon (5 ml) cumin
- 1 teaspoon (5 ml) homemade Curry Powder (see Index)
- ½ teaspoon (3 ml) asafoetida (see Aromatics and Special Ingredients)
- 5 tablespoons (75 ml) brown sugar

1 tablespoon (15 ml) red-wine vinegar
½ teaspoon (3 ml) salt

To Assemble:
½ cup (125 ml) raw peanuts
3 small- to medium-sized waxy new potatoes, boiled, cooled, peeled, and cut into ½-inch (12-mm) cubes
1½ medium-sized onions, chopped
3 to 4 jalapeños, thinly sliced
½ to ¾ cup (125 to 180 ml) cilantro, coarsely chopped
1 cup (250 ml) plain yogurt

1. To make the sev: Combine chick-pea flour, rice flour, curry powder, cayenne pepper, cumin, salt, and 3 tablespoons (45 ml) vegetable oil. Mix until it forms granules. Stir in ⅔ cup (170 ml) water and mix, adding more if dough does not hold together. It should be firm enough to hold together, but not too wet, or mixture will fall apart as it fries.

2. Heat oil for deep frying. Test a tiny bit of the dough in the oil. If dough falls apart into small bits while it cooks, then it is probably too wet and you should add a bit more chick-pea flour.

3. Form the noodles by pressing through a spaetzle maker with holes about ⅛-inch (3-mm) wide directly into the hot oil. (I use a strainer with holes this size and press the mixture through with a spoon. Many Indian and Middle Eastern grocery stores sell gadgets to make these noodles.) The noodles should be about 2 inches (50 mm) in length. They fry very quickly, so allow only 1 or 2 minutes on each side until golden brown. Do not let them get darker, or they will have a burnt flavor.

4. Remove from hot oil and drain on paper towels. Repeat until dough is used up. By the end, as I am losing patience, I often force the dough between my fingers, which results in larger, unusually shaped fried crisps. They taste great, though their appearance is somewhat uneven.

5. To make the sauce: Place tamarind in saucepan with 2 cups (500 ml) water. Boil for 10 minutes, then strain. Discard the tamarind solids and reserve the liquid. (Instead of boiling and straining the tamarind you may instead use tamarind concentrate added to the 2 cups [500 ml] water.)

6. Sauté onion and garlic gently in butter until softened. Add spices and cook 1 or 2 minutes. Add tamarind liquid, bring mixture to a boil, add brown sugar, vinegar, and salt to taste.

7. Place about ¼ cup (60 ml) of the sev in serving bowls. Top with 1 or 2 tablespoons (15 or 30 ml) of the raw peanuts, several tablespoons of the diced potatoes, 1 or 2 teaspoons (5 or 10 ml) of the chopped onion, and a scattering of the jalapeños and cilantro, then add 2 tablespoons (30 ml) each of yogurt and tamarind sauce. Serve immediately.

ADVANCE PREPARATION: Each ingredient may be prepared separately ahead of time—the noodles will last in a tightly covered container at room temperature for up to 1 week, the tamarind sauce will last in the refrigerator for up to 2 weeks, and the potatoes could be cooked up to 2 days ahead. Chop the raw ingredients just before serving.

Garlic Flatbreads

I got the idea for these garlic flatbreads one day while preparing the chewy, crisp Chinese green onion pancakes, *ts'ung yu ping*. Why not use garlic instead of the green onion? The traditional method of rolling and coiling the dough forms many layers inside the pancake after it's flattened out. They fry to a golden, brown-speckled disc, the layers inside tender and infused with garlic.

Chewy flatbreads are enjoyed in many cuisines, especially in those of the East and Middle East. You could accompany these flatbreads with any savory, spicy dish or simply with a tomato-and-feta-cheese salad as a snack or light meal.

Flatbreads are extremely easy to prepare, but the dough should be made the day before so it can become tender and elastic.

Yields 4 flatbreads

> 2 cups (500 ml) unbleached white flour
> ⅔ to ¾ cup (170 to 180 ml) water
> 3 tablespoons to ¼ cup (42 to 56 g) unsalted soft butter
> 8 to 10 cloves garlic, coarsely chopped
> 1 teaspoon (5 ml) salt, or to taste
> 3 tablespoons (45 ml) vegetable oil

1. Place flour in bowl and make a well. Slowly add water, mixing with a fork until it becomes a thick dough. When it becomes too difficult to mix with a fork, use your fingers. When dough is no longer sticky, knead until it feels smooth, about 2 minutes.

2. Wrap in plastic wrap and chill overnight.

3. Divide into 4 pieces. Roll a piece into a rectangle about ⅛-inch (3-mm) thick with a rolling pin.

4. Spread the rectangle with about 1 tablespoon (15 ml) butter, then sprinkle with one-quarter of the coarsely chopped garlic and a pinch of salt. With your hands tightly roll the dough into a sausage shape, enclosing

the butter and garlic, then coil that sausage shape into a circle as if it were a snake or a coiled rug. Roll the coil flat into a ¼-inch (6-mm) pancake, about 6 inches (150 mm) in diameter. Repeat with the other 3 pieces of dough.

5. In a flat skillet or griddle, heat about 2 teaspoons (10 ml) of oil. One by one, fry each pancake until it is golden and flecked with brown spots, then turn and cook on other side. It should take about 3 to 4 minutes. Add more oil as needed per pancake.

6. Drain on a paper towel, cut into quarters or wedges, and serve immediately.

VARIATION 1: For an Indian flavor, use half whole-wheat flour combined with the unbleached white flour.

VARIATION 2: Ts'ung Yu Ping
For the traditional Chinese chewy onion flatbread, use thinly sliced green onions, allowing about 1 green onion per flatbread.

Olive and Rosemary Bread

Italy

Aromatic with fresh rosemary and punctuated with salty green and black olives, this is a special loaf. It is not necessary to bake one's own bread in the Mediterranean lands. Even the smallest of villages has a bakery that offers crusty, honest bread. There, it is truly the staff of life: No meal is really complete without it.

This is a bread tasting of olives and herbs, to eat with pungent cheese such as Appenzeller or fontina, to accompany a tomato salad or roast chicken.

Yields 2 loaves, 5¼-by-9¼ inches (131-by-231 mm),
or 1 large free-form loaf

¼ cup (60 ml) lukewarm water
1 package dry yeast
2 cups (500 ml) warm (room temperature) water
2 tablespoons (30 ml) olive oil
2 teaspoons (10 ml) sugar or honey
1 teaspoon (5 ml) salt
6 to 6½ cups (1500 to 1625 ml) unbleached flour

    1 heaping tablespoon (15 ml) fresh rosemary leaves, lightly
       crushed (do not substitute dried; use instead 2 teaspoons [10
       ml] dried thyme leaves)
  10 black Greek-style olives, pitted and halved
  10 Greek- or Italian-style green olives, pitted and halved

1. Pour ¼ cup (60 ml) warm water into bowl; add yeast and stir to dissolve. Then add 2 cups (500 ml) warm water, olive oil, sugar or honey, and salt.

2. Stir in 4 cups (1000 ml) of flour, 1 cup (250 ml) at a time, and beat until dough is smooth and elastic. Then mix in 1 cup (250 ml) of flour to make a stiff dough.

3. Flour a board with the remaining flour and knead the dough on it until smooth and no longer sticky, 5 to 10 minutes. It should be fairly elastic. The mixing and kneading may all be done in a food processor.

4. When dough is kneaded, add the rosemary and olives and knead into dough.

5. Let rise in greased bowl, covered with a damp towel in a warm place until almost doubled in volume, 1 to 1½ hours.

6. Punch down and squeeze out any air bubbles. Form either two small loaves or one large one. Place small ones into lightly greased baking pans, 5¼-by-9¼ inches (131-by-231 mm), or if making a large loaf, place on a lightly greased baking sheet. Let rise until almost doubled, about 45 minutes.

7. Preheat oven to 400° F. Place a shallow pan filled with hot water on the floor of the oven. Bake the bread until crusty and brown, about 40 minutes. Loaves should sound hollow when tapped.

ADVANCE PREPARATION: Dough may be kneaded and left to rise the first time, then refrigerated for up to 3 days. Remove from refrigerator and add olives, herbs, and let rise for the second time; then bake.

VARIATION: While I usually eschew convenience foods of any sort, a good-quality commercial bread dough may be used in this recipe, the olives and herbs kneaded in, left to rise, and baked.

Some Simple Sandwiches

Po'Boy Try this decadent way of making Po'Boy sandwiches: Pile fried oysters or catfish onto a crusty roll, slather with aïoli, then serve.

Summer Sandwich   Toast thick, sliced bread, rub with garlic. Top with tomato slices, basil leaves, Jack or mozzarella cheese, and drizzle with olive oil. Broil until cheese is bubbly.

Spread pungent, creamy Blue Castello cheese inside a long, thin baguette, sliced lengthwise. Add lots of fresh, whole basil leaves, close up, and serve immediately with a glass of rustic red wine.

Sun-dried tomato hors d'oeuvre   Spread thin slices of baguette with Montrachet, Lezay, or California goat cheese, top with a slice of sun-dried tomato and a leaf of basil. Serve immediately. This is probably the best way to eat goat cheese, sun-dried tomatoes, or basil.

Cucumber-Herb Cheese Tartines   Mix half cream cheese and half goat cheese together with lots of finely chopped garlic, green onions, and parsley. The mixture should be almost as green as emeralds. Season with a pinch of thyme, then spread on thin slices of baguette, and top each slice with one or more slices of peeled cucumber. Serve immediately.

Asparagus Prosciutto and Aïoli   Generously slather garlicky aïoli onto a baguette sliced lengthwise. Add cooled al dente asparagus, as much rosy prosciutto as you like, and chopped fresh basil. Close up tightly. If you like, you could add the basil to the aïoli for a fragrant, lovely green sauce. Enjoy!

Roast poblano or anaheim peppers, then peel. Marinate at least 15 minutes in olive oil, vinegar, oregano, garlic, and a dash of cayenne pepper. Drain and enjoy on crusty bread spread with goat cheese, as is or lightly broiled.

Another delectable goat-cheese combination is Royal Provence or Lezay combined with pungent, green Italian-style olives (pitted, of course).

Open-faced cheese sandwiches are sensational when generously seasoned with chopped garlic, green pitted olives, and pickled or roasted peppers. Broil to bubbling and serve with your favorite mustard, if desired.

Rich pâté makes a delicious sandwich on crusty French bread paired with lots of fresh-tasting peppery watercress.

A FEW SWEETS

The sun-drenched meals do not usually end with elaborate sweets. Those kinds of sweets are usually eaten at a café or bakery, or at friends' homes for tea, to be savored when the palate is not already satiated with flavors and the stomach not overwhelmed with food.

Of course, on a special occasion you will find a meal ending with a rich cake or syrup-dripping pastry, but usually the meal ends with fruit: sun-sugared nectarines, blood oranges from North Africa, juicy melons, or exotic mangos. Sometimes the fruit will be poached or marinated in syrup or wine, or baked and served with a dab of fresh, slightly whipped cream.

Most "real sweets" are purchased from a pastry shop, where they have the time and equipment to create these elaborate productions. The sweets made at home are comfy puddings such as rice and tapioca or egg-rich crème caramel, full of flavor but not overly complicated.

I have here a collection of a few of these sweets: a chocolate cake more dense and chocolaty than you ever imagined, and so simple as to be almost crude (I learned to prepare it in an old stone kitchen in the south of France). There are also lots of dishes and ideas for dishes made with fruit. And, of course, there is always my favorite: ice cream topped with sliced fresh fruits, doused generously with brandy or liqueurs. What a nice way to end a meal or a day.

Fresh Fruit in
Fraises de Bois Sauce

France

This simple, fresh fruit compote, glistening in lovely hues of scarlet, amber, green, and off-white, is heady from the brandy and Fraises de Bois liqueur. Fraises de Bois, made from wild strawberries, is rich with berry taste. Try it sometime, drizzled over strawberry ice cream slathered with sliced strawberries.

Serve this tipsy fruit bowl for brunch with a glass of champagne, or as a light dessert with a very simple cookie or fresh fruit sorbet or sherbet.

Serves 4 to 6

> 2 medium-sized bananas, medium-ripe
> 2 to 3 kiwi fruits
> 1 medium-sized orange
> 1 pint (500 ml) hulled strawberries
> 2 tablespoons (30 ml) brandy
> 2 tablespoons (30 ml) Fraises de Bois liqueur
> 1 tablespoon (15 ml) sugar

1. Peel bananas, kiwi fruits, and orange. Slice each fruit into slices ½-inch (12-mm) thick, including the strawberries.

2. Toss with brandy, Fraises de Bois, and sugar. Chill for ½ to 1 hour. Do not let stand for too much longer as the color from the Fraises de Bois will discolor the kiwi. Serve immediately.

Amarena Cherries over Crushed Ice

Italy

Walking along the heat-baked streets in Rome, I came across a stand selling freshly shaved ice topped with a huge variety of colorful syrups. There was green mint, milky almond, a pink syrup tasting of roses. A rainbow of bottles filled with orange, lemon, anise, or lime syrup lined the shelves. My favorite was amarena cherry, small intense fruits macerated in syrup. Nothing else came close to the pleasure of cooling off from the sticky, hot day than a glass of this crushed ice melting in its sweet syrup.

In Rome the ice I had was shaved by hand by a large muscular man with a mustache. I've gotten a similar consistency by first lightly crushing the ice by hand, then whirling it about in a food processor.

Enough ice cubes to fill 4 cups (1000 ml)
Amarena cherries and syrup to taste, about 3 tablespoons (45 ml) per person

NOTE: Amarena cherries are much like syrupy preserves. They come in bottles and attractive jars. Greek sour cherry preserves may be used instead, with the addition of a tiny bit of almond extract.

1. Prepare shaved ice by placing the ice cubes in a plastic bag and giving it a few light whacks with a mallet or by using a metal ice crusher.
2. Place partially cracked ice in processor and process until finely crushed.
3. Fill each glass with crushed ice and top with amarena cherries and syrup. Serve immediately.

VARIATION: Any of the Italian-type syrups, alone or in combination, may be poured over the ice instead of amarena cherries.

Shrikhand

Strawberry and Rose-Flavored Yogurt

India and the Middle East

Eaten at Indian festivals, shrikhand is a dish of creamy, aromatic yogurt, often spiced mysteriously. Similar dishes are enjoyed throughout the Middle East. I particularly like the addition of strawberries and rose water— just the tiniest bit so that the dish does not taste like roses or perfume, but enhanced by the flowery aroma of strawberries.

Serves 4 to 6

3 cups (750 ml) plain yogurt
1 to 2 teaspoons (5 to 10 ml) rose water
½ teaspoon (3 ml) almond extract
¼ cup (60 ml) sugar, or to taste
2 cups (500 ml) strawberries, cleaned and sliced

1. Mix together yogurt, rose water, almond extract, and sugar. Stir until smooth.

2. Add strawberries and chill.

VARIATION: Instead of strawberries add several tablespoons of coarsely chopped, unsalted pistachio nuts and a pinch of ground cardamom.

Mango and Gooseberry Fools

Australia

A fool is that British bit of sweet fluffy whipped cream blended with mashed fruit. Almost any fruit is delicious in a fool—whatever is at the height of freshness and flavor. The exotic mango and traditional gooseberry are favorites in the sunny land of Australia.

Serve these pastel creams of sweet-tart fruits, pale green and orange, nestled next to each other, in long-stemmed champagne glasses or balloon wine glasses.

Serves 4 to 6

1 cup (250 ml) gooseberries (see Note)
½ cup (125 ml) sugar, or to taste
2 ripe sweet mangos
2 cups (500 ml) whipping cream
8 ripe red strawberries (optional)
4 sprigs mint (optional)

NOTE: No need to clean gooseberries of their leaf or stem ends when making fool; once cooked and pureed they are not noticeable. This should really be made with fresh gooseberries, but may be made with canned gooseberries, well drained.

1. Cook gooseberries in very little water until tender. Drain and puree, then cool to room temperature. Add ¼ cup (60 ml) sugar, or to taste.

2. Peel mangos, pit, and puree. Add ¼ cup (60 ml) sugar, or to taste.

3. Whip cream until it forms fluffy, firm peaks. Divide into two parts and fold half into the pureed gooseberries and half into the mango puree. Chill.

4. Serve chilled, several spoonfuls of each, spooned into a long-stemmed

flat champagne glass. Decorate with a few strawberries and a sprig of mint if desired.

VARIATION: Mash ripe strawberries and spoon over or into fool.

Poached Peaches in Strawberry Puree with Mint

France

The peaches are poached in a simple syrup, then cooled and served swimming in a puree of sweetened strawberries. The golden spheres look enticing lying in the pink pool of liquid berries, garnished with the bright green of fresh aromatic mint (a dollop of softened vanilla ice cream would not be bad).

Serve as dessert, following Panzanella and Petti di Pollo alla Sorpresa (see index for both). They'd be nice for brunch as well.

Serves 4 to 6

4 to 6 ripe but firm medium-sized peaches
1½ cups (375 ml) sugar
2 cups (500 ml) water
Juice of 1 lime or lemon (2 tablespoons [30 ml])
1 pint (500 ml) strawberries, hulls removed
Additional sugar to taste, if needed
Fresh mint leaves to garnish, 2 to 3 per serving

1. Peel peaches by submerging in boiling water for just a second. Remove immediately and peel skin. It will come off easily. Leave peaches whole.

2. Combine sugar and water and bring to a boil. Cook over medium-high heat for 5 minutes, then stir in lime or lemon juice.

3. Add peaches to syrup. Cook over medium heat for 10 minutes on one side, then turn over and cook on the other side so that all sides of the peach are simmered in the sweet liquid.

4. Let cool in the syrup. You will have more syrup than you need; use the excess for fresh fruit compotes, cool fruit drinks, wine punches, sorbets, and so on.

5. Take ½ cup (125 ml) of the peach poaching liquid and puree it with the strawberries. Add extra sugar to taste. Serve each poached peach in a bowlful of pureed strawberries, garnished with a sprig or a few leaves of mint. Serve immediately.

ADVANCE PREPARATION: Poach the peaches and prepare the puree 1 day ahead. Combine them to serve at the last minute.

VARIATION: Fresh, sweet oranges may be sliced and served in a pool of the pureed strawberries, replacing the peach poaching liquid with orange juice plus 2 tablespoons (30 ml) sugar, or to taste. Garnish with 2 tablespoons (30 ml) coarsely chopped fresh mint.

Middle Eastern Fruit Compote with Pistachios

Middle East

Sweet fruit, so refreshing in the hot, dry Middle East, is here combined with other tastes of this region for a light, fragrant dessert. Pistachios add crunch, and rose water subtly perfumes the fruit. This is a typical Arabian compote. Any fruit in season can be used with an eye to balancing taste and texture. Since this dish depends upon the fruit, choose the ripest and most flavorful.

Serve for brunch, followed by Pastelle de Tortillas; or enjoy for dessert after Roast Cumin Lamb (see Index for both).

Serves 4

> 1 sweet, ripe but firm bosc pear, peeled, cored, and diced
> 1 large ripe banana, peeled and diced
> 1 pint (500 ml) strawberries, hulled and sliced
> 1 orange, peeled, seeded, and diced
> 1½ tablespoons (23 ml) honey at room temperature, or to taste (depending on sweetness of fruit)
> 1 teaspoon (5 ml) rose water (see Aromatics and Special Ingredients)
> 2 tablespoons (30 ml) coarsely chopped, unsalted pistachio nuts

NOTE: This fruit salad would sadly wilt if prepared too far ahead. Because it is easy and quick to put together, I recommend preparing it just before serving.

1. Combine pear, banana, strawberries, and orange. Drizzle in honey and toss with fruit, then add rose water.
2. Serve immediately, topped with pistachio nuts.

Glace aux Poires avec Praline de Noisettes

Pear Ice Cream with Hazelnut Pralines

France

Ice-cream tasting is my idea of the perfect profession. I would travel all over the world dipping my spoon into freezers and containers as I traveled, proclaiming which was smoothest, which was the most flavorful, and which demanded another taste. As it is, I am making an amateur's search for the perfect ice cream. I remember particular locales by the quality of their ice cream and consider that ample reason to relocate, if only for long enough to enjoy a bowlful.

Glace aux Poires is one of the best ice creams I've eaten, inspired by my favorite ice cream in Paris, Bertillon. It tastes like a frozen essence of pear, and topped with the sweet crunchy hazelnut praline mixture, it is sublime.

This recipe makes a lavish amount of the hazelnut praline, more than you'll use for the dish. Save it and sprinkle it over store-bought ice creams, sandwich it with whipped cream between layers of sponge cake, or eat it out of hand for a rather indulgent snack.

Serves 4 to 6

2 cups (500 ml) sugar
2 cups (500 ml) water
1 cup (250 ml) hazelnuts
4 egg yolks
1 cup (250 ml) whipping cream
4 to 5 ripe Bartlett pears, pureed
3 tablespoons (45 ml) brandy

1. Heat sugar and water together to make a syrup. Boil over medium heat until it reaches a soft-ball stage, that is, it does not disintegrate but flattens out when a small amount is added to a glass of cold water. The sugar syrup should reach the temperature of 240° F. on a candy thermometer. This takes about 30 to 40 minutes.

2. While the syrup is cooking: toast the nuts in a dry frying pan over medium heat until lightly flecked with brown, tossing and turning them so that all sides toast. You may wish to taste one to see if it has developed the characteristic hazelnut flavor.

3. Let cool, then remove skins by rubbing a handful back and forth between your palms. The friction will remove most of the skins. Wrapping

the nuts in a clean towel while you rub them helps, also. Place nuts in a metal bowl.

4. Beat egg yolks, cream, and brandy together.

5. When syrup reaches desired temperature and consistency, add half to the nuts and toss quickly to coat, then pour onto a buttered cookie sheet and cool. Beat egg yolk-cream-brandy mixture into the rest of the syrup and mix well. Cool

6. Peel and puree the pears. When cream syrup mixture is cool, add to pureed pears, then freeze in ice-cream maker or in freezer, removing after several hours to stir, then returning to freezer to refreeze. For a lighter ice cream, you should do this twice.

7. In processor, coarsely chop praline. Serve ice cream with an accompanying bowl of praline for each person to sprinkle on top or stir in before serving.

ADVANCE PREPARATION: Homemade ice cream does not keep as long as store-bought; store, tightly covered in the refrigerator, for up to 2 weeks, but it really is best eaten within 2 days.

VARIATION: The combination of juicy peach and meaty walnut is superb. Substitute peaches for pears and walnuts for hazelnuts.

Several Sorbets

Called *sorbet* in France, *sorbetto* in Italy, and *sharbat* in the Middle East, these cool ices with bright flavors are easily put together and frozen in your home freezer. Any fruit juice (I love pineapple with lots of tart lime juice) makes a lovely sorbet, as does strong, black, slightly sweetened coffee or tart, sweet lemonade. Pureed watermelon, cantaloupe, or honeydew makes a light, refreshing ice.

A jolt of something alcoholic is quite wonderful in these frozen desserts, but with alcohol these sorbets do not stay frozen long at room temperature. No problem, though—they melt into delicious icy drinks. Provide straws if you wish.

Coconut Rum Sorbet

West Indies

Creamy and exotic, with a good shot of rum, this makes a great finish to a spicy, flamboyant meal. Try it following Pollo Pibil or Thai Grilled Chicken with Peanut Sauce (see Index).

Serves 4

½ cup (125 ml) water
⅔ cup (170 ml) sugar
2 cups (500 ml) coconut milk
¼ cup (60 ml) dark Jamaican rum
1 teaspoon (5 ml) vanilla

1. Heat water and sugar until liquid boils. Add coconut milk, rum, and vanilla.
2. Cool to room temperature. Freeze in ice-cream maker or freezer tray. As it cools and freezes, the coconut milk will separate from the rest of the liquid. Do not be concerned; just stir together, and it will recombine.

Sonoma Apple Sorbet with Blackberries

California

Before Sonoma county's proliferation of wineries and vineyards, the area was well-known for its juicy apples. Wild blackberries also grow in great profusion in the sunny valley, and you have only to amble down a few country roads, or along the banks of a cool creek with an empty bucket during berry season to find enough berries for dessert.

This icy apple sorbet flavored with a hint of blackberry brandy is a perfect accent for those sun-sugared berries, and a lovely, light ending to a hearty meal.

Serves 4 to 6

1½ cups (375 ml) apple juice
½ cup (125 ml) sugar
3 tablespoons (45 ml) blackberry brandy
2 tablespoons (30 ml) lemon juice
½ cup (125 ml) milk or cream
1½ cups (375 ml) blackberries

1. Heat apple juice and sugar until sugar melts and liquid comes to boil. Add blackberry brandy, lemon juice, and milk or cream. If liquid appears to curdle, simply stir well. When it cools, before it freezes, simply discard any solids that sink to the bottom.

2. Let liquid cool to room temperature, then place in ice-cream freezer and freeze; or freeze in a metal tray or pan. Homemade sorbets, especially those containing alcoholic beverages do not freeze as hard as commercial ones do. They also melt faster at room temperature.

3. Serve in champagne glasses on top of a few tablespoons of blackberries, or serve with the blackberries on top of the sorbet.

Pear Sorbet

France and Italy

Ripe, sweet pears make my favorite sorbet (*sorbetto* in Italy)—light and clear tasting, like a grove of pear trees ripening in the Provençal or Tuscan sun. I especially like pear sorbet served next to a scoop of rich vanilla or hazelnut ice cream, and maybe a crisp cookie or two.

Serves 4 to 6

5 to 6 ripe and fragrant Bartlett or bosc pears
Juice of ½ lemon (1 tablespoon [15 ml])
½ cup (125 ml) sugar, or to taste (depending on sweetness of fruit)
3 tablespoons (45 ml) pear liqueur or brandy
¼ teaspoon (1.5 ml) almond extract

1. Peel and core pears, then puree and add lemon juice.

2. Combine pureed pears with sugar, pear liqueur or brandy, and almond extract. Freeze in ice-cream maker or freezer, removing once or twice to scrape ice crystals away from sides of bowl.

3. Serve as desired.

ADVANCE PREPARATION: Homemade ices do not keep as long in the freezer as store-bought ones do; enjoy within 3 days for maximum flavor. Keep tightly wrapped in freezer.

VARIATION: Peach Sorbet

Substitute 8 ripe, firm peaches for the pears and peach brandy for the pear brandy. Also delicious topped with in-season sweet raspberries.

Gâteau au Chocolat

French

This dense flourless chocolate mixture is an old French cake of the type that's become popular here as "sin," "decadence," and so on. Dark and chocolaty, it is everything a forbidden sweet should be—bittersweet, deep melt-in-your-mouth flavor and covered with rich cream and fresh fruit.

It's hard to believe that anything this special could be so simple.

Serves 6

1 pound (450 g) bittersweet chocolate chips
½ cup (125 ml) very strong, very hot coffee (or substitute 2 teaspoons [10 ml] instant, dissolved in ½ cup [125 ml] very hot water)
¼ cup (60 ml) sugar
2 sticks (224 g) unsalted butter, at room temperature, plus extra for buttering pan
4 large eggs
Pinch salt
2 teaspoons (10 ml) vanilla
1 cup (250 ml) whipping cream
3 tablespoons (45 ml) confectioner's sugar, or to taste
Fresh strawberries or raspberries for garnish

1. Preheat oven to 350° F.

2. Place three-fourths of the chocolate chips in a bowl; pour the hot coffee over it and let stand for 5 to 10 minutes or until the chocolate has melted. Stir, and let stand until it becomes slightly warmer than room temperature.

3. Into the warm chocolate, stir the sugar, butter, eggs, salt, and 1 teaspoon (5 ml) vanilla, beating until smooth. Stir in remaining chocolate chips.

4. Generously butter a round or square 8-inch (200-mm) cake pan. Pour in the chocolate mixture and bake 30 to 40 minutes or until a crust forms on top. Remove from oven, cool, and then loosen sides of cake from pan with a knife. Remove from pan by inverting, carefully, onto a plate. If any

of the bottom comes off (it always does for me) just press it back on—it will be covered with cream anyway and no one will see it. Chill until ready to serve.

5. When ready to serve, whip cream until firm peaks form, then flavor with confectioner's sugar and vanilla (or flavor cream with brandy or liqueur). Spread over cake and serve surrounded by fresh berries. If berries are not in season, make a sauce by pureeing slightly softened, frozen berries, add a dash of berry liqueur, and sweeten to taste (if the berries are sweetened, add no extra sugar).

ADVANCE PREPARATION: Keeps extremely well, tightly wrapped in the refrigerator, for up to 1 week, and may also be frozen. Top with cream just before serving.

Teresa's Mexican Chocolate Cake

Mexico

This recipe is from Teresa Chris, my literary agent, whose palate for chocolate knows no international boundary. She believes that each chocolate cake has its season. While fluffy cream-billowed ones are satisfying on a winter's day, this cake is for the sunny days. Its flavor conjures up the image of a walk through the streets of a sun-slaked Mexican village. It is fragrant with cinnamon, as Mexican chocolate so often is, and the dense cake and fudge frosting are delicious after a spicy, savory meal, with a cup of strong coffee, or to tote along on a picnic.

Yields 1 8-by-14-inch (200-by-350-mm) flatcake

Enough unsalted butter or lecithin spray to coat an 8-by-14-inch (200-by-350-mm) pan

Cake:
1 stick (112 g) unsalted butter
½ cup (125 ml) vegetable oil
½ cup (125 ml) cocoa
1 cup (250 ml) water
1½ teaspoons (8 ml) distilled white vinegar
½ cup (125 ml) milk
2 cups (500 ml) sifted flour
1 teaspoon (5 ml) baking soda
Pinch salt
2 cups (500 ml) sugar

2 eggs, beaten
1 teaspoon (5 ml) cinnamon
1 teaspoon (5 ml) vanilla extract

Fudge Icing:
   1 stick (112 g) unsalted butter
   1 box (approximately 4 cups [500 ml]) confectioner's sugar
   ⅓ cup (85 ml) cocoa
   ⅓ cup (85 ml) milk
   1 teaspoon (5 ml) vanilla
   1 cup (250 ml) coarsely chopped pecans or walnuts

1. Preheat oven to 350° F. Combine butter, oil, cocoa, and water in a saucepan and heat until cocoa has melted in.

2. Mix vinegar and milk and set aside to sour.

3. Combine flour, baking soda, salt, sugar, eggs, sour milk, cinnamon, and vanilla in large bowl. Then combine with the first mixture; it will be soupy. Pour into the buttered cake pan and bake for 20 to 25 minutes. The cake will pull away from the sides of the pan when ready. Cool for 5 minutes in pan, then let cool on rack.

4. When cool, prepare Fudge Icing.

5. To make Fudge Icing: Heat butter until it melts, then continue heating it over medium heat until it comes to a boil and gets foamy. Remove from heat and immediately add powdered sugar—this gives it a burnt sugar flavor—and beat together until creamy and thick; then add cocoa, milk, and vanilla.

6. Add pecans or walnuts and quickly spread on top and sides of cake. Work quickly, as it hardens very fast as it cools. Dip knife into hot water to facilitate spreading.

ADVANCE PREPARATION: This is a sturdy cake, and it keeps well, tightly wrapped and refrigerated, for several days. It also freezes extremely well.

VARIATION: Forget the cake and make the icing for a pan of fudge.

Mandorlata

Italian Almond Coffee Cake

Italy

The sweet scent of almond in this cake is seductive indeed. Tender and moist, covered with a layer of sliced toasted almonds and sugar glaze, this is just one of the myriad almond cakes enjoyed throughout the Mediterranean. Deceptively plain looking, these cakes perch on the shelves of bakeries from Milano to Málaga, appearing nowhere near as fancy as are the other cakes. Ah, but just one bite of this indecently good cake is all you need to become a devotee.

It's better the second day, and the third, and the fourth, or for as long as it lasts. The brandy mellows, and the cake firms up by the second day. Perfect to prepare the night before a brunch, or even several days before serving. Enjoy with a cup of strong coffee or a small glass of wine.

Yields 1 8-by-8-inch (200-by-200-mm) square cake

        1 cup (250 ml) raw unblanched almonds
        1 cup (250 ml) flour
      ½ teaspoon (3 ml) baking soda
      ½ teaspoon (3 ml) baking powder
      ¼ teaspoon (1.5 ml) salt
        1 stick (112 g) unsalted butter, at room temperature
        1 cup (250 ml) sugar
        1 egg
      1½ teaspoons (8 ml) almond extract
      ¾ cup (180 ml) sour cream
      ½ cup (125 ml) brandy
      ½ cup (125 ml) confectioner's sugar
        2 tablespoons plus 2 teaspoons (30 ml plus 10 ml) milk
        1 cup (250 ml) sliced almonds, toasted in an ungreased pan
          until lightly browned

1. Grind raw almonds in nut grinder, blender, or food processor until mealy in consistency. Set aside.

2. Mix flour with baking soda, baking powder, and salt. Set aside.

3. Cream butter with sugar. Beat in egg, then add 1 teaspoon (5 ml) almond extract, sour cream, brandy, and ground almonds.

4. Combine flour mixture with butter-sugar-almond mixture, stirring only enough to make a thick batter. It should retain some lumps. They will bake away, and overstirring will toughen the cake. Pour into buttered and

floured 8- or 9-inch (200- or 225-mm) square cake pan, top with sliced almonds, and bake at 350° F. for 40 to 45 minutes.

5. Mix confectioner's sugar with milk and remaining almond extract. Remove cake from oven, pour confectioner's sugar mixture over cake, and return to oven for another 5 minutes or until cake seems firm and not runny inside. (A knife or cake tester will not emerge clean from this cake since it is so moist.)

ADVANCE PREPARATION: This cake tastes best prepared the day before, and continues to stay moist and delicious for 3 days. It could possibly last longer, but in my home it is gone by then.

Simple Fruit Dishes and Ideas

Oranges and strawberries, both sliced, tossed with honey to sweeten, and sprinkled with orange-flower water and cinnamon.

Make sorbet from wine-poached pears or peaches.

Soak dried apricots in sweet white wine until they plump up drunkenly and are very good to eat, about 3 days.

In southwest France, Armagnac or other brandy is sprinkled onto sweet, ripe melon; the brandy enhances the ripe melon flavor. It doesn't really work if the melon is underripe, however.

Naranjas al vino tino   In Spain, slices of sweet orange are sprinkled with sugar, drizzled with red wine, and allowed to marinate an hour or so. In Sicily, it is blood oranges, marinated with Marsala.

Moroccan perfumed orange juice   For each glass of orange juice, allow 1 teaspoon (5 ml) orange-flower water, 1 teaspoon (5 ml) sugar, and a dash of cinnamon. Mix together and serve over crushed ice. I like a bit of vodka in mine every so often.

SOME SUGGESTED MENUS

Salad of Mango, Chile,
   and Peanuts
Weta Ki
Steamed Rice
Sonoma Apple Sorbet with
   Blackberries

Tomatillo Guacamole
Pollo Pibil
Black Bean–Chipotle Puree
Warm Corn Tortillas
X-Nipek
Coconut Rum Sorbet

Salade Auvergne
Canard aux Olives et Vin Rouge
Crusty bread
Fresh Fruit in Fraises de Bois
   Sauce

Minestra alla Zingara
Insalata Gorgonzola
Crusty bread and a bowl of
   Niçoise olives
Glace aux Poires avec Praline
   de Noisettes

Gratin Varaire
Rôti de Porc Provençal
Les Fruits Rouge-a selection of
   berries, strawberries,

raspberries, and blackberries,
accompanied by a shaker of
sugar and a bowl of crème
fraîche

Pasta Basilico
Vitello con Peperoni e Olives
Amarena Cherries over Crushed
   Ice

Karnabit bi Tahini
Hameen with Salata
Middle Eastern Fruit Compote
   with Pistachios

Pastelle de Tortillas
Basket of Ripe, Juicy
   Strawberries
Mandorlata
Café au lait

Puree of Artichoke Soup à la
   Alice B. Toklas
Petti di Pollo alla Sorpresa
Ripe sweet figs
Pear Sorbet

Alecha
Sarish Bata
Tamatar Chatni
Pear Sorbet or Shrikhand

INDEX

INDEX

Chocolate Cake, Teresa's Mexican,
218–219
Chocolate cake, dense and rich
(Gâteau au Chocolat), 217–218
Cilantro, 5
Clams, Curried, 151–152
Coconut milk, 11
Coconut Rum Sorbet, 215
Confit of Duck, 142–143
Confiture de Tomates, 188–189
Corn husks, 12
Couscous, 12
Crab, Peas, and Buckwheat Pasta,
155–156
Crostini, 196–197
Cucumber Dressing, 33
Cumin and Garlic Lamb, 172
Curry Paste, Thai Green, 183–184
Curry Powder, Homemade, 182
Curry-Baked Lemon Pork, 166–167

Dahl, Lemon-Curry, 85–86
Dried chiles, 12
Duck
and goose fat, 7
and sausage gumbo, 140–141
confit, 142–143
cracklings, 143
leftover, in salad with potatoes and
olives, 144
roasted with olives and zinfandel,
139–140

Eggplant
in spicy-tart sauce, 33–34
pickles, 191–192
stuffed with tomatoes, onions, and
eggplant, 78–79
rich and spicy stew with green
beans, 74–75
Eggs
coated with spicy meat and served
with peanut sauce, 70
in watercress-tarragon sauce, 147
layered vegetable omelet, 59–60
omelet with cilantro-spice puree
and feta, 67–68

scrambled with tortilla strips, 66–67
sandwich of egg and watercress, 71
with peppers, Basque style, 68–69
with tortillas, tomato sauce, black
beans, peas, ham, and banana,
90
with tomatillo sauce, 71
Endive, with Roquefort, 41
curly, with tarragon and olives, 41

Faire Chabrot, 57
Fattoush, 24
Feta cheese, 12
Fish
chopped and steamed in banana
leaves, 150–151
fillets with mustard seeds, 149
Sea Bass with Lime-Ginger Cream,
146
with olives, 148
Fools, Mango and Gooseberry,
210–211
Fresh Fruit in Fraises de Bois Sauce,
208
Fudge, 219
Ful Midammis, 90–91
Ful misri, 13

Garlic, 5
Garlic Flatbreads, 203–204
Garlic-Mashed Potatoes, 75–76
Garlic Soup, Cold, 43–45
Garlic-Herb Oil, 179
Garlic-Saffron Scallops, 155
Gâteau au Chocolat, 217–218
Gingerroot, 13
Glace aux Poires avec Praline de
Noisettes, 213–214
Gnocchi, Ancho, in Corn Cream,
105–106
Goat Cheese, Wrapped in Vine
Leaves with Green Olives,
63–64
Grape leaves, 13
Gratin Varaire, 76–77
Guacamole, with Tomatillos, 184–185
Gulai Malabar, 74–75

226

Potatoes *continued*
  spicy, with green beans and
    tomatoes, 88
  with confit, 144
Poulet au Vinaigre, 123–124
Poulet le Midi, 122–123
Poulet Mistral, 123
Prosciutto and Olive Butter Sandwich,
  197–198
Puree de Carottes Provençale, 48–49
Puree de Pommes de Terre à l'Ail,
  75–76
Purslane, 6

Radicchio, 6
  in salad with fennel and orange, 21
Raspberry Vinegar, 17
Ravioli di Gorgonzola con Radicchio,
  109–110
Ravioli in Casserole with Tomato
  Sauce and Fresh Rosemary, 119
Red Beans and Rice with Broccoli
  and Xinxim, 80–82
Red Bell Peppers
  roasted in salad with fennel, 38
  roasted in salad with chick peas,
    carrot, and anchovies, 39–40
  pureed in soup with lemon cream,
    45–46
Rice flour, 17
Rice noodles, 17
Rice, Cardamom-Scented Sephardic
  Style, 116–117
Ricotta al Forno, 69–70
Risotto Giardino e Mare, 117–119
Risotto with Asparagus and Shrimp,
  117–119
Risotto with Squash Blossoms, 119
Risotto with Sun-Dried Tomatoes and
  Artichoke Hearts, 119
Roghetta, 6
Romaine Lettuce, Shredded with Dill,
  41
Rôti de Porc Provençal, 161–163

Saag Pakoras, 199
Sabzi Khordan, 21–22

Sage, 6
Sajoer Lodeh, 51–53
Salads
  Greek cabbage, 37–38
  Indian potato and yogurt, 30–31
  of cucumber, tomato, mint, parsley,
    and pita bread, 24
  of duck, potato, and olive, 144
  of fennel, orange, and radicchio, 21
  of greens and gorgonzola, 26–27
  of herbs, tomato, cucumber, and
    feta, 21–22
  of lettuce, roghetta, tarragon,
    prosciutto, and foie gras, 36–37
  of mango, chile, and peanuts, 40
  of potato, mint, and capers, 25–26
  of roasted red peppers and fennel,
    38
  of roasted red peppers, anchovies,
    chick peas, and carrot, 39–40
  of tomatoes, herbs, olives, and
    bread, 27–28
  of warm cheese-stuffed peppers,
    22–23
  Provençal Chicken Salad with aïoli,
    28–30
  Southeast Asian Vegetable Salad,
    32–33
  Thai, 34–36
Salade Auvergne, 36–37
Salata Feta, 62–63
Salata, Relish of Mint, Tomato, and
  Lemon, 116
Salmon with Watercress-Tarragon
  Sauce, 146–147
Salsa, Chipotle, 188–189
Salsa, with Orange, Lime, and
  Cilantro, 186–187
Sandwiches
  asparagus, prosciutto, basil, and
    aïoli, 206
  blue cheese with basil, 206
  egg salad and watercress, 71
  ful, tahini, and salad in pita, 91
  goat cheese and roghetta, 196
  melted mozzarella with tomato,
    basil, garlic, and olive oil, 206

Acknowledgments

To:

Janice Gallagher, editor and friend, who shared both the enthusiasm and work on *Sun-Drenched Cuisine* and *Hot & Spicy* and who believed in me from the beginning

Teresa Chris, agent, supporter, and confidante

Jeremy Tarcher, esteemed publisher

Gretchen Woelfle, for her hard work and good ideas

Esther Novak, whose kitchen and friendship have survived the testing of two cookbooks

The following friends who've tasted and tested, offered recipes, advice, and support: David Aspin and Paula Levine, Mariano Basso, Esther and Walter Franco, Rachel Goldberger, David and Sari Jeffries, Loni Kuhn, Jonathon Leichtling and Wendy Stern, Zabel Meshiyan, Noah and Dinah Stroe, Judy and Phillip Schaeffer, and Giovanni Tempesta

Fran Grant, Jeanne McElkhatton, Patrick McGregor, and Leslie Blumberg for sharing their knowledge and expertise

My parents, Isadore and Caroline Smith, and my grandmother, Sophia Dubowsky, who is the most enthusiastic cook I know

Leah and Gretchen Spieler, who good naturedly ate their way through the writing and testing of this book when often what they really wanted was a hamburger